KU-716-468

H.E.P. Woodcock.

GORDON

By the same author

I Saw for Myself (1957)
Disarmament (1959)
Europe will not wait (1960)
Lawrence of Arabia (1961)
The Arabs (1964)

GORDON
martyr and misfit

By
ANTHONY NUTTING

THE REPRINT SOCIETY LONDON

First published in Great Britain 1966
This edition published by The Reprint Society 1967
By arrangement with Constable & Company Limited
Copyright © Anthony Nutting 1966

Printed in Great Britain by Richard Clay (The Chaucer Press), Ltd.,
Bungay, Suffolk

Acknowledgements

The author wishes to acknowledge with grateful thanks the help given to him by Miss A. J. Lewis and the Manuscript Department of the British Museum in providing access to General Gordon's letters, diaries and memoranda.

The portrait photograph of Charles George Gordon, the statue of Gordon by Hamo Thornycroft, 'Chinese Gordon', the statue of Gordon at Khartoum, and Li-Hung Chang, are reproduced by permission of Radio Times Hulton Picture Library.

The drawing of Gordon's head being shown to Slatin Pasha, and the portraits of Sir Evelyn Baring and the Mahdi, are reproduced by permission of the Mansell Collection. The map of the defences of Khartoum is taken from *The Royal Engineers in Egypt and the Sudan*.

ILLUSTRATIONS

Between pages 144 and 145

MAPS

CONTENTS

CHAPTER 1

MAN OF DESTINY

ON February 11, 1885, the news reached London that Charles George Gordon had been speared to death when Khartoum fell a fortnight before to the revolutionary armies of the Mahdi after a long and painful siege. Seldom in Britain's history has the death of one of her sons called forth so emotional a reaction on the part of public opinion. The Mahdi was denounced as a savage, notwithstanding the fact that he had offered to set Gordon free if he surrendered and had given the strictest personal orders that he was to be taken alive. The British Government was arraigned for failing to send relief in time and the Prime Minister was called a murderer. And Gordon himself—already a hero in the public's eye for his exploits in China against the Taiping rebellion and for his efforts to suppress the slave trade in the Sudan—became a modern symbol of the soldier-saint and Christian martyr. The gallantry of his stand against overwhelming odds, combined with the high religious principles which guided his life, evoked from Parliament and Press encomiums containing every superlative in the English language. 'A hero of heroes,' Gladstone called him, while Queen Victoria, in a letter of condolence to his sister, Augusta Gordon, referred to him as 'Your dear, noble, heroic brother.' And for the next twenty years or more his memory was to remain 'dear, noble, heroic' to his fellow-countrymen, who held him up to succeeding generations as the perfect example of courage, patriotism, and godliness. In token of this public reverence, the inevitable statues were erected in London, Aberdeen, at the Royal Engineers' Depot at Chatham, and, after the British conquest of the Sudan fourteen years later, in Khartoum itself. More usefully, a school, later to become a University College, was established in his memory at Khartoum; and homes for the training of boys for the Army were founded in England.

But then, as the fashion changed and the Victorian era gave way to one which held somewhat different values, the denigrators got to work, and somebody had to start chipping at the masonry of his public pedestal. The laurel wreath of greatness, it was now said, was undeserved and the halo of sanctity a piece of camouflage. Gordon was a humbug whose professions of piety were a cloak for his weaknesses. Instead of the warrior-saint struggling to uphold righteous causes against barbarism, a new picture emerged of the charlatan sitting in his tent in darkest Equatoria, with a Bible in one hand and a brandy bottle in the other, too drunk to shoulder the responsibilities of leadership even when his camp was attacked by hostile tribesmen, yet vain enough to claim the credit for the achievements of his expedition.

Clearly, neither of these pictures—the warrior-saint or the drunken charlatan—gives any real insight into Gordon's true character and motives. Both are caricatures and, as such, misleading and deficient. But it is as delusory to call him a saint as it is tendentious to accuse him of drunkenness. And even if either description were true, it would not answer any of the questions which Gordon's life, and death, have left to be resolved. Why did he never marry? Why did he hate living in England and prefer to soldier under the banner of some foreign potentate? Why did he quarrel with all his superiors, British or foreign? Why was he so ruthless, so self-contradictory and incapable of sticking to any decision?

Neither godliness nor humbug can explain any of these essential riddles in the life of Gordon. Still less can they point the answer to the most pregnant questions of all: Why did Gordon stay in Khartoum and die a martyr's death when he could have saved himself and the garrison which he went there to save? And why, when he heard that the British relief force was on its way, did he declare in terms that he would not be rescued, but would send the garrison away and 'fall with the town and run all risks'?

His instructions were to evacuate as many of the Egyptian garrisons as was possible before they were cut to pieces or captured and sold into slavery by the avenging hordes of the Mahdi's nationalist followers. Not only did he agree to carry out these orders; he also personally helped to draft them, and himself insisted on adding words to the effect that the policy of evacuation 'should on no account be changed'. Yet from the moment when he reached Khartoum he ignored his instructions completely and, although hopelessly outnumbered, changed the policy of evacuation to a policy of all-out resistance or, in his own pungent phrase, of 'smashing up the Mahdi'.

What prompted this violent change of mind and the resulting suicidal stand at Khartoum has never been explained. Certainly no one could be more unpredictable or changeable than Gordon where material issues or questions affecting his fellowmen were concerned. He was forever resigning his posts and then withdrawing his resignation, and he never ceased to make snap judgements about people which further acquaintance forced him to change. To those on the receiving end of his letters and despatches he must have seemed more often than not to be veering from one course to another like a stricken ship in a storm. But where the innermost searchings of his soul were concerned, he knew what he was doing and, in the final analysis, he was determined at all costs to go through with it. From his early adult years he had chosen his destiny, and through all the vicissitudes of his subsequent life and service his every action was directed and designed to fulfil this predetermined purpose.

In contrast to his external relationships, there was no vacillation here. On the contrary, right up to the end he never wavered from his unalterable guide-line. And the very doubts and inconsistencies which afflicted him in the discharge of his duty to the world around him were in all probability themselves due to the inevitable conflict which so single-minded, even selfish, a pursuit of his destiny had wrought with the safety and well-being of the people he served.

For some unexplained reason, his previous biographers have elected either to conceal this crucial choice or to dismiss it as being of no account. Yet there can be little doubt that therein lies the key to the enigma of Charles Gordon and the only rational explanation as to how this eccentric irregular soldier came to be numbered among history's most remarkable martyrs.

CHAPTER 2

THE MARTYR IN THE MAKING

THE man who was destined to be known through most of his adult life as 'Chinese Gordon' and to find immortality as 'Gordon of Khartoum' was born into this world on January 28, 1833, a younger son of a family of eleven, steeped in the traditions of the British Army and claiming descent from a warrior clan of Scottish Highlanders. His father was later to become a Lieutenant-General, as was his eldest brother, Henry, and his grandfather and great-grandfather were also distinguished Army Officers. His mother, on the other hand, came of Puritan rather than military stock and was the daughter of Samuel Enderby, a shipowner who plied his trade on both sides of the Atlantic Ocean, in London and New England. Thus, with a long tradition of military discipline on one side and of Puritanism on the other, it might be expected that at least in his early years Gordon would have grown up as a strict conformist to Victorian convention, who was scared stiff of his elders, never dared to step out of line, and was always 'seen and not heard'.

In fact, the contrary was the case. And in his boyhood, much of which was spent at Woolwich, where his father was Inspector of the Carriage Department at the Royal Military Academy, he was a high-spirited imp who indulged in all manner of mischief and practical jokes. A favourite prank was breaking windows with the aid of missiles which fired heavy screws from cross-bows and were manufactured by friendly workers in the Royal Arsenal. Sometimes the R.M.A. would be selected for attack by young Charlie Gordon and his brothers. And when they were around, no instructor at the Academy could feel entirely safe from having his lecture interrupted, to the delight of his cadet-students, by the sudden splintering of glass as one of these missiles struck home. At other times the Arsenal storehouses would be the target or, to enliven a dull Sunday afternoon, there would be a round of bell-ringing at the neighbours' front doors.

Yet, just as in later life Gordon was never able completely to sever the bonds of British military tradition, so in his boyhood he was drawn towards the Army, which had formed his family background over the three previous generations. As a child he owned hundreds of lead soldiers which he 'drilled' for long hours at a time. Also, mischievous imp though he was in his out-of-school hours, he showed an early promise in such useful military arts as map-making and drawing. And before the age of fifteen he left his boarding school at Taunton and, following in the footsteps of his eldest brother, Henry, enrolled in September 1847 as an enthusiastic young cadet in the same Royal Military Academy which he had earlier subjected to such constant attacks from his cross-bows.

In his studies young Gordon had no trouble at all. The early promise which he had shown at Taunton in draughtsmanship continued to prosper, and the examples of his work at the R.M.A., which are to be found in the Royal Engineers' Museum at Chatham, show a truly astonishing artistry and eye for detail. In fact, his drawings of guns and forts stand to this day as model examples in the Royal School of Military Engineering. But in his general conduct he did not do so well. For the first time in his life, he found himself subjected to the rigours of military discipline, against which he often reacted with a rebelliousness and quickness of temper which he was never to lose in adult life. He was nearly expelled for butting a senior cadet in the stomach and knocking him down a flight of stairs. On another occasion, when he was hauled before the Commandant and punished for an offence which he had not committed, he angrily tore the corporal's stripes off the sleeves of his tunic and flung them at the feet of his astonished superior. And, finally, towards the end of his four and a half years at Woolwich, he suffered a loss of seniority for losing his temper with a junior cadet and hitting him on the head with a clothes' brush.

The effect of this setback was to lose him the vacancy as a subaltern in the Royal Artillery for which he was hoping. And when he eventually passed out of the R.M.A. in June 1852 he had to be content with a commission in the less popular of the two corps for which Woolwich catered—the Royal Engineers. So at the age of nineteen Charles Gordon received the traditional posting for all R.E. subalterns at the start of their career and was sent to the corps' depot at Chatham. Eighteen months later, with a good report on his work, he was posted to Pembroke Dock in Wales, where he was to assist in the construction of a chain of forts, designed to protect the naval base against a sea-borne attack. Eleven years later he was to be engaged in supervising the building of what he regarded as an equally useless group of forts at Gravesend. But whereas then he found compensation in establishing himself as a kind of one-man Salvation Army, at Pembroke he was hard put to it to discover any diversions. Being of slight build, with penetrating blue-grey eyes, an engaging smile, a soft and gentle voice, and a face that was handsome to the point of being almost feminine in the exquisite delicacy of its features, he was in considerable demand for the local social round and much admired by his superiors' and fellow officers' wives. But even as a young subaltern Gordon hated dinner-parties, dances, and small talk; and so he found no compensation in the social life of Pembroke.

The nearest that he came to forming any great friendship was with a Captain Drew, a deeply religious man who was also something of an evangelist. This association was to exercise a permanent influence on Gordon's life and thinking. Hitherto he had had little, if any, appetite for religion, which, like many a schoolboy and adolescent, he had looked on as just another irksome routine discipline. He had stubbornly refused Confirmation, although his family were regular churchgoers and partakers of Holy Communion. And if he showed any consciousness of his mother's Puritan background, it was to regard it as another of those stuffy traditions to be rebelled against. But something about Captain Drew made him change his attitude towards religious worship and prayer. Perhaps it was the fact that his new-found mentor was not himself a member of any established church, a nonconformist without capitals, which meant that he could combine being a rebel with being a good Christian. Perhaps also a sense of loneliness at this first unhappy exposure to regimental duties and social life in Britain impelled young Gordon to seek solace in contemplation. At any rate he became a different man, once he had put upon himself this new 'greatcoat', as he was later to describe his religious beliefs. Even the dreariness of Pembroke Dock seemed suddenly transformed. 'Now I would not wish for a prettier place,' he wrote to his sister, herself

16

a deeply devout and religious person. And in his innermost self he felt a better man, who had 'turned over a new leaf' and wanted Augusta to pray for him. He even asked her if she thought that he could help their parents to 'think of eternal things'. Although he spoke only rarely of his conversion over the next ten years, undoubtedly it formed a watershed in his life. And if the resulting stream flowed for a while hidden and underground, it only required the inevitable natural calamity of his father's death for the torrent of his faith to come gushing to the surface, whence for the rest of his days it was to irrigate and regulate his thinking on every issue. The mystic sense that was to grow in him in later years until it came to dominate his life undoubtedly had its origins in this chance encounter with the evangelical Captain Drew.

However, no sooner had this mysticism taken root than young Gordon's attentions were diverted to another sphere. In March 1854 Britain had cast her lot with Turkey against Russia in that bloody by-product of a dispute between the Roman and Greek Churches over the custody of certain shrines in the Holy Land— the Crimean War. British opinion was strongly Russophobe at the time; and when Russia invaded Turkey's Balkan provinces following the Sultan's decision to award custody of the shrines to the Roman Church and to disallow the Russian-sponsored Greek Orthodox claims, the British Government leapt at the opportunity to teach Tennyson's 'o'ergrown Barbarian of the east' a salutary lesson and, in particular, to deny Russian influence in the Balkans and warships in the Black Sea.

Caught up in the prevailing wave of Russophobia, Gordon itched to join his British Army comrades serving in the Crimea. His eldest brother, Henry, was already in action there with his infantry regiment, and the young Engineer subaltern lost no time in volunteering for service overseas. But here he was to discover for the first time in his life that the wheels of officialdom grind slowly. Weeks passed, lengthening into months, with no response to his application; and eventually he was driven to seek the intervention of an old friend of his family, Sir John Burgoyne, who was currently Inspector-General of Fortifications at the War Office. This produced the desired result and, in December 1854, Gordon finally received his orders to proceed immediately to the Crimea.

Such impatience to get into action seems natural enough in a young soldier at a moment when his country was at war. But although he does not appear to have said anything of it at the time, we know from letters which he wrote to a parson friend of his nearly thirty years later, as well as to his sister, that there was a deeper psychological impulse than youthful patriotism which drove him to join in this notoriously messy conflict. To quote his own words, 'I went to Crimea, hoping without having a hand in it to be killed.' And from his letters to his family from the battle-front, it was clear that, thanks to his new-found faith, he considered himself already 'prepared' for death. Certainly no one tried harder to get himself killed than young Lieutenant Gordon. Time and again he would expose himself quite unnecessarily to enemy fire, carrying out reconnaissances of the Russian fortifications, unarmed and without an escort, or supervising the digging of rifle-pits far in advance of the front-line trenches and only a few yards from the enemy's picket-lines. And, as his Crimean diary shows, his main, and almost only, complaint was for those periods, so inevitable in war, when 'we are at a standstill ... we are doing nothing'. For the sufferings of the allied armies he had little sympathy. He declined to receive any parcels of food or clothing from home, insisting that the officers had nothing to complain about, while the men had only themselves to blame if they endured privation, for they were quite unable to look after themselves. And he spoke with utter disdain of those officers who welcomed the periods of standstill, or in any way failed to share the hazards of war with their men.

Yet, despite his efforts to get himself killed, Gordon survived with only a flesh wound, which did not keep him out of action for more than ten days. He was present at the greater part of the Siege of Sebastopol and took part in the attack on the Redan and, when the Russians eventually withdrew after setting fire to Sebastopol—which he described as a splendid sight—he spent four months helping in the systematic demolition of Sebastopol's docks, in furtherance of Britain's determination to cripple Russian maritime supremacy in the Black Sea. In February 1856 the work of destruction was completed, and in the following month the Crimean War officially came to an end with the signing of the Treaty of Paris. Gordon received the British war medal with clasp, plus a medal from Britain's Turkish ally and the French

18

Legion of Honour—an ironic reward for one who had never concealed his contempt for the French Army, who talked a great deal, yet whose courage he found wanting by comparison with their Russian enemies. In addition, he was cited in the list of R.E. subalterns who had particularly distinguished themselves in action.

For a junior officer in those times it was not an unreasonable 'hand-out'. Yet he could not resist a scornful dig at the 'shower of decorations and promotions which fell upon senior officers'. 'What easily earned C.Bs. and majorities there have been in some cases,' he commented, while at the same time denying that he was ambitious for any personal recognition! Not for the last time in his life, Gordon was carping at the rewards bestowed upon his fellows while disclaiming, somewhat disingenuously, any feelings of personal jealousy. But if he resented the success of his living superiors, he could also be most charitable about the dead. Writing of the much-maligned Commander-in-Chief, Lord Raglan, who died in the Crimea, as Gordon put it, 'of tear and wear', he said that his death was 'universally regretted as he was so kind, although not a good Commander-in-Chief which we could not expect from his age'. And in a postscript which, for Gordon, spoke a volume of sympathy, he added, 'I hope he was prepared.'

Gordon stayed in the Crimea until May 1856, when he was posted to Bessarabia, on the borders of Russia and Rumania, to assist in delimiting the frontiers laid down by the Paris peace settlement. A year later he was sent to Erzerum in Turkey to do a similar job on the Armenian border. No doubt because he felt himself entitled to a spell of home leave, he asked to be excused from serving on the Armenian Frontier Commission. But his request was refused by the War Office and, although he managed to spend a few months with his family at the end of 1857, it was not until October in the following year that he was released to return home on the completion of his work on Turkey's Asian borders.

This experience of fifteen months in the wild highlands of Armenia and the Caucasus was to exercise an influence upon Gordon's life and tastes almost as great as that of the religious faith which he had found at Pembroke. Forced to live in tents, because the houses of even the local princes were to his mind unfit for human habitation, and surrounded by lawless tribes who owed allegiance to no official authority, he developed a taste for life in the wild, open spaces and an aversion to civilized habits and social conventions which he was never to lose. One sentence taken from a letter to his family shows how he had now begun to identify himself with those who dwelt outside the boundaries and disciplines of man-made laws and customs. Writing to say how deeply he admired, and 'trusted', the wild Kurdish tribesmen in these parts, he described them as 'lawless as ever, they go from Turkey to Russia and back again as they like; they are fine-looking people, armed to the teeth'. And this from an official member of the Armenian Frontier Commission whose job was to fix the posts that marked the very boundary which these Kurds held in such complete contempt!

Small wonder that, as he returned home after these experiences, he wrote to his parents to say, 'I do not feel at all inclined to settle in England and be employed in any sedentary way.' And it is no less surprising that in 1860—a year after he had been promoted to captain and appointed as Adjutant to the R.E. depot at Chatham—he volunteered to join the British force which was then being gathered together at Shanghai with the object of forcing the Chinese Emperor to ratify the Treaty of Tientsin. The lure of strange places and far-off, inhospitable lands which had started to attract him in Armenia was now to draw him still further afield. And although he could not have known it at a time when he was merely asking to join a British punitive expedition against Peking, his action was to involve him in far more adventurous engagements than forcing the hand of the Manchu Emperor.

In particular, it was to involve him as an active opponent of one of history's strangest rebellions—the Taiping revolt against the Manchu Dynasty, led by a former school-teacher, Hung Hsiu-chuan, a self-confessed convert to Christianity, who for fourteen years held the Yangtze River valley in thrall in an attempt to substitute himself for the Tartar Emperor and the Christian faith for the established Buddhist tradition. So little has been made in books about Gordon of the course which this extraordinary uprising took and of the successes it achieved long before Gordon arrived in China, that it has come to be regarded as a momentary affair which, when it threatened British persons and property in Shanghai, was promptly and effectively crushed by the so-called Ever Victorious Army under Gordon's leadership. So far is this interpretation from the truth that an account of the origins, aims, and initial triumphs of the Taiping revolt has been interposed in the following chapter, if only to get the record straight and to enable the student of Gordon's life to judge correctly and impartially his role in helping the Chinese Imperial armies to put an end to the pretentions of Hung Hsiu-chuan, which efforts won for the young Engineer captain nation-wide acclaim, plus the pseudonym of 'Chinese Gordon'.

China—Taiping Campaign

CHAPTER 3

THE TAIPING REVOLT

THE leader of the Taiping revolt, Hung Hsiu-chuan, was born in January 1814 near Canton in southern China, the son of a village headman of the Hung clan of the Hakka tribe. Twenty thousand strong, the Hakkas were a tall, tough, and independent mountain people who kept their own language and traditions, disdaining such customs as foot-binding for women. Hung, who was originally named Huo-hsin, or 'Fireflash', grew up fast in the Taoist tradition of Puritan reaction to Confucianism a gay, straightforward and quick-witted boy. And his father soon realized that he had produced a scholar for whose schooling money must somehow be saved, so that Hung might be educated to hold office under the Imperial régime, as had some eighty members of the Hung clan in days gone by. Some of these ancestors had been married to members of the Ming Dynasty, which ruled China until it was ousted in the seventeenth century by the Manchu Dynasty of Manchurian Tartars, and out of loyalty to their Ming relatives had frequently used their positions under the current régime to fan the embers of resistance to 'foreign' rule. For while the Manchus had on the whole become accepted in the north of China, they had never really won the support of the south, where a nostalgic sympathy for the old and a bitter hatred for the new régime smouldered on into the nineteenth century and found expression in a number of secret societies and petty rebellions.

There was indeed much to hate and rebel against in the Manchu régime. Corruption was rife at all levels of society. And, as Hung soon discovered, his quick wits and studious application were not enough to secure for him the necessary 'studentships'. Success in examinations required a bribe for the examiners. And although at the age of sixteen he took on the post of village schoolmaster to earn enough money for this purpose, taxation wiped out his savings, and he was forced to abandon the quest for government office.

This act of renunciation preyed on his mind to such an extent that he soon became gravely ill. The Taoist priest was summoned to recite prayers for his recovery, but to no avail. Delirious with fever, he began to dream the wildest dreams, in which he was borne on wings up to the 'Thirty-third Heaven', where he found himself face to face with the Venerable-in-Years, who girt him with a sword and ordered him to exterminate the demon-worshippers who had rebelled against God's rule on earth. Hung was then named Hsiu-chuan, 'the Accomplished and Perfected', and was led to the edge of a veranda which looked out on the world, where he saw revealed beneath him all the sins of men. A moment later he sank back to earth and awoke from his dream. But almost immediately he collapsed into another trance, where he found himself doing battle with demons and evil spirits, brandishing his sword on the battlements of the heavenly city, aided by a young man of friendly and noble countenance, who called himself the Son of God. And when all the demons had been killed or driven out, Hung found himself once more in the presence of the Venerable-in-Years, who told him to return to earth to serve His cause and to be of good courage, 'for you are My son'.

When Hung had recovered from his fever, a remarkable physical change came over him. No longer was he stooped as if permanently bowed down by the burden of study and long hours of teaching. Now he carried himself erect and with a new and noticeable dignity. He began to compose poetry, depicting himself as the hand and voice of God, newly sent to 'slay the depraved ... and to relieve the people's distress'. And, bolder still, he tried his hand at writing proclamations in red—the colour reserved for the use of the Emperor alone—which outlined 'the noble principles of the Heavenly King, Hung Hsiu-chuan'. Then as he began to ponder the problem of overthrowing the corrupt but all-powerful demons of the Manchu régime, a significant development occurred, which suggested that perhaps the Tartars were not so powerful after all. This was the outbreak of the Opium War between Britain and China, when a handful of British sailors and marines routed the Imperial Chinese Army and forced the Emperor to cede Hong Kong to Britain and allow European trading communities to be established in Shanghai and several other ports. It was a crushing blow to the prestige of a dynasty which for two centuries had denied the establishment of diplomatic relations with the European powers by insisting that any foreign envoy should 'kow-tow' to the Dragon Throne in recognition of China as the supreme power in the world. And Hung was duly and deeply impressed. If a small British force could pull off so easy a victory over the Manchus, how much more easily could a popular movement, united in faith and purpose, get rid of them altogether?

As he turned these possibilities over in his mind he came across a bundle of papers which had been handed to him by a bearded stranger on a recent visit to Canton, and which he had put away at the back of a bookshelf on returning to his village. The papers were a set of extracts from the Christian Bible, and their bearded distributor was a young Chinese convert to Christianity who worked for the London Missionary Society in Canton. Now, as Hung started to read the Book of Genesis, the memory of his celestial visitation took on a new significance. Here was the Venerable-in-Years revealed as the Creator of the universe. Here too was the true Shang-ti, the Supreme Ruler, to whom the Taoists had taught him to offer his kow-towing obeisance. To this simple-minded school-teacher, far from raising any conflict with the traditional dogmas on which he had been reared, this new doctrine explained as nothing had ever done before who it was who received the written prayers, which as a child he used to burn in the belief that they would ascend to Heaven and be heard by Shang-ti. Here from the pages of the Christian Bible God spoke in words almost identical to those which the Venerable-in-Years had used to address him: 'They have rebelled against me', 'I girded thee, though thou hast not known me', 'In chains shall they come over and ... they shall make supplication unto thee.' Here then was proof that he had been girt with a sword in order to act, according to the Scriptures, as 'a revenger to execute the wrath upon him that doeth evil', and 'to wrestle against principalities, against powers, against the rulers of the darkness in this world, against spiritual wickedness in high places'.

Curious to discover more of this exciting new faith, Hung went to Canton to visit the Baptist mission. But when he told the missionaries of his celestial visitations he was dismissed as a crank and denied any proper instruction. Left to his own untutored interpretations of Christianity, he evolved a curious theology which he tailored to win maximum popular support, and hence to serve his political designs against the régime. His version of the Holy Trinity consisted of God the Father, Christ the Son and Elder Brother, and Hung himself as the other son of God and Younger Brother of Christ. The New Testament became known as the 'Former Testament' and Hung's revelations became the 'New Testament'. The ritual of baptism omitted any mention of the Holy Ghost and included burning and sending aloft to Shang-ti a written confession of each candidate's sins, which were thereby 'washed away'; and in accordance with Taoist ritual all prayers were written down and then burned.

Such falsifications of Christian beliefs and practices were greatly to shock many Western missionaries in China. But Hung had no difficulty in selling his peculiar brand of religion to the simple villagers of southern China, whose rebellious nature made them ready converts to any faith that promised to lift the curse of poverty, extortion, and corruption from their brows. As with the Communist revolution of Mao Tse-tung after World War II, so with the rebellion of Hung Hsiu-chuan the wretched peasantry flocked to join the leader who vowed to liberate them from their wretchedness. Rejoicing in the discovery that they could safely discard their ancient superstitions and no longer had to pay their hard-earned savings to placate the evil spirits and to purchase peace and good health for their families, the new converts ranged far and wide, smashing the idols in the Confucian temples and cursing all established authority. Hung was their only ruler, the instrument appointed by God to work His vengeance on the hated Tartars and to withdraw the Heavenly Mandate from the usurpers of Manchuria who had seized the Dragon Throne.

An important element in this incipient rebellion was, as Hung knew very well, the long-standing sympathy of many southern Chinese for the Ming Dynasty. And if the movement he had started was to succeed in toppling the Manchus, it was imperative to co-ordinate action with the most powerful of the several secret societies then existing in China—the Triads, or Heaven and Earth Society, who were pledged to secure a Ming revival. To this end Hung went to Canton, where from the Triad leader, a lapsed Buddhist monk named Chu, he gathered the important intelligence that the Triads were planning an uprising in Kwangtung

Province in twelve months' time. He could not have hoped for better news. Now he would be able to come out in the open and to strike the Imperialists with a united force of Christian and Triad followers. Returning home to Kwangsi, he assembled an army of 10,000 over the next twelve months and equipped them with spears, halberds, a few ancient muskets and home-made bullets and gunpowder. Then when the Triads struck in July 1850, a group of his followers abducted Chu and brought him to Hung's headquarters in Kwangsi. The Triads were then told that their leader had joined forces with Hung, whereupon a large proportion of them hastened to join Chu, leaving only a token force to harass the Imperial armies in Kwangtung.

With Chu and the majority of his army in his own camp, Hung set about ensuring for himself the undisputed leadership of the combined revolutionary forces. His stratagem was to swear an oath of blood-brotherhood with the Triad Leader, which made him as acceptable to the partisans of the Ming Dynasty as if he had himself been born of the true blood. And since Chu, a weak creature whose greatness had been thrust upon him, was only too ready to defer to his stronger partner, whom he called 'Elder Brother', Hung was able to neutralize his only possible rival and to secure the undivided loyalty of the large mixed bag of armies now under his command. Henceforth he could appear as the son of God to his Christian followers and a scion of the Mings to the Triads. In short, he was all things to all his men. And, exploiting his undisputed leadership, he parcelled out the command posts in his army to those of his closest friends and relatives who had been his first converts and disciples. The army was divided into four commands—north, south, east, and west—and each commander was given the title of prince. His brother-in-law, Yang, was appointed eastern prince and senior commander, with a cousin named Feng as his deputy and southern prince. The northern prince was Wei, a wealthy landowner who had financed Hung's movement from the start, and the western command went to Hsiao Chou-kwei, another brother-in-law and a farmer in Kwangsi who had done sterling service in recruiting for Hung's cause.

Considering that the Imperialist garrisons in Kwangsi and Kwangtung numbered nearly 100,000 soldiers, the ease with which Hung was able to plan and carry out his rebellion seems

27

astonishing. But there was then no such thing as a standing army in China, nor was there any centralized command structure for the provincial garrisons. Also, despite their numbers and equipment, the morale of the Imperialists was low, corruption was rife among their leaders and, whenever a town was threatened by an insurrection, rather than defend themselves by force of arms, the civil authorities more usually bribed the insurgents to take themselves to the next town and, when the besiegers had departed, ingratiated themselves with the provincial viceroy by announcing a great victory for their armies. In his turn, the viceroy, to save himself the trouble of investigating such claims, would pass on the good news to Peking. And, since the size of China made it impossible for any central authority to impose itself in the provinces, no investigations would be made to check the veracity of these reports. Occasionally a rebellion would get out of hand and, after several months, news would filter through to the Emperor. Heads would then fall and new brooms would be despatched to sweep up the rebels. But the very severity of these ultimate sanctions only made the provincial authorities all the less inclined to anticipate trouble in the pious hope that the rebellion would die out and the danger pass.

This was certainly the case with Hung Hsiu-chuan. And in January 1851, with the stage set for revolt, he issued his first Order of the Day, an injunction to his troops to obey all orders, to observe the Ten Commandments, and to remember that all believers would be saved to enjoy honour in this world and everlasting happiness in the next. Then, at a court levee for his officers, he made his supreme gesture of defiance against the Manchus. Mounting a splendid throne and wearing the Dragon Robe of Imperial yellow satin embroidered with golden dragons and hung with the gold and lapis lazuli trimmings and trappings of the Emperor, he proclaimed himself the Tien Wang, or Heavenly King, and gave to his movement the title of Taiping Tien-kuo, or Heavenly Kingdom of Great Peace. And, telling his commanders to show the courage and ferocity of tigers, he ordered them to advance on Peking, there to usher in a new golden age for all of China. The civil war had started and Hung had burned all his boats. From now on it was to be war to the death and there could be no turning back. For he had committed the two crimes for which not even the Emperor could commute the mandatory death sentence—high treason and wearing the Imperial robe.

*   *   *

Since Hung's objective involved a march of over 2,000 miles, from one end of China to the other, his strategy clearly had to be one of rapid and constant movement. Any captured towns had to be abandoned as soon as the required stores of food, money, and arms had been requisitioned. Discipline, both military and spiritual, had also to be strictly enforced, not least because it was essential to avoid provoking the local population at each stage of the march. To this end, looting was prohibited on pain of death, as were also rape, prostitution, adultery, opium-smoking, and, of course, desertion. To keep his followers constantly in fear of divine vengeance, Hung proclaimed from time to time that God or Jesus Christ had descended from Heaven to speak to him. The strictest discipline was also kept in the routine training of the Taiping armies. After a long day of instruction in spear and sword-drill, boxing and musketry, there followed several hours of religious teaching. Failure to learn the Lord's Prayer and the Ten Commandments within three weeks of enlistment could result in the execution of the unfortunate recruit. And even when all this intensive training and instruction was over for the day, the Taiping soldier could not relax and enjoy a drink or a smoke or a flutter at some game of chance without risking a severe flogging with bamboo rods.

After the first eight months of the revolt had witnessed an unbroken succession of Taiping victories, the provincial authorities tried to offer terms for Hung's surrender. But he contemptuously declined to treat with them, claiming that the Heavenly Mandate had been withdrawn from the Manchus, who were 'descended from an insignificant nation of foreigners', and entrusted to him, the Tien Wang. Thus provoked, the Imperialists attempted stronger measures and for a while succeeded in bottling the rebels up in the city of Yungnan, where Hung lost 2,000 of his men, including the Triad leader, Chu, before he was able to break out. For the next six months the going was extremely tough, until in April 1852 the Taipings broke out of the mountain ranges of the south and began the long descent towards the great valley of the Yangtze River. Thereafter they could make use of the rivers that flowed conveniently northwards through the province of Hunan. But as they advanced by river towards Hunan's capital, Changsha, disaster struck when they were ambushed by Imperialist troops and Feng was killed. A few months later another 'prince'— Hsiao—was killed besieging Changsha, blown into fragments by the explosion of an antiquated artillery piece.

Nevertheless, undaunted by these losses, Hung pressed on towards the Yangtze valley, and in early December seized the city of Yiyang on the Tungting Lake, where he requisitioned a large fleet of boats and set out across the lake to Yochou. Without pausing for breath, the Taipings then careered on down the broad canal linking the lake with the Yangtze River and by mid-January had captured the Triple City of Hanyang, Wuchang, and Hankow, that great commercial centre and staging post for the trade that flowed down the Yangtze to the sea.

There was now no concealing the real danger of the Taiping rebellion to the Manchu Dynasty. This was no local brush-fire which would burn itself out in due course, but a real conflagration whose flames might soon be licking at the Dragon Throne itself. Nobody realized this better than the Empress Yehonala, who had graduated by means of a remarkable combination of beauty and brains from the status of a lowly concubine to be the Emperor's wife. And because she not only had a great influence over her husband, but also possessed a shrewd judgement of men, Yehonala prevailed upon the Emperor to appoint as virtual Commander-in-Chief of the Imperial Armies in Central China the man who, more than any other, was responsible for ultimately destroying the Taiping rebellion and saving the Manchu Dynasty.

Tseng Kuo-fan, a former minister in the Imperial Government, was then living in retirement on his estates in Hunan. A scholarly Chinese with no Tartar blood, he accepted the Manchus with resignation, taking comfort from the fact that these 'foreigners' from Manchuria had become converted to Chinese customs and traditions. As a believer in Confucianism, he had no use for the so-called Christian Taipings, and when Hung's armies invaded his native province he formed a private militia to resist the rebels and equipped it with a fleet of river-boats for greater mobility. His commanding personality and unimpeachable integrity soon overcame the inherent reluctance of the Chinese peasantry to accept any form of military service, and within a short time he had gathered together, under the title of the Hunan Braves, an army superior in morale and fighting skill to any of the regular Imperial garrisons.

At this point Hung changed his entire strategy and decided to make Nanking his capital city and to limit his operations against Peking to a kind of punitive expedition. Turning eastwards, he headed down the Yangtze valley towards the sea, and two months later came within sight of the massive red sandstone walls of his objective. Nanking's civic leaders promptly took to their heels and, with the aid of a well-placed mine to blow a large breach in the ramparts, the Taipings took possession of the city in the name of the Heavenly Kingdom of Great Peace, celebrating their triumph with a massacre of Nanking's defenders on a scale so great that the corpses thrown into the Yangtze blocked the passage of the ceremonial Dragon Boat which brought the Tien Wang to claim his newest conquest. Then, two months after his success, Hung despatched a force to take Peking. Setting out on May 12, 1853, the Taipings headed northwards at breakneck speed and had covered nearly half the distance to Peking within five weeks. But they soon overreached themselves, and when the Emperor summoned up reinforcements from Mongolia they were caught between a Mongol army and an Imperialist force 150 miles south of the Manchu capital. Due to over-confidence, Hung had miscalculated badly the extent to which the Manchus would fight to save themselves. And with no Taiping army in reserve to draw the fire of the encircling Mongols and Imperialists, his men were cut to pieces.

The Taiping threat to Peking was removed, never to be remounted. But in the meanwhile Hung was pressing onwards east of Nanking. Chinkiang at the mouth of the Yangtze had fallen to one of his Triad commanders and great alarm had been caused in Shanghai among the Chinese population and the European community, who had heard with horror of the Nanking massacres. To calm this atmosphere of trepidation, the British Governor of Hong Kong, Sir George Bonham, decided to pay a visit to Taiping headquarters, partly to see for himself what type of people these strange Christian rebels were and partly to make it clear to them that Britain would only take sides against them if her subjects were themselves attacked. But his observations were anything but reassuring. He was not received by the Tien Wang and, in response to his assurances of British neutrality, he was handed a written communication which claimed for the Taipings the right to control and regulate British trade with China and suggested that Britain should 'achieve the merit of diligently serving our Sovereign'. Bonham duly retorted that he could not accept that 'the English are subordinate to your Sovereign', reminded the Taipings that Britain traded in China by right of a treaty with the Imperial government, and threatened that, if British subjects or property were attacked, Britain would seize Nanking. But, oblivious to European reactions, Hung repeated his claims when Bonham's mission was followed up by representatives of France and the U.S.A.

No doubt Hung felt he could afford to strike such a haughty attitude. For soon afterwards a force of his Triad allies seized the treaty port of Amoy and, more spectacular still, another group of Triads captured Shanghai in September 1853. Amoy was retaken by the Imperialists after five months; but in Shanghai the Triads resisted a Manchu siege for fifteen months. And it was not until December 1854, when French naval units lying offshore were provoked into joining the Imperialists by the Triads' refusal to remove a gun emplacement threatening the French compound, that the rebels were finally blasted into submission. Nevertheless, the Taipings made a grave mistake in antagonizing the representatives of the Christian West. Admittedly, many Europeans and Americans dismissed the Tien Wang as a brutal blasphemer and revolutionary, whose Christian professions were a blind to secure Western help to overthrow the Manchus. But there were also a number of Western missionaries, plus some officials, who felt that the Taipings might, 'if more perfectly instructed, become the pioneers of the pure gospel of Christ, or, if neglected, degenerate into the most ignorant of mere fanatics and iconoclasts'. And Hung's arrogance only served to alienate such potential sympathizers and to hasten the day when Britain, France, and America would cast aside the cloak of neutrality and commission Charles Gordon to help the Emperor's armies to destroy the Taiping rebels.

By the beginning of 1855 a stalemate had been reached between the rebels and the Imperialists. Tseng had retaken the Triple City in the previous autumn but, try as he might, he could not dislodge the Taipings along the middle reaches of the Yangtze, still less from their capital and stronghold of Nanking. And Hung, having failed to capture Peking and lost Hankow and Shanghai, had adopted a largely defensive strategy. As for the foreign powers, Britain's interests seemed to lie with the Imperialists; but the Crimean War had decided her against getting involved in any Far Eastern imbroglio for the time being, and she had declared a policy of strict neutrality in China's civil war. America and France had followed suit.

It was the lull before the storm; but the storm when it finally broke took a totally unexpected form. In September 1856, in a mad orgy of internecine conspiracy and vengeance, the Taiping movement succeeded in dismembering itself when first its Commander-in-Chief, Yang, and then the northern prince, Wei, were put to death for treason. The rot was started by Wei, who had long been intriguing to replace Yang as head of the Taiping armies and to become the power behind the Heavenly Throne. Wei used the lull to pour his poison into the Tien Wang's ears, suggesting that Yang was plotting to displace him and win the throne for himself. Hung proved a ready listener, for Yang had recently humiliated him by publicly reproving him in the name of Shang-ti for alleged harshness to his wives. At the same time Wei sought to provoke Yang by suggesting that the Heavenly King had been less than generous in rewarding his triumphs in the field. Goaded by Wei, Yang was persuaded to demand from Hung the title of 'Immortality', which by ancient tradition belonged to the Emperor alone. Stunned by this apparent confirmation of Wei's tales, Hung sent for Wei, who subtly suggested that, since most of the Tien Wang's troops were then out of the capital on various campaign duties, Hung should play for time and grant his brother-in-law's demand. With a deep sense of humiliation, Hung accepted the advice, went to Yang's palace, and there publicly conferred on him the Emperor's traditional title. But, as Wei had planned, he secretly nursed an irremovable grudge and, when Wei informed him that enough of his troops had returned to Nanking, he willingly agreed to Yang being put to death. The Commander-in-Chief was then invited to Wei's palace and there murdered by his guards.

Now Wei revealed his true colours and, disregarding Hung's order that only Yang should suffer for his treasonable presumption, ordered his soldiers to carry out a systematic massacre of all Yang's relatives and adherents, including his wife, Hung's own sister. Several thousand people are said to have perished by this butchery, including many of the finest soldiers of the Taiping armies. But Hung was temporarily powerless to stop the massacre. With Wei in command, he was virtually a prisoner in his own palace, the only troops in Nanking being those of Wei's army. Indeed, had it not been for the courage and loyalty of a Taiping general, Shih Ta-kai, who volunteered to escape from Nanking and summon help, Hung might himself have met the same end as Yang. In the nick of time, Shih Ta-kai returned with forces adequate to overthrow the treacherous Wei. The populace now turned upon the usurper and Wei was done to death.

In a few weeks of crazy savagery the Taiping movement had lost its two ablest generals, together with several thousands of its best troops. Of the four original princes of the north, east, west, and south, none now remained. Feng and Hsiao had been killed in action, Yang and Wei had destroyed each other. The Taipings had written their own death warrant in the blood of their best commanders and nothing would ever be the same with the Heavenly Kingdom of Hung Hsiu-chuan.

*   *   *

Within a few days of the final act of this bloody drama, the wheel of Fate began to turn in a succession of episodes which were ultimately to spell doom and disaster for the Tien Wang. The first of these episodes arose out of a personal clash between the British Consul in Canton, Harry Parkes, and the Chinese Viceroy, a brutal Manchu potentate, named Yeh, who boasted of having executed some 70,000 'rebels' as a reprisal for the Triad rising in Kwangtung. A ship flying the British flag was arrested by the Canton authorities on suspicion of smuggling opium. Parkes, a determined imperialist of the old school, seized upon the incident to get his own back for a host of petty harassments which he and the European traders of Canton had suffered at Yeh's hands. The Crimean War was now over and Britain no longer felt the same inhibitions about getting involved in China; hence, when the Chinese authorities rejected Parkes' ultimatum demanding satisfaction for the arrest and an end to the restrictions on foreigners, he was able to summon British naval forces from Hong Kong to bombard Canton. Thereupon Yeh, who was as determined a fighter as Parkes, responded with threats against the lives of the European residents. And, since the Consul had neither the authority nor the troops to take any stronger action, the issue lay in abeyance for several months until the arrival in September 1857 of Lord Elgin, the son of the collector of the 'Elgin Marbles', in the capacity of a special ambassador, supported by a force of Indian and French troops and equipped with full powers to bring the Chinese to heel. Elgin repeated Parkes' ultimatum and, when Yeh renewed his threat to the Europeans, ordered a bombardment lasting for more than twenty-four hours and then sent in his troops. Yeh was seized and Canton was taken under Allied military occupation.

The news of this British action caused great rejoicing in Hung's capital. At last, it seemed to the Tien Wang, the British and French had decided to cast their lot with their Chinese co-religionists against the idolatrous Tartars. But the Taipings' joy was short-lived. Six months after taking Canton, Elgin went on to Tientsin and, under the threatening muzzles of British and French naval guns, persuaded the Manchu Emperor's plenipotentiaries to sign a treaty of peace and friendship, under which the European powers received the right to trade upon the Yangtze River as far as Hankow as soon as the peace presently 'disturbed by outlaws . . . shall have been restored'.

It was a bitter blow for Hung. Gone now was all hope of an alliance with the British and French, whose interests lay explicitly in restoring peace along the Yangtze in favour of the Manchus. To make matters worse, Tseng had received reinforcements from the south and his Imperialist forces were closing in on Nanking. Desperately Hung sought to retrieve his position by inviting Elgin to his court at Nanking. Elgin refused for himself and sent a deputation from his staff. But the visit proved no less harmful for the Taiping cause than the previous visits of Western officials; and the general impression left on Elgin's staff was that the Taipings were no more than pirates, and that the sooner they were dispossessed of their Yangtze conquests the better it would be for Britain and all civilized nations.

The British had made up their minds to have no dealings with the Taipings. But they were soon to discover that their new-found 'friendship' with the Manchus was not going to be all plain sailing. Almost exactly a year after the signature of the Tientsin Treaty, Elgin's brother, Sir Frederick Bruce, and the French Minister were ambushed by Imperialist forces while on their way to Peking to secure the Emperor's ratification of the Treaty. Three British gunboats and several hundred men were lost under a murderous point-blank fire directed by the Chinese from the Taku forts at the mouth of the river route to Peking; and the rest of the allied fleet withdrew to Shanghai, taking Bruce and his French colleague with them.

Such treachery could not be allowed to go unpunished, and Britain and France duly set about preparing yet another punitive expedition, which was this time to march on Peking and teach the Manchu Emperor a lesson in international good manners. After a long delay, the expedition, consisting of 12,000 British and 6,000 French troops, led by Elgin himself, set out for Peking in July 1860. The Taku forts were taken after a stiff fight, and when the Allies reached Tientsin at the end of August the Manchu commander, seeing that he was outgunned, offered a truce. But when Elgin's emissaries reached the meeting-place they were seized, together with their escort of Sikh infantry, and carted off to prison in Peking. Elgin promptly ordered an advance on the Manchu capital, whereupon the Emperor fled; and on October 6 the Anglo-French force took Peking and occupied the great Summer Palace of the Manchus.

When Elgin's troops arrived, four of the captured emissaries were found to have been done to death by torture. To Elgin's mind, such a crime demanded a punishment which would serve as a permanent reminder that war still had some rules that could not be broken. Declining to punish innocent Chinese citizens by such devices as levying a fine on the population of Peking, he struck at the Emperor himself and ordered that the Summer Palace should be burned to the ground. And after this great Manchu monument had been reduced to a smoking pile of rubble, he demanded and obtained the official ratification of the Tientsin Treaty.

Meanwhile, in Nanking hope of securing Western support had dwindled almost to vanishing point. Suffocated by the blockade that Tseng Kuo-fan's troops had thrown around their capital, the Taipings had broken out in the early spring of 1860 in a desperate effort to recapture Shanghai, and had taken Soochow, some fifty miles inland from Shanghai. The break-out was commanded by Li Siu-cheng, otherwise known as the Faithful Prince, who became Hung's effective Commander-in-Chief after the blood-bath of Nanking. A different type altogether from the ferocious Yang and the treacherous Wei, the Faithful Prince not only spared the lives of Soochow's defenders, but provided the civic and military chiefs of the city with funds and transport to return to their homes in Manchu territory. And as he advanced towards Shanghai, swallowing up Quinsan, Taitsan and Kahding as he went, he treated their populations with similar leniency. Like-wise, when he arrived outside the walls of the city, he asked for a truce to discuss the situation with Bruce and other Western representatives. But Bruce had made up his mind that there could be no parley with the Taipings, and the only response was a hail of heavy artillery fire from British and French guns.

Now, convinced that there was no hope of talking the Euro-peans into any arrangement, nor of capturing Shanghai against such superior fire-power, the Faithful Prince withdrew, but not before he had sent Bruce a threatening letter, telling him that if he continued to side with the Imperialists, he must expect inter-ference with British trade along the Yangtze River. Now more than ever convinced that British and Taiping interests were irreconcilable, Bruce despatched a delegation, headed by Harry Parkes and supported by a naval escort, to demand an under-taking from the Taipings not to threaten Shanghai. Hung's ministers duly agreed, although they limited the guarantee to a period of twelve months. They were also forced to permit a British gunboat to be stationed off Nanking, ostensibly to mark the navigable channel for trading ships, but in reality to prevent gun-running for the Taipings. Parkes then went even further and, proceeding upstream to Hankow, delivered a severe warning to the Taiping commander that any attempt to retake the Triple City would incur Britain's grave displeasure and possible sanc-tions.

How much effect these threats had on the Taipings' resolution at this stage is impossible to assess. But shortly afterwards, on the death of the Emperor in August 1861, a *coup d'état* in Peking placed in power the widowed Empress Yehonala, whose first act was to promote Tseng to be Commander-in-Chief of all the Imperialist armies. Tseng was henceforth able to bring all necessary reinforcements to bear to drive the Taipings back down the Yangtze and bottle them up in the Nanking area. There he planned to make use of the British and their allies by pushing the rebels eastwards in the direction of Shanghai, which manoeuvre could not fail to arouse the European powers in defence of their interests. Not only were British and French troops now stationed in Shanghai, but the Shanghai merchants had recently financed the creation of a corps of Chinese mercenaries under an American soldier of fortune, Frederick Townsend Ward, which was later to be known as the Ever Victorious Army and to be commanded by Charles Gordon. And it was Tseng's hope that the Europeans would be goaded by the proximity of the Taiping threat into lending the Imperialists active military aid, and so providing the eastern lever of the nutcracker with which he planned finally to crush the rebellion.

Tseng's plan was put into operation in September, and before the end of the year 1861 he could afford to congratulate himself on its success. Beaten back from the Triple City, the Taipings lost Anking and, falling straight into the trap, lunged eastwards to seize Hangchow and Ningpo. The latter was a treaty port with important European trading interests only 100 miles south of Shanghai and, as Tseng anticipated, it was not long before a British warship moved in to help to recapture it. Better still, the Faithful Prince, from his battle headquarters in Soochow, made no secret of his plans to attack Shanghai when the twelve months' truce expired in February 1862.

The effect of these threats on the Chinese and European population of Shanghai was electric. The British authorities announced that, while remaining neutral in the broader conflict between the Manchus and Taipings, they would defend to the death any place within a thirty-mile radius of Shanghai. But the Taipings were now much too desperate to heed such warnings, and at the end of January 1862 the Faithful Prince advanced from Soochow across the thirty-mile perimeter to within fourteen miles of the city. They were immediately engaged by Ward's mercenaries, and as they cut their way through to Shanghai, British, French, and Imperialist forces joined in the fight. The Taiping advance was halted, and four months later the Faithful Prince was ordered to withdraw and return to Nanking. Tseng had by now mopped up the whole Yangtze valley to the west and the Tien Wang was closely besieged by an overwhelmingly superior Imperialist army. Morale was dangerously low and the Taipings were going over to the Imperialists in large numbers. General Ching, one of their best commanders, had deserted and become deputy commander to Li Hung-chang, Governor of Kiangsu Province and commander of the Imperial forces in the east.

Moreover, the Faithful Prince's return to Nanking brought no relief to Hung, and his efforts to break Tseng's stranglehold throughout the rest of the year were in vain. When direct assaults had failed, in a forlorn attempt to lure the besiegers away from his capital, he ordered a feint advance in the direction of Peking. But Tseng was not to be drawn by such stratagems. His plans were working out well and the bell was tolling for the Taipings. All that was now needed was for the Europeans to close in on the east and squeeze the nutcracker tight around Nanking. And as the year 1863 dawned, this was what Captain Charles Gordon was about to do.

CHAPTER 4

THE EVER VICTORIOUS ARMY

GORDON had reached Shanghai from England on September 17, 1860—rather late, he feared, 'for the amusements'. But he was still in time to join up with Elgin's expedition a few days after it had occupied Tientsin. And it fell to him to direct the work of burning the Summer Palace. Although never a great amateur of works of art, the destruction of such priceless treasures upset him profoundly. For he had been greatly surprised to find in a Tartar Emperor's mansion 'as much splendour and civilization as you would see at Windsor'. Still, he was also sufficiently incensed by the murder of defenceless hostages to fall in with the prevailing view among Elgin's officers that this singular act of vandalism was just punishment for such barbaric behaviour.

When the Anglo-French expedition withdrew after the Emperor's brother had agreed to Elgin's terms, 3,000 British troops were left behind at Tientsin, to ensure payment of the Chinese indemnity. The force was commanded by General Staveley, Elgin's military commander, whose sister had married Gordon's eldest brother, Henry. Gordon was attached to this force as Senior Engineer in charge of constructional work. Here he kept himself busy conducting surveys of the country around Tientsin and riding prodigious distances on horseback—seventy-two miles to Taku and back was nothing to this astonishingly tough and energetic young soldier. He also explored up to the Great Wall of China, an area never before traversed by Europeans, to find out whether there were any passes through this mountainous region by which Russia might attack China. Although the work was hard, he thrived on it, and wrote regularly to his mother to reassure her that the climate was excellent, and that he was in good health and happy to be largely his own master. He got on well with his seniors, including Staveley, although he thought him 'an essentially selfish man', who 'looks after No. 1'. And in March 1862 he wrote home to say: 'I am settled here for another year in all probability and cannot say I regret it. The climate, work and everything suits me and I am ... happy both in mind and body.'

In fact, he only stayed a few more weeks. During that time the Taipings launched their second attack on Shanghai. And General Staveley, who had been promoted meanwhile to C.-in-C. British troops in China, decided that he must spare some of the Tientsin force to strengthen the city's garrison, which consisted only of 1,000 Indian troops, a similar number of French, a small naval squadron and half a battery of artillery. Two regiments of infantry were therefore sent down with a group of Engineers under Gordon, who arrived in Shanghai in May 1862.

By this time the Faithful Prince's thrust in the east had been halted. And, since the Western powers' official neutrality did not permit British or French troops to operate outside the thirty-mile radius, Gordon's energies were mainly devoted to constructing new defences for Shanghai. For several months the nearest he got to seeing any real action was when a week after his return from the north, he conducted a survey, under enemy fire, of the town of Tsingpo on the western boundary of the thirty-mile perimeter. Thanks to his close personal observations, which he committed to his ever-ready sketch-book, he knew exactly where the weak points in the town's defences were, how many boats would be required to bridge the surrounding creek and how far the attacking force would have to charge across open ground to storm the breach that would be made by their supporting artillery. And the information which he was able to pass on to General Staveley was instrumental in securing the fall of Tsingpo with a minimum of effort by British arms.

But his passive role was not to last for very long. Five months after Gordon came to Shanghai, Ward, the Ever Victorious Army's commander, was killed leading his men in pursuit of the Taipings retreating southwards from Tsingpo. The command of the force devolved upon Ward's deputy, a man of partly American and partly French origins, H. A. Burgevine. If Ward was an adventurer, Burgevine was a blackguard who, before the Ever Victorious Army was formed, had sold arms to the Taiping rebels. He was also quite callous about human life, and after capturing Kahding, on the northern edge of the Shanghai perimeter, celebrated his promotion by allowing his troops not only to loot their fill, but also to kill their Taiping prisoners by blowing them out of guns. These atrocities profoundly shocked General Staveley and other Western officials, and when the story figured in such newspapers as the *Times of India*, a public outcry was caused.

Inexorably the finger now began to point towards Gordon as the only possible successor to Ward. Except for an American, Colonel Forrester, who had returned home after Ward's death, all of the Ever Victorious officers were out for personal gain. Added to this, both the British Consul in Shanghai and General Staveley favoured the appointment of a British Army officer, and the commander of the Imperialist forces in the area, Li Hung-chang, saw in the nomination of a British successor to Ward an opportunity to involve the British in fighting for the Manchu cause. Both he and Tseng had received offers of troops from Russia, but neither of them would risk accepting such help from a nation that had too often shown itself greedy for Chinese territory. Russian troops could all too easily become a deadly 'fifth column' in the event that Russia decided to take a bite at Manchuria or Mongolia. But the British were an altogether different bet, for they seemed only interested in trade, and the sooner the Taipings were finished off the more trade they would be able to do with China. Besides, Britain had the best armaments, and if a British officer were to command a force that was subject to Chinese authority—the Ever Victorious Army was nominally under Li's overall command— then the British would have a greater interest in supplying him and the Chinese Imperial armies with the best modern equipment.

But there was a diplomatic problem to be overcome. As a corollary to the official British policy of neutrality in China's civil war, the British Government had ordained that no officer in the Queen's service could serve the Manchu Emperor. Bruce—now British Minister at Peking—had stretched the neutrality policy a long way because he was convinced that the Taipings could never establish a real and proper administration in China. But it might be stretching it too far for Ward's force to be taken over by a Britisher. Still, there really was no suitable alternative to Gordon and, rather than risk the Ever Victorious Army disintegrating and possibly deserting to the Taipings for lack of an effective leader, Bruce was prepared to recommend to London the appointment of a British commander at least as a provisional step. Besides, he saw the strength of Staveley's contention that

Ward's force might ultimately be used to Britain's long-term advantage. Although the Chinese had mobilized a very large number of men to fight under Tseng Kuo-fan against the Taipings, there was still no provision for a regular national army, a lacuna which could prove a serious threat to the growing commercial interests of Britain in China. The Taipings would probably soon be crushed, but who could tell when some other rebellion might not arise and, in the absence of any regular Chinese force, seize the treaty ports and the Yangtze valley and throw the British out of China? Staveley therefore felt that the Ever Victorious Army, especially if commanded by a British officer, might help to provide the nucleus from which a regular national army could be created after the Taipings had been finished off.

The weighing of these arguments and counter-arguments inevitably took some time. And after waiting for several weeks, Li, whose determination to secure a British commander was matched by his growing dislike and distrust of Burgevine, decided to force the issue and remove the blackguard from his position of temporary authority. Like a true mandarin, he went to work to destroy his enemy. First, he ordered Burgevine to march his army to the Nanking area. And when, as he had anticipated, Burgevine refused to move so far from his base, he arranged with the bank from which the Ever Victorious Army was paid to withhold payments for a while. Walking straight into the trap, Burgevine lost his temper and with an escort of roughs marched to the bank, assaulted the banker and seized the cash. He was instantly dismissed. A short while later, in January 1863, the British Government responded to the arguments of Bruce and Staveley and announced that British officers could be seconded for service with the Manchu Emperor. The way was now open for Gordon to take command of the Ever Victorious Army. Li had achieved his purpose and, to make sure that Gordon would be more than merely theoretically under his orders, he insisted on a Chinese officer serving as a joint commander of the force, which would henceforth be paid by him as Provincial Governor and no longer by the Shanghai merchants. In return for these concessions to his authority, he agreed that the force would not operate beyond the thirty-mile perimeter without the express approval of the British and French authorities in Shanghai.

Gordon's reaction to this strange and challenging appointment was typical of his pernickety sense of duty. At the time he was engaged on a survey of the terrain within the Shanghai perimeter, and on learning that he had been selected, he refused to take up his new post until he had finished his survey. Not that he was unenthusiastic about his appointment. On the contrary, he was itching for action, and confided to a young officer with whom he shared rooms that he anxiously hoped for Ward's command. But his meticulous attention to detail told him that he must familiarize himself with every acre and every town and village in the area in which he was going to fight.

Pending Gordon's arrival, another British officer, Captain Holland, who had served under Burgevine in the capture of Kahding, was placed in temporary command of Ward's force. But when Holland led his men against the fortified town of Taitsan, to the north-east of Kahding, he met with a costly defeat, due to poor staff work, faulty intelligence and lack of ammunition. The reverse took a serious toll, not only of lives, but also of morale. Burgevine's dismissal had given rise to much discontent in the Ever Victorious Army. The officers feared that with a British regular soldier in command they would be replaced, and the men suspected—rightly as it turned out—that they would be placed under strict discipline and forbidden to loot. The Taitsan defeat had aggravated an already dangerous situation, and there was a possibility that it might lead to mass desertions. Staveley therefore dismissed Holland forthwith; and on March 26, 1863, Gordon, now promoted to Brevet-Major, assumed command of the Ever Victorious Army and became, as he wrote to his mother, 'now a mandarin'.

Gordon immediately set about trying to transform this relatively undisciplined force of mercenaries into a small professional army. How much success he achieved in this direction is debatable. Certainly they soon looked to be a better organized force. But, although Gordon used to the full his qualities of personal leadership and reckless courage, he had to suppress two mutinous revolts and lost over one-half of his force from desertions before final victory was won.

At this point, the Ever Victorious Army consisted of around 3,500 men divided between five and six regiments and two batteries of field and four of siege artillery. For small arms, they were mostly equipped with smooth-bore muskets, although a few had

44

British Enfield rifles. The officers—Americans, Germans, Spaniards, Frenchmen, Scandinavians, and a few Britishers—were, according to Gordon, 'reliable in action ... [but] troublesome in garrison and touchy to a degree about precedence'. The artillery officers, and men too, were 'by far superior to any other arm of the force', possibly because they got between 10 and 20 per cent. more money than the infantry. As was to be expected in an army of mercenaries, pay was by current standards excellent. From the inception of the force, all recruits had been offered more pay than any other contemporary army and twice as much as the Chinese Imperial forces. Otherwise it would have been impossible to persuade any Chinese to serve under European officers and to expose themselves to public mockery as 'foreign devils' for wearing an alien uniform—brown tunics and green turbans.

Nevertheless, military discipline and training had always been extremely lax: during harvest-time many of the men returned to their villages, leaving their regiments dangerously under strength. Nor was there any proper control over the force's deployment by the Chinese authorities. A system of bonus payments for every town or city captured by the force put the Imperialists at the helpless disadvantage of having to haggle over the exact amount every time the Ever Victorious Army was due to go into action. At the same time, the Shanghai merchants were not always very prompt in paying the force, and officers and men had been allowed to make up for the lack of regular pay with whatever plunder, especially of opium, gold, and girls, that they could lay their hands on.

Gordon made it clear from the outset that all this was to be changed. All ranks would have to undergo proper training and regular drill. The bonus system would cease and the force would take its orders from Governor Li and General Staveley. Prompt and regular payments would be made in future from the Chinese Imperial Treasury, and looting would be strictly forbidden. Trading in opium and women would be stopped forthwith, and the penalty for desertion or drunkenness in action was death. Ward's former officers were told that they would be kept on if they behaved themselves, but that any indiscipline or inefficiency on their part would be punished by instant dismissal. Wenching in between military operations was tolerated, for Gordon knew well enough that neither officers nor men would submit to the fullest rigours of his Puritanical ideas. But to demonstrate his disapproval of these licentious ways, he lived and ate apart from his officers and troops, except when actually engaging the enemy.

Gordon also devoted much time and energy to revising the tactics of the Ever Victorious Army, and introduced a new approach to the problem of mobility. His survey work had taught him to use boats to traverse the network of canals and waterways in this part of China, instead of marching in single file along the narrow paths that lined the rice-fields. Roads were then non-existent, and, apart from slowing down the rate of march, these paths, often knee-deep in mud, did not permit the passage of artillery and so reduced the fire-power of an advancing army. Gordon therefore collected a flotilla of gunboats and river steamers, among which was the *Hyson,* which had rendered sterling service in the capture of Tsingpo. The steamers, each equipped with a 32-pounder gun and a 2·8-inch howitzer and commanded by American captains chosen for their experience of river navigation in the United States, were powerful enough to strike terror in the hearts of the rebels, and manoeuvrable enough to use their paddle-wheels like the caterpillar tracks of a modern tank to drag themselves along the canal bottoms when the water was too shallow for them to float. And the smaller gunboats could take advantage of the high canal banks to ferry large numbers of troops to within a short distance of their objective unseen by the enemy's observation posts.

Helped by this new mobility and the superior fire-power of his flotilla, Gordon felt sufficiently confident to assure Li that he could crush the Taipings in his theatre of operations within eighteen months. According to his intelligence reports, the local population was becoming convinced that the Imperialists were now on top and, although Taiping atrocities and terror tactics were neither as frequent nor as frightful as the vengeance of the Manchu armies, popular feeling was becoming increasingly ready to condemn cruelties practised by the likely losers and to condone the atrocities of those who seemed to be winning the struggle. And, in the hope of further impressing public opinion, Gordon gave orders that no prisoners taken by his troops were to be executed, as had frequently happened in the past, and that all captured Taipings were to be encouraged to serve in the Ever Victorious Army.

Li was much impressed and not a little relieved by the apparent improvements wrought by Gordon's new régime. Though a confirmed zenophobe, after his first contact with his new commander he was constrained to write in his diary that he found him 'a direct blessing from Heaven.... He is superior in manner and bearing to any of the foreigners I have come into contact with and does not show outwardly that conceit which makes most of them repugnant in my sight.' And in token of this new-found confidence he straight away ordered the Ever Victorious Army to undertake an expedition to relieve the town of Chanzu on the Yangtze estuary, which was then resisting a fierce Taiping siege. The 8,000-strong garrison had formerly been part of the Tien Wang's forces, but had recently changed sides and delivered Chanzu into the hands of the Imperialists, thereby blocking one of the few remaining supply lines for running guns and ammunition up to Soochow. The Faithful Prince, on his return to the Yangtze theatre from the north, had heard of their defection, and had promptly despatched a force to Chanzu to teach these deserters a savage lesson in loyalty, and to wrest this strategically important town back from the Manchus.

Early in April Gordon's steamers arrived at the mouth of Fushan Creek, a narrow waterway connecting Chanzu with the Yangtze estuary. Penetrating up the creek, the Ever Victorious Army met with brief opposition from some of the beleaguering force, but a few blasts from one of the steamer's guns soon silenced the Taipings' fire and, as the relieving force pressed on up to Chanzu, the besiegers withdrew without offering any further resistance. It was Gordon's first victory, and an easy one at that, which did not reflect any particular credit or discredit upon either winners or losers. But it served to raise morale in the Ever Victorious Army; it proved that one 'fire-ship', as the Chinese called Gordon's armed steamers, was the equivalent of 3,000 troops equipped as the Taiping armies were; and it earned for Gordon himself the Order of the Yellow Button as a token of the Imperial Government's appreciation of his prompt and successful action.

But no sooner had Gordon received his decoration than a curious episode occurred which threatened to bring about his removal from the Ever Victorious Army. Burgevine had not taken his dismissal lying down and had hastened to Peking, where he appealed to the British and American Ministers to persuade the Prime Minister, Prince Kung, to reinstate him. Bruce and his American colleague were completely taken in by Burgevine. Convinced that he had been ill-used and to establish 'the principle that a foreigner who does his duty by this government shall not be thrown over by it at a moment's notice without sufficient cause', they requested Prince Kung to order Li to reinstate the American. But Li was not the kind of man who would tamely accept the countermanding of his orders and appointments. Claiming his rightful measure of autonomy under the Chinese system, he adamantly refused Prince Kung's request. Burgevine had proved his demerit and Gordon had proved his merit, and Li was not going to let any government—Chinese, British, or American—tell him who should command his troops. For good measure he promoted his English commander to the rank of a General of Division in the Chinese Army.

There was nothing more to be said. But the episode had considerably nettled Gordon, whose reaction foretold that he was never going to find it easy to rise above any threat to his position or dignity. For on the very day that Li informed him that Burgevine would not be reinstated under any circumstances and that he had the fullest confidence in his new commander, Gordon wrote to the Secretary of the British Legation in Peking to say: 'I must distinctly decline any further doings with any Chinese forces.' However, after further reassurances from Li, he changed his mind, and a few weeks after his victory at Chanzu he was on the move again. This time he was ordered to march on Taitsan, where the Imperialists had just suffered an unexpected reverse. Thinking he had reached an agreement with the Taiping commander in Taitsan, who had offered to desert with his garrison, Li sent a force to take over the town. But as they entered Taitsan they were furiously attacked and lost thirty killed and 300 prisoners.

Immediately Li turned to the Ever Victorious Army to avenge this treachery. Gordon promptly mustered his full force—3,000 men with supporting artillery transported in sixty small gunboats, each armed with a 9- or 12-pounder gun and supported by the paddle-steamer *Hyson* with a 32-pounder in the bow and a 12-pounder in the stern—and headed for Taitsan. On May 1 the Ever Victorious Army's artillery, supported by the *Hyson*'s 32-

pounder, opened up a murderous fire on the stockades outside Taitsan, as a prelude to what was to be the fiercest battle of Gordon's campaign. The Taiping garrison knew that they were held to be guilty of treachery by the Imperialists and could expect no quarter if they surrendered. And since Gordon quickly surrounded the town and blocked all but the eastern exit, which led towards the sea, escape would be a fruitless undertaking. For the Taipings therefore there was no alternative to fighting it out, despite the superior fire-power of their attackers.

Gordon's plan was to move his guns steadily closer to the walls and, when a breach was made, to rush his infantry forward in their gunboats and through the breach. The guns did their work well and after three hours' bombardment a gaping hole had been torn in the ramparts. But as the infantry poured from their boats into the breach, the walls seemed to explode with a hail of bullets and spears. As they wilted and withdrew, Gordon ordered two 8-inch howitzers to blast the Taiping defenders from the walls. Once more his men tried to force the breach, but the Taitsan garrison still held on. As fast as one lot were wiped out by Gordon's howitzers, another lot rushed to take their place and by desperate hand-to-hand fighting somehow managed to force the attackers back from the walls. Then on the third attempt Gordon, armed as always with no more than a rattan cane, led a fresh contingent into the breach; and although for a moment it looked as if this attack would be similarly repulsed, these reinforcements managed to turn the tide. With one final charge they broke through the Taiping ranks and into the town.

The battle was won—at no small cost to either side. For, although Gordon made light of his losses in a letter written to reassure his mother, in fact his casualties ran to 10 per cent. of his force. The courage and fidelity shown by both sides in this fierce engagement made a deep impression on him. And it was no doubt with the capture of Taitsan in mind that Gordon later described the Chinese soldiery as 'very patient, easily satisfied, easily governed, apt to learn, anxious to be taught, and very quick to appreciate the object in view.... Their bravery is passive, they require to be led to the attack, when they will follow, but in some instances ... they would outdo even foreigners in bravery.'

Li now planned to close in gradually on Soochow, the main

Taiping stronghold east of Nanking. And his next objective was Quinsan, twenty miles west of Taitsan and on the main waterway heading to Soochow from the coast. But before undertaking any further operations, Gordon insisted on returning to his base at Sungkiang to regroup his force. His decision was much appreciated by his badly battered troops. But when they found that instead of enjoying a spell of leave, as was customary after an important victory, they were to get straight down to intensive training for the assault on Quinsan, there was much grumbling in the ranks. First they had been prevented from looting at Taitsan, and now they could not even spend a bit of leisure in their favourite brothels. For a while they carried out their duties with dumb hostility. But when the force was about to start for Quinsan three weeks later, every officer sent in his resignation, and when Gordon ordered the force to parade in marching order on the following morning, only his bodyguard obeyed. Every other non-commissioned officer and man refused to parade. Immediately a number of the non-commissioned officers who were suspected of goading the men to indiscipline were arrested and put in chains, whereupon resistance began to crack. Several officers asked to be allowed to withdraw their resignations, to which Gordon acidly replied that he was leaving forthwith for Quinsan with his bodyguard, that he would halt halfway there and that anyone who failed to join him by the afternoon roll-call would be dismissed. Gordon had won another round in the battle of wills between his ideas of discipline and the heritage of disorder that had been left to him. But there were other and tougher rounds still to come.

On May 27 Gordon joined General Ching, the Taiping defector, who was now Li's principal general, outside Quinsan, and at once found himself at odds with his ally. Ching wanted to attack the east gate of the town, but Gordon objected that the east was the most strongly fortified side of Quinsan and that strategy required that the Taiping defenders should be prevented from withdrawing westwards to reinforce Soochow. It seems that they agreed to differ, for at this point Gordon left Ching to guard the east gate and took the *Hyson* and about eighty gunboats round to the western side of Quinsan. Before he reached his objective, the Taipings began to leave the town, seeking to make a break for Soochow. Leaving half his force outside the west gate to prevent any further breakout, he set off in pursuit of the retreating Taipings. But as darkness began to fall he was forced to call off the chase and return to Quinsan. Then as he drew level with the detachment which he had left to block the western exit, a furious fusillade began and he saw approaching through the darkness a vast mass of humanity. It was the rest of the Taiping garrison, numbering about 8,000 men, fleeing from Quinsan. Gordon immediately gave orders for the *Hyson* to sound her whistle and to fire her guns into the oncoming mass. The effect was total consternation in the Taipings' ranks. Panic seized them and they broke and ran in all directions, screams of terror mixing with the shrill screech of the *Hyson*'s whistle and the wails of the dying and wounded.

It was a massacre at point-blank range, and when Gordon ordered a cease-fire just before dawn a terrible scene of carnage met his eye. Fifteen hundred of the enemy lay dead or maimed by this murderous fire. And although Quinsan surrendered without further resistance, Gordon was to carry this slaughter on his conscience for the rest of his campaign. In his report he made the excuse that 'Matters were in too critical a state to hesitate, as the mass of the rebels, goaded into desperation, would have swept our small force away. We were therefore forced to fire into them and pursue them towards Quinsan, firing however very rarely and only when the rebels looked as if they would make a stand ... and though humanity might have desired a smaller destruction, it was indispensably necessary to inflict such a blow on the garrison of Soochow [*sic*] as would cause them not to risk another engagement.'

But this explanation was not enough to silence the chorus of criticism which now arose from those Europeans in Shanghai and elsewhere who were inclined to look upon the Taiping rebels with a kindly eye because of their Christian professions. In a letter to the *Shanghai Shipping News*, he sought to answer his critics by asserting that 'over 1,500 rebels were killed by the populace in their retreat from Quinsan'. But his effort merely provoked a chorus of denunciation that he was trying to shift the blame for the slaughter on to the local population. And from now onwards he became as troubled by these attacks as he was by the growing disloyalty and indiscipline of his force.

Because of this, Gordon tried, soon after the fall of Quinsan, to play the honest broker with the Taipings and to offer his 'good offices towards any arrangements they might be inclined to enter into with the Imperialists by which any more fighting might be avoided'. As he saw the situation, the rebels' position was worsening rapidly, and if they did not make terms the Imperialists would very soon refuse to treat with them. Nothing could then avoid a massacre on an infinitely greater scale than Quinsan and, as a general in the Chinese army, he would be indissolubly associated with the bloodshed. But the attempt was abortive and, as far as is known, the Taipings did not even bother to reply to his proposal.

Thus frustrated in his efforts to make peace and attacked for his methods of waging war, Gordon tried to remove the other thorn in his flesh—his nagging doubts about the loyalty of his force. In the hope that new surroundings might induce a better atmosphere within the Ever Victorious Army, he decided to sever connections with Sungkiang, where too much fraternization with the local inhabitants had upset discipline, and set up his headquarters at Quinsan. But this decision, too, was ill-starred. For at the first parade in their new quarters, the artillery regiment not only absented themselves, but issued a proclamation threatening to turn their guns on their European officers and on any of the Chinese other-ranks who sided with them. This was mutiny, and Gordon had to act decisively. Ordering the artillery men to parade, he demanded to know who had inspired the proclamation and, when no one came forward, he announced that he would have one in every five men shot. A loud groan followed from the assembled ranks, whereupon Gordon seized hold of a corporal who was groaning the loudest, dragged him to the front and ordered a member of his bodyguard to shoot him on the spot. The order was summarily carried out and Gordon, addressing the dead man's astonished comrades, told them that they were all under arrest and that, unless the ringleader's name was given to him within an hour, he would carry out his threat and execute every fifth man.

Within the hour the culprit was uncovered, and the mutiny was over. But Gordon's troubles were not. For in the next few days some 2,000 of his force deserted, rather than submit any longer to such severe discipline, and Gordon was driven to replace them with Taiping prisoners taken in his recent operations.

This was a crushing blow, and Gordon, who, as his later career was to show, never failed to react with almost childish petulance to the smallest flouting of his authority or criticism of his actions, decided that he could tolerate no more. The mass desertions, coming on top of everything else—the massacre at Quinsan, the sniping in the Press, and two mutinies—were as much as he could stomach. And, on the pretext that the Imperialist paymasters were falling into arrears with the payment of his force, he wrote to Li, resigning his command, which he claimed had become 'derogatory to my position as a British officer'.

But no sooner had he returned to Shanghai than a crisis arose which was to change his mind completely. Burgevine had gone over to the Taipings, taking with him some 300 Europeans whom he had secretly recruited in Shanghai. Gordon at once decided that only his continued leadership of the Ever Victorious Army could prevent the force following its erstwhile commander and deserting *en bloc* to the rebels. 'I am really the only stay of the force, and on my life hangs its existence,' he had written home after the capture of Quinsan.

Leaving aside the question of how he reconciled this assertion with his petulant decision to remove that 'only stay' by resigning, it is probably fair to say that his belief in his indispensability was true in the sense that he was by far the best soldier on the strength. But, as was shown by the desertion of more than half his men after the Quinsan mutiny, his ability to hold the force together was highly questionable. And if the Taipings' prospects had not looked so black as they then did, it is hard to believe that Gordon alone could have stopped the rest of his force following Burgevine into the Tien Wang's camp. For the Ever Victorious Army, he had taken all the fun and profit out of campaigning, and there was little left for them to gain by fighting for the Imperialists except regular pay and the certainty of being on the winning side at the finish.

But Gordon not only believed that he alone could hold the Ever Victorious Army together; he was also convinced that only he could persuade Burgevine to return to his own side and become a loyal supporter. He had earlier gone bail for the American when rumours were rife that he was planning to join the Taipings and, on Burgevine's written assurance that these rumours were false, had told the authorities in Shanghai that he

53

would stand as guarantor of his good behaviour. It was therefore doubly important to get the renegade back as soon as possible and so to redeem his pledge. Bruce in Peking was taking the line in his despatches that, by Li's refusal to reinstate Burgevine, 'a friend has been converted into a dangerous enemy'. And there was no knowing how London might react to this comment.

In the event, Burgevine did return in due course to the Imperialist camp, although not out of any liking or respect for Gordon. He had expected to be greeted with open arms by the Taipings and to be appointed to some high post in the Tien Wang's armies. But, to their credit, Hung and the Faithful Prince had little time for him and still less inclination to give him an important command. He had failed to deliver a consignment of arms that he had promised to bring with him, and let it fall into the hands of the Imperialists; and in any case they did not trust him. With no work to occupy him, Burgevine soon reverted to his heavy drinking habits, thereby alienating himself still further from the Puritanical Taipings. And as week after dreary week went by, he began bitterly to regret his defection, until one day in September, two months after he had joined the rebels, he sent Gordon a secret message from Soochow asking for help to rejoin his old comrades. Then, when he had made good his escape, to Gordon's outraged amazement he proceeded to suggest that the two of them should join forces, declare themselves independent of the Imperialists and of the Taipings and advance with the Ever Victorious Army on Peking. There they would seize the Dragon Throne and instal themselves as the rulers of China. The proposal was probably inspired more by drunkenness than by calculated treachery. But Gordon was taking no more chances and Burgevine was sent back to Shanghai with a safe-conduct and a request to the American Consul to see to it that he left the country without delay.

CHAPTER 5

TRIUMPH AND TREACHERY

WITH Burgevine out of the way, Gordon was able to devote all his attentions to the final phase of the Ever Victorious Army's operations—the capture of Soochow. Although the city was well beyond the thirty-mile perimeter, a new British War Office ruling had just been issued which allowed any British officer in China to undertake any action necessary to protect Shanghai, provided that he were on half-pay and in the service of the Chinese Government. Tseng's nutcracker strategy was, moreover, working well; Nanking was tightly invested, and it was undoubtedly to Britain's advantage to crack the Taiping nut as soon as possible and so to resume the flow of trade up and down the Yangtze River. And if this required the capture of Soochow, nobody was going to refuse Gordon the green light to go ahead.

Indeed, at this point the Taipings' situation could scarcely have been more critical. After having dominated an area almost as big as Western Europe, they had been gradually pinned by Tseng's armies into a narrow rectangle 100 miles long by forty wide. Their Yangtze supply route was blocked by Imperialist forces commanding the estuary, and their last outpost of any strength—Soochow—was rapidly becoming encircled. To the east lay Quinsan, now in Imperialist hands; to the south the route had been cut since July when Kahpu and Wokong surrendered with scarcely a shot fired, and Gordon was soon advancing from these towns with his steamers to take Patachiao, less than five miles from Soochow's south gate; and to the west was Lake Taihu, on which Imperialist gunboats and armed steamers plied a constant patrol. The Taipings' only escape route lay to the north, and, after beating off two rebel attempts to retake Wokong, Gordon moved up at the end of October to cut this off and complete the encirclement of Soochow. Blasting his way through the Taiping defenders with his heavy guns and mowing down rebels once again at point-blank range, by mid-November he had seized every position commanding the exits from Soochow and placed a ring of steel around the city.

Meanwhile, inside Soochow morale had sunk to zero. Realizing that they could neither defend the city against Gordon's guns nor break out and run for it, all but one of the Taiping chiefs favoured surrender on terms, and sent word to this effect to General Ching. The one dissentient was Moh Wang, a ruthless and exacting Taiping leader who made a habit of executing any of his commanders who surrendered a position to the enemy. Secretly, his fellow Wangs agreed on a plan that when the Imperialists attacked they would make a sortie behind the redoubtable Moh Wang. Then they would immediately return to the city, shut Moh Wang out of Soochow, and surrender with the garrison of 30,000 men. Hearing through his spies that treachery was being planned, Moh Wang summoned his fellow Wangs to the council chamber and made it clear to them that he knew of their plots. But his brave defiance was his death warrant. A moment later he fell to his knees with a knife in his back and a well-aimed sword-cut sent his head rolling across the floor. His executioners lost no time in making contact with Ching. And on December 5 the Imperialists occupied the east gate, and there took over the city on the promise that the lives of the Wangs and their garrison would be spared.

Soochow was by far the most valuable prize taken by the Imperialist armies in the east, and immediately its surrender was announced Ching's men fell to looting the city, abducting the women and girls, and killing any of its inhabitants who tried to defend their families or property. But Gordon was determined to prevent the Ever Victorious Army joining in the mêlée, for fear that such a breach of regulations would lead to a total breakdown of discipline. And to this end he marched his men to Li's advance headquarters—aboard a steamer on the canal linking Soochow with Quinsan—to demand a bonus of two months' full pay for every man on his strength. Li agreed in principle, but declined to sanction more than a month's pay. And when Gordon so informed his men, there were so many cries of protest, accompanied by threats to take the law into their own hands and seize Li's headquarters, that he felt the only safe course was to order his second-in-command to take the Ever Victorious Army back to Quinsan. Li invited him to attend the ceremony on board his steamer at which the Soochow Wangs were formally to surrender their city. But Gordon was reluctant to witness such public humiliation of the Taiping chiefs, for whom he had a sneaking admiration; and, refusing Li's invitation, he returned to Soochow to do what he could to protect at least the Wangs and their families from being butchered by Ching's victory-crazed soldiers.

As things turned out, Gordon could not have made a greater mistake than to send his own troops back to Quinsan and, further, to refuse to attend the surrender ceremony. And it was not long before he realized his fatal blunder. Returning to Soochow, he was in time to see the Wangs leaving for Li's head-quarters. At first he was moderately reassured by their evidently buoyant demeanour as they rode their ponies out of the city. But a while later, as he watched their arrival from a vantage-point on the wall over the east gate, he was disturbed to see a large and excited crowd of soldiers gathering around the Wangs. Then as the crowd broke up, the soldiers made for the east gate, shouting triumphantly and firing their rifles in the air. Descending from the city wall, Gordon soon found himself face to face with Ching, who was clearly much disconcerted at meeting his British col-league. And when he was asked how the ceremony had gone off, Ching at first tried to pretend that the Wangs had not gone to Li's headquarters, and then stated that they had run away, after making impossible demands that they be left in command of the city.

Unable to shake Ching from this obvious lie and now highly suspicious that the Wangs had met with foul play at Li's hands, Gordon went to see for himself. As he made for the east gate he found that one of the chief Wang's palaces had been sacked by the Imperialist troops, and when he went to inspect the damage he was seized by the owner's terrified family and held as a hostage against further violence by Ching's soldiers. It was only with the greatest difficulty that he managed to persuade his captors to re-lease him so that he might go to Li and insist, if necessary under the threat of bombardment by the *Hyson*'s guns, that the Im-perialist soldiers be placed under proper restraint. Then, as he approached Li's headquarters, his worst suspicions were con-firmed when one of his American officers told him that a boy, claiming to be the son of one of the Wangs, had taken refuge in his tent, saying that his father had been beheaded and that he feared for his life. Under cross-examination, the boy repeated his story, pointing to a spot across the waterway where he said that his father had been done to death, and when Gordon went to investigate for himself he discovered the bodies and severed heads of nine Wangs lying on the ground where they had been executed. Gordon's rage and disgust now knew no limits and, seizing the head of the boy's father as proof of Li's treachery, he stalked off to his gunboat determined to avenge this barbarous breach of faith.

His first thought was to seize Li, confront him with the grisly evidence of his treachery, and demand that he resign all his commands. But, remembering that he had dismissed his own men, whereas Li was protected by several thousand Imperialist troops, he decided to put his reproaches and demands in a letter. And an extraordinary and revealing letter it was too. First, Gordon demanded Li's resignation, asserting that he would have him charged with treachery before the highest Imperial authority; then he went on to threaten that, if Li refused to resign, he would have nothing more to do with him and would return to the Taipings all the towns that he had captured from them.

That Gordon had every right to be furious over Li's treachery cannot be denied, for, rightly or wrongly, he believed that 'if faith had been kept, there would have been no more fighting, as every town would have given in'. That he should even order his own superior to resign is also in the circumstances understandable, if presumptuous. But this threat to hand over captured towns to the enemy would have been none other than treasonable blackmail, if Gordon had been able to carry it out. As it was, with the possible exception of Quinsan, he was not in a position to hand over any to the Taipings, since the garrisons of all captured places were Li's and not Gordon's troops. Yet it would be a mistake to attribute Gordon's empty threats merely to that childish petulance which he had shown before, and was to show again, when he was crossed by his superiors. His letter to Li also revealed that curious incapacity for objective judgement in matters affecting himself which he never overcame. For while he expected other British officers and officials, such as Bruce in China and later Baring in Egypt, to be more understanding and tolerant of foreign ways and weaknesses, he never ceased to require, where he was concerned, a respect for what he considered English standards of conduct on the part of those whom he served and those who served him. And that his Chinese superior should have fallen so far beneath such standards was for him, at the time, entirely unforgivable.

Perhaps fortunately, Li never learned the full contents of this imperious letter, since his British liaison officer discreetly informed him only that a letter had been received from Gordon which was clearly written under great emotional stress and which contained a number of angry reproaches for the murder of the Wangs. To which Li responded with an offer to take the full blame for what had happened and a reminder that, since Gordon had not himself drawn up the surrender terms, he could not be held in any way responsible. At the same time, Li claimed that the Wangs had made impossible demands on him and that he had killed them to prevent further trouble. But Gordon was not to be mollified, and on returning to his base at Quinsan, still carrying the grisly relic of the murdered Wang's head, he continued to fulminate about placing Li under arrest.

At this point, General Brown, who had succeeded Staveley as C.-in-C. British troops in China, appeared on the scene to try to patch things up between Gordon and Li. But Gordon was adamant. Li must be publicly executed for his treachery. Brown therefore went in search of Li; but, far from achieving any reconciliation, he returned from his interview almost as indignant as Gordon. Li had refused any explanation of his conduct and had treated Brown as an interfering busybody. And Brown had angrily informed him that Gordon would henceforth be instructed to suspend all further operations on behalf of the Imperialists and that the British Government would in all probability withdraw their support for the Manchu cause, recall Gordon, and disband his army. Brown then returned to Shanghai and reported his stormy interview to Bruce in Peking, who informed the Imperial Government that Gordon could have no further dealings with Li.

Gordon was now able to sulk in his tent on official authority. And for six weeks he remained at Quinsan with the Ever Victorious Army, declining to take part in any further operations against the Taipings, while Li's troops continued their advance north-west from Soochow. After two weeks of this inactivity, the Imperial Government, prompted by Li, sought to break the deadlock by sending Gordon a decoration and a handsome bribe of 10,000 taels, which were delivered in person with a covering letter from the Emperor, wrapped in yellow silk and proclaiming the thanks of the Dragon Throne for his assistance to the Imperialist cause. Gordon sent the gift and the medal back with a letter explaining that after what had occurred at Soochow he was 'unable to receive any mark of His Majesty the Emperor's recognition'.

But while he might decline to be bought with cash or cajoled by praise, other influences were at work which were soon to win him over to a more co-operative frame of mind. Foremost among these influences was the fact that the inactive life at Quinsan was beginning to have its effect on his force and, as always happened when they were not fighting, the officers became slack and the men got sick from smoking too much opium. An added problem was that Li had authorized bonuses amounting to £40,000, and the Ever Victorious soldiers, for once, had too much money to spend in search of pleasure. So difficult did Gordon find it to keep his force together and disciplined during these weeks of idleness that he had to dismiss sixteen of his officers for insubordination. Moreover, far from receiving any indication that the British Government backed his decision to resign his command, he was being continually reminded by Bruce in Peking of the overriding need to 'keep the force from deserting and to preserve Shanghai'.

So, two months after the Soochow incident, Gordon went to see Li and, on the Governor's undertaking to make a public announcement accepting the sole responsibility for the Wangs' murder, he agreed to co-operate with the Imperialist army in further operations against the Taipings. Writing to Bruce to explain his volte-face, he accepted that he would be open to 'very grave censure' for his decision. But he claimed that, if he had left the Imperialists to fend for themselves, hostilities might have lasted another six years, whereas 'I do not apprehend the rebellion will last six months longer, if I take the field.' Bruce, for his part, was only too happy to support Gordon's decision to take the field again. Britain's Minister in Peking had personally taken a fairly cynical line about the execution of the Wangs, which he judged by Chinese standards as being justifiable precautions taken in the heat of the battle *pour encourager les autres*. He had also refrained from demanding Li's dismissal, and confined himself to asking for an enquiry into his conduct at Soochow, knowing perfectly well from his experience over the Burgevine affair that, so long as the Governor continued to win victories and so long as his patron, Tseng Kuo-fan, remained Commander-in-Chief of the Imperial armies, any request for disciplinary measures against Li would be ignored by the Dragon Throne.

Bruce was, after all, a British diplomat accredited to a foreign government, and his job was to serve British political and commercial interests. Some of China's richest silk-producing acres were in the area between Soochow and Nanking, together with a vital stretch of the Grand Canal linking the Yangtze River with Shanghai, and the sooner these acres could be restored to cultivation and the Grand Canal cleared, the better would Britain's interests be served. And as Gordon and his Chinese ally came together once more and closed in on this area, the British Minister's letters both to and about the Ever Victorious Army's commander became noticeably warmer. After the fall of Soochow, he had written to the Foreign Secretary praising to the skies the man whom a few months ago he had been prepared to sacrifice to appease Burgevine. 'His tact,' he said, 'in dealing with the difficulties arising from the jealousy and suspicion of the Chinese authorities, in rescuing Burgevine and the misguided foreigners serving in the Taiping ranks and in thereby obviating the risk of this foreign adventurer element uniting with them, has been no less conspicuous than his personal gallantry and military skill.' And to Gordon himself, he wrote: 'Your ability and tact is beyond praise. You have no more sincere admirer of what you have done than myself.'

There were other reasons, apart from recapturing the silk districts and the Grand Canal, why Bruce now wanted Gordon to resume operations with the Ever Victorious Army. On political grounds, he had come to the view that Gordon could be used to prove to the Chinese how much they needed such 'wisdom and instruction' as Britain alone could provide in the creation and maintenance of an army drilled and trained on European lines. (Bruce had tried to foist on to the Chinese a similar experiment for creating a Chinese navy under the command of a Captain Sherard Osborne, R.N., but the project had failed because Osborne insisted on trying to break down the system of decentralization and to deal directly with the Imperial Government on all matters.) There was also the problem of what might happen to the Ever Victorious Army if Gordon left it. As the Taipings' fortunes waned, Bruce's anxiety lest the force should desert to the rebels gave way to a new fear that they might turn to brigandage and threaten British and other foreign interests and property in China.

At the same time Bruce had to take account of those factions in the British Press and Parliament who, taking their cue from Gordon's critics in China, resented the participation of a British officer in operations, and atrocities, on behalf of an idolatrous tyranny against a Christian rebel movement, were waxing stronger every day. And they were able to raise such an outcry against his resuming operations on behalf of the Imperialists after the Soochow massacre that the Government was forced to revoke the Order in Council which permitted British officers to serve with the Manchu Emperor's forces. But while there was method in Bruce's flattery, for Gordon to inform the British Minister in Peking that the Taiping rebellion would continue for six years if he quit and only for six months if he carried on was clearly a gross overstatement of his contribution to ultimate victory. He may have been 'the only stay of the force', but the force had scarcely proved itself 'the only stay' of the Imperialists. (It was not even the only force of its kind in the Imperial armies. At the same time as the Ever Victorious Army was formed, a Franco-Chinese brigade had been created to clear the Ningpo area of Taipings.) Undoubtedly it helped to save Shanghai and cleared the eastern theatre of Taipings. But it was the armies of Tseng Kuo-fan who bore the brunt of the fighting over twelve long years and now stood poised to deliver the *coup de grâce* against the Taipings' stronghold of Nanking.

Moreover, Gordon's latest contention was totally at variance with his earlier estimates of the likely duration of the rebellion. From his days at Tientsin, he had been at pains in his letters home to belittle the Taipings' chances of success, or even of survival. In August 1862 he had written to his mother: 'I think the rebellion is on the decline and that the end of '63 will see its suppression.' Again, in September he wrote: 'I do not think the rebellion will last long, it is nearly extinguished,' adding that the Taipings 'are certainly a very harmless enemy ... once defection begins I do not think much time will elapse before the break-up.' And when he got to Shanghai and saw the rebels in action against

British troops, he was full of contempt for the way 'they bolted' and described them as 'very despicable'. For a while after he took on the Ever Victorious Army he seemed to be in some doubt as to which were the more despicable, the Taipings who bolted, or the Imperialists, who he claimed were never ready to follow up a success; and his letters home showed much resentment for Britain's non-intervention policy, which he felt, by leaving the issue to the Imperialists, kept the rebellion going and prolonged the misery and starvation of the people whose rice was plundered to feed the rebel armies. But after taking Quinsan in May 1863 he was asserting once again that 'four or six months might settle the rebellion.... The rebels ... show they are decidedly sharply declining and defection has commenced in their ranks which will no doubt spread rapidly.'

It would not, however, be fair to charge Gordon's claim that the rebellion would be over in six months, if he took the field again, entirely to conceit on his part. He badly needed an excuse for his volte-face, which, as he suspected, was received with horrified astonishment by the European consuls in Shanghai, who had denounced the Wangs' execution as 'extreme treachery, abhorrent to human nature'. He knew that uncharitable people in Britain would be only too ready to accuse him of having been in this, and all other incidents involving the massacre of Taiping rebels, the willing agent of Governor Li. In anticipation of this outcry, he had insisted with the Imperial Government through Bruce that 'in future operations in which a foreign officer is concerned, the rules of warfare, as practised among foreign nations, are to be observed'. And although this remarkable demand was, even more remarkably, accepted by the Peking authorities, who agreed to instruct Li accordingly, Gordon remained sensitive to criticism of his role in China right up to the moment when he returned to his own country.

So ended the Soochow incident. Honour had been adequately satisfied, Gordon had been publicly exonerated and Li had taken the blame. But whether justice had been done was another matter. For in a dramatic postscript to this bloody episode, Li's British liaison officer was later to reveal that Ching had admitted, shortly before he was killed in action the following April, that he and not Li was responsible for ordering the executions of the Wangs. Ching would have hardly lied to protect Li, for whom he had little, if any, feeling of friendship. Besides, as Burgevine told Gordon in a letter from his exile in Japan, Ching had made 'many overtures to return to his old standard'—the Taipings—and therefore had every reason to silence the Wangs before they informed on him to his Imperialist masters. And Burgevine was not only in a position to know of any such overtures by Ching from the time that he spent with the Taipings in Nanking, but also had less motive than anyone to shield Li, the man who had sacked him from his brief command of the Ever Victorious Army. That Gordon himself later came some way to accepting this view seems clear from a letter written in June 1864 to his brother Henry, in which he stated: 'There were many reasons to exculpate the Futai [Governor] for his action which is not at all a bad act in the eyes of the Chinese. In my opinion ... Li Futai is the best man in the Empire, has correct ideas of his position and for a Chinaman has most liberal tendencies.'

Finally, it is difficult to acquit Gordon of some negligence in this affair. He was invited by Li to be present at the surrender ceremony, yet he refused. And, added to this, he had sent his Ever Victorious Army back to Quinsan. True, he had done so to stop them taking their revenge on Li for refusing to pay the full bonus to which they considered themselves entitled. But his action only proves that he was not in control of his men. Had they been under proper discipline and had Gordon attended the surrender ceremony and kept them in close attendance while doing so, there can be little doubt that neither Ching nor anyone else would have dared to put the Wangs to death. But although he had personally experienced treachery at Ching's hands and was aware that Ching had beheaded prisoners before, and although he knew that Li was emotionally distraught because his brother had recently been killed fighting the Taipings, Gordon absented himself from the ceremony and trusted in the good faith and humanity of the Imperialists. Thus, however he may have been publicly exculpated, he cannot escape some element of indirect responsibility for what happened. And while no one could fail to share his sense of outrage at the execution of these defenceless prisoners, the almost hysterical nature of his subsequent threats against Li suggests that once again Gordon was suffering from a sense of guilt. Certainly he seemed to be at a loss to explain matters to his family. For, having written regularly to his mother throughout the previous ten months' campaigning to give her graphic accounts of his engagements, accompanied by detailed sketch-maps, he told her virtually nothing of the Soochow incident, and hardly wrote to her between the end of December 1863 and the following April. And when he resumed his regular correspondence, he scarcely referred to the matter and offered no explanation whatever of his conduct, either at the time or subsequently.

*   *   *

When Gordon took the field again with the Ever Victorious Army the civil war was almost over. Ever since July of the previous year, when Tseng's army occupied the Taiping stockades around Nanking and brought up the Yangtze a powerful fleet of gunboats and armed steamers bought from the British, Hung's capital had been effectively surrounded and cut off from all hope of relief. The Faithful Prince had returned from his attempted diversion in the north with only a fraction of his army, having lost tens of thousands of men from exposure and starvation, desertion and enemy fire. There was no other army left for the Tien Wang to call in aid. His Triad allies had long since been mopped up and their battle-grounds in the south and east, around Canton and Shanghai, had become a vast execution yard. And the few Taipings who still survived to the east of Nanking were mere isolated pockets of resistance unable to hold any cohesive line, let alone to break the ring of steel with which Tseng was gradually strangling and starving the life out of the Tien Wang's capital.

Realizing the hopelessness of the situation, the Faithful Prince told Hung that there was nothing for it but to try with what troops remained to break out of Nanking and strike inland into the hills north of the Yangtze. But Hung, whose hair and beard had gone grey with the weight of failure and defeat, was now on the verge of insanity. Utterly rejecting these counsels, he proclaimed that he had been made ruler of the Empire by Shang-ti, that he was the lord of all nations, that he held the Empire in an iron grasp and that, if the Faithful Prince no longer supported him, there were others who would do so. 'You say there are no soldiers,' he raved, 'but my heavenly troops are more numerous than the firmament.'

Meanwhile, as Li's army continued its advance from Soochow,

first one and then another town surrendered without a fight, and in the south the isolated Taiping garrison of Hangchow capitulated to the Franco-Chinese brigade. By the end of March 1864, the only town of any size left in Taiping hands was Changchow, nearly half-way between Soochow and Nanking, and this was being attacked by Li's troops. Here the Faithful Prince's son was in command of a rebel brigade, and, not to be outdone by his courageous father, the young Wang broke out of the town with 7,000 men, smashed his way through the besiegers' lines and marched eastwards in a desperate attempt to recapture Quinsan and Chanzu and reopen a corridor to the Yangtze estuary.

Gordon was far away to the west attacking Kintang, forty miles from Nanking, when news of this threat to his base came through. To add to his problems, he had been wounded in the leg while leading his men in an assault on the town's defences. Nevertheless, with characteristic endurance, he promptly headed eastwards to cut off the Taiping advance. And two weeks later his heavy artillery caught the Faithful Prince's son unawares and sent him and his force scuttling back whence they had come. Gordon then joined forces with Li's Imperialist troops and moved on Changchow.

Here, for once, his superior fire-power did not seem to do the trick and after the usual breach had been made in the walls, two assaults by a total of four regiments were beaten off with nearly 300 casualties. An attack by Li's troops on another side of the town had suffered a similar rebuff. But Gordon was not a Royal Engineer for nothing. If he could not attack the breach across open ground without exposing his men to deadly rifle fire, he would dig trenches with breastworks through which they could creep unobserved to within a few yards of their objective. After the necessary work had been done under cover of darkness, Gordon's artillery greeted the dawn with another furious bombardment, which continued throughout the morning. Then as the guns ceased fire, the Ever Victorious Army poured out of their concealed positions under the town walls and, with Gordon at their head, swept through the breach. Yet the moment of triumph all but ended in tragedy. For as the Ever Victorious troops poured across the rubble of the ruined ramparts, they and their commander found themselves looking down the muzzle of a 32-pounder gun only 150 yards away. The gun belonged to the *Fire-*

fly, one of the Imperialists' armed steamers which had been captured in a daring Taiping raid on Shanghai six months earlier, and had been removed from the steamer to strengthen the defences of the town. But the hand of Providence that had protected Gordon in earlier hand-to-hand encounters reached out once more to save him. At this critical moment the gun jammed and, as the exultant wave of Ever Victorious soldiers crashed down upon the gun-crew, he claimed his last victory in the service of the Manchu Emperor.

Only Nanking now remained to be reduced, and for this the Ever Victorious Army's help was superfluous. Not only was the Taiping capital surrounded by 80,000 of Tseng's troops, but the situation inside the city was growing daily more desperate. The food supplies seized from the surrounding countryside were almost exhausted. Rice had risen to prohibitive prices, and the starving inhabitants were too weak to man the ramparts. Hung himself, now completely mad, was subsisting on a self-brewed concoction of leaves and grass, which he called 'sweet dew' from Heaven and which he told the Faithful Prince would sustain and nourish his people if they ate it with true faith. Day and night the explosion of mines tore holes in the city's fifty-foot thick walls, shattering what remained of the defenders' morale, and, like rolls of funeral drums, proclaiming impending doom for the last stronghold of the Taiping rebellion. Nothing could now save Nanking. And by the middle of June even Hung himself had come to accept that its fall was merely a matter of time and that the Heavenly Mandate had been withdrawn from him and handed back to the Manchus.

According to Chinese tradition, there was only one honourable course for him to pursue, only one way to expurgate his disgrace and failure to fulfil the duty allotted to him by Shang-ti. With his vermilion brush Hung wrote out his last edict, proclaiming even in this hour of final defeat his everlasting faith in the Christian God: 'Now I hereby declare to heaven, earth and men that God the Heavenly Father is alone most excellent, who was from the spreading out of the heavens until now the exceeding great creator of all things.' Then he nominated his sixteen-year-old son as Tien Wang, mixed a fatal dose of gold leaf with a goblet of wine and with a last pathetic cry that he had failed 'the Heavenly Father', drank the mixture down to the last drop. He died shortly after midnight on July 1 after writhing in agony for several hours, and was buried secretly in a corner of the palace garden, where on the following morning his wives committed suicide by hanging themselves from the trees.

For the next sixteen days his death was kept secret by his family and the Faithful Prince, who feared that public knowledge of their ruler's suicide would start an uncontrollable panic. Meanwhile, Tseng's sappers moved into position to lay the great mine which was finally to breach the city walls. Twice the Faithful Prince led a sortie in an attempt to drive them away, but each time in vain. And by July 19 the mine was ready and the Imperialists were poised for the onslaught. The fuse was blown and with it 40,000 lb. of gunpowder exploded against the ramparts. A sixty-yard breach was made, and through the smoke and dust and rubble Tseng's men swept across the wall and into the city. Then the slaughter began. For, despite their starving condition, not one of the garrison surrendered without a fight. Of those who were not killed defending the city street by street, 7,000 were put to death after capture and most of the rest committed suicide either by their own swords, by burning themselves to death in their own houses or by throwing themselves into the Yangtze.

In the mêlée of fire and fighting the Faithful Prince was able to escape with Hung's son, the new Tien Wang. But he was soon caught by Tseng's cavalry and brought back to Nanking. There, while awaiting the decision of the Empress as to the manner of his execution, he spent his days confined in a cage, writing what was supposed to be the traditional 'confession' of a captured rebel to the Dragon Throne, but which turned out to be a totally unrepentant autobiography. Living up to his title, he refused to confess to treason for having served what he believed to be a higher cause than that of any emperor. His dignity and fidelity were indeed so remarkable that Tseng was moved to decide that, whatever Peking might ordain, he should die as merciful a death as possible. And when word came from the Imperial Government that the Faithful Prince was to be executed 'by a slow and ignominious process', Tseng quickly ordered that his prisoner be beheaded and pretended in his report to his Manchu masters that he had done so before he received the Imperial edict, because he feared that the Faithful Prince might be hailed as a martyr if he had been tortured to death. His head, together with that of the exhumed body of Hung Hsiu-chuan, were sent to Peking, where they were set on spikes above the city gate as a warning to other potential rebels against the Dragon Throne.

So ended that extraordinary episode in history known as the Taiping rebellion. For more than twelve years a Christian convert and former school-teacher had held the Yangtze River valley in thrall, defying all the efforts of the mighty Manchus to overpower him. And in those years more people are said to have perished than in the holocaust of World War I, either by death in action or massacre, or by starvation resulting from the depredations inflicted on the country to feed the Taiping armies. Even for a nation so nurtured in the traditions of bloodshed as China, it had been a cataclysm of rare moment. But for Gordon it was to have a peculiar significance, in that it brought him face to face with a movement of religious fanaticism dedicated to the destruction of an established order which it was his duty to uphold—a situation which was to repeat itself twenty years later, although with a very different outcome.

CHAPTER 6

'CHINESE GORDON'

WHILE Tseng Kuo-fan was preparing for the fall of Nanking, Gordon, impulsive as ever, took it upon himself to disband the Ever Victorious Army without so much as a word of consultation with either Bruce or General Brown. Not that he minded by-passing either of his British superiors—he considered Brown to be unfit for his command and Bruce to be something of a humbug. But his precipitate action seems oddly at variance with his earlier belief, in line with Bruce and Staveley, that the Ever Victorious Army should form the nucleus from which a regular Chinese army might be created to protect British interests in China after the Taiping rebellion had been crushed. Suddenly, and conveniently, forgotten were Gordon's claims that his force was an indispensable arm of the Imperialists. Now they were just a bunch of dangerous, low-class mercenaries who had to be pensioned off, and quickly, with substantial bribes and bounties.

'This force,' he wrote in explaining his arbitrary decision, 'has had ever since its formation in its ranks a class of men of no position.... Ignorant, uneducated, even unaccustomed to command, they were not suited to control the men they had under them.' Relating how these 'uneducated' officers had twice mutinied and throughout the campaign 'needed to be continually watched and kept in motion against the rebels', he added that it was only by exploiting their mutual jealousies and playing one off against another that he was able to carry on with the command. 'In short,' he contended, 'it can be easily understood that both men and officers ... were not a force which it would be advisable to keep during peace times.... After the fall of Chang-chow both men and officers were quite fagged out and sick of the service. . . . The Futai, disgusted by the conduct of some of the officers and by the hanging back of the men ... was willing to pay £100,000 for their disbandment.... It was necessary to take immediate action as otherwise both officers and men might refuse to leave.... To have waited and discussed the question would have thrown the onus of the dissolution of an American [sic] force on our government. By acting on my own responsibility the field is now clear for any arrangements that may be considered necessary. I consider the force even under a British officer a most dangerous collection of men, never to be depended on and very expensive. In my opinion more would be done by a force of Chinese under their own officers, who do not want for bravery when properly instructed.... Do not let us try to govern their own men by foreigners but, keeping these latter as instructors, make them create their own officers....' This, he now concluded, was the only way to set about forming a Chinese regular army, for if a force such as the Ever Victorious Army were kept in being, not only might it turn against the régime and become a threat as dangerous as the Taipings, but the Mandarins would have no incentive to establish any kind of standing army if it appeared that the job was being done for them by a foreign power. And to prove his point he promptly attached himself to the Imperialist army as an instructor.

It was a remarkable somersault even for a man as full of contradictions and sudden impulses as Gordon. And it would have been more understandable if, from a yearning to return home, he had simultaneously decided to sever all his connections with China. But that he had no such yearning was soon shown by the enthusiasm with which he immediately threw himself into the task of teaching the Imperialist forces how to 'create their own officers'. One can only conclude, therefore, that he had finally come to realize that, notwithstanding his successes in action, he had failed to transform this band of mercenaries, and its multinational collection of officers, into a disciplined force capable of setting the necessary example to the Chinese. Therefore, the sooner the whole thing was disbanded and forgotten the better. Accordingly, he seized on Li's £100,000 offer and dissolved the force in a matter of a few days, with a gratuity to all officers and men sufficient to set them up in civilian life as shopkeepers, small traders, hotel-keepers or smallholders. For which gesture, designed as it was to buy these unscrupulous mercenaries off turning to brigandage at the expense of foreign property, he received a letter of fulsome thanks from the Shanghai merchants.

From his own Government he received promotion to the rank

71

of Colonel and a C.B. And from the Dragon Throne came the award of the rank of Ti-tu, or Commander-in-Chief of a Provincial Army, together with the Order of the Yellow Jacket, with the right to wear the peacock feather of a mandarin, the highest distinctions attainable in the Emperor's service. In presenting these decorations, the Imperial Government requested Sir Frederick Bruce to inform Queen Victoria of its high regard for Gordon 'in evidence of the desire of the Chinese Government by its consideration of General Gordon's merits and its bestowal of rewards to strengthen the *entente cordiale*'. The Chinese Government also offered a large money gift, but this Gordon declined on the grounds that he could not accept any financial reward while so many millions of Chinese were living at starvation levels, due to the deprivations resulting from the Taiping rebellion.

No such inhibitions, however, prevented him from accepting the other awards. On the contrary, from an unpublished note in Gordon's handwriting now in the Royal Engineers' Museum at Chatham, it appears that he had long coveted the distinction of the Yellow Jacket. This 'decoration' dated from the days when the first Manchu Emperor was marching on Peking to overthrow the Ming Dynasty and, fearful of being singled out and killed by the Ming armies, dressed his personal bodyguard of forty men in the same yellow jackets as he wore himself. And when later the jacket became a decoration for services to the Manchu emperor, the number of those entitled to wear it were by tradition limited to forty. Hence its conferment was a highly-prized honour. And although Gordon gave the impression at the time that he would prefer not to be rewarded for his services to such a barbarian régime, he is on record as having written about his Yellow Jacket: 'The Chinese tried hard to prevent me having it; but I said either the Yellow Jacket or nothing; and they at last yielded.'

But perhaps the greatest of all the distinctions he gained was the appellation of 'Chinese Gordon', by which he was generally to be known until his death at the hands of the Mahdi's warriors won him immortality as 'Gordon of Khartoum'. For with his supporters, as with his detractors, the Press reports of events in China over the previous twelve months had created the impression that the Taiping rebellion had been crushed by the almost unaided efforts of the Ever Victorious Army. 'Major Gordon captured

Soochow on December 5' ran the laconic announcement in the London *Times* of January 22, 1864. And it is fair to say that, until the Ever Victorious Army came under British command, the public at home knew nothing of its existence and precious little of the civil war which had been raging in China for twelve years.

It was something more than ordinary patriotic sentiment that led the British Press and public to take such an exaggerated and one-sided view of Gordon's role in the Taiping rebellion. Victorian England was building what Sir Winston Churchill once called the 'Second British Empire'. The great migration of people to Canada, South Africa, Australia, and New Zealand that started towards the end of the Industrial Revolution was gaining momentum. In the thirty years after 1850 no less than $6\frac{1}{2}$ million people out of a population of 26 millions had left the British Isles to seek their future in the colonies. In the East, since the suppression of the Indian Mutiny in 1858, British policy had become overtly imperialist, and Britain ruled over her Indian empire with the sword, dispensing impartial justice and efficient government in the name of the Queen Empress. After the infamy and disaster of the Crimean War, she was recovering her pride. The island race that had triumphed over Napoleon and had conquered vast territories in every quarter of the globe was on the march again, and was proving what everybody had known all along—that one Britisher was equal to at least twenty 'fuzzy-wuzzies'. (Elgin's demand for an indemnity from the Manchus for the murders of his truce negotiators bears eloquent testimony of the current valuation of a Britisher's relative worth—£10,000 for any Englishman not returned alive and £500 for each native soldier!) As Lord Elton put it in his biography of Gordon: 'This was ... an age in which, it almost seemed, any stray detachment of the British Army could be relied on ... to produce a junior officer capable of pacifying a frontier, quelling a rebellion or improvising and administering an empire.' And there was nothing so popular in this age of heroics and George Alfred Henty as a story which proved through some personal triumph or act of bravery that the British were superior to every other race. In a word, Victorian England was looking for English heroes—and Gordon was available.

It is therefore understandable that the Victorians should have lionized Gordon as the almost sole architect of the victory in China. What is extraordinary is that so many of his more recent biographers should have unquestioningly followed suit. True, the Ever Victorious Army played an important part in prosecuting Tseng's nutcracker strategy which crushed the Taipings' last stand. True, too, they suffered heavy losses in the relatively small number of hotly contested engagements which they were called upon to fight—107 officers and 1,458 men killed and wounded out of a total force that never exceeded 4,000, and 57 officers and 1,300 men dead of sickness. But when Gordon took over the command the Taiping rebellion had only another seventeen months' life left in it. And it is a matter of inescapable historical fact that the lion's share of the credit for defeating the Taipings belonged to Tseng Kuo-fan and his armies, who doggedly held on while Hung carried all before him, and whose inexorable pressures gradually forced the Taipings to abandon their conquests one by one. Yet so hypnotized have Gordon's biographers been by the aura of heroism with which Victorian legend has surrounded their subject—his rattan cane, the 'Wand of Victory', his reconnaissances under heavy enemy fire, his personal leadership in fierce hand-to-hand fighting—that, whether consciously or not, they give all the credit to Gordon and ignore Tseng Kuo-fan, in some cases not even mentioning his name.

Of course, the self-esteem in which Gordon held himself for his Chinese exploits did nothing to dull the glamour that surrounded his name. Both in his reports to Bruce and in his letters home he consistently claimed to be the mainstay of the Ever Victorious Army, and contended that only his force among the Imperialist armies could be relied upon to take places from the Taipings and hold on to them, and then only after he had taken command. He even sought to imply that his leadership had prevented mass desertions from the Ever Victorious Army to the Taipings. And as late as July 1864 he was writing to his brother to say what a relief the fall of Nanking was to him, for 'as long as it held out, my late officers held themselves ready to join the rebels if there was a chance of success'.

All this suggests that Gordon was a man of overweening conceit who held himself infinitely superior to his fellows in the soldierly virtues of courage, leadership and tactical skill. Yet this would not be a true picture of this strange soldier of fortune. Conceit he certainly possessed, but it was the prevailing conceit of a British officer serving in foreign parts, whose every instinct told him that the British were the only truly superior race. 'The Chinese trust us,' he proudly asserted to his mother after he took on the Ever Victorious Army, 'but never ask any favours from the French.' In the same vein he had written from the Crimea to complain that the French were not playing their part, and in China he poured scorn on the Franco-Chinese force which was engaging the Taipings to the south of Shanghai. As for the Imperialist army, this was to Gordon a mere rabble—under Chinese command. But with British officers—any British officers—to lead it, the 'excellent fighting material' within its ranks could be licked into shape and transformed into an almost invincible force. In the simple thinking of this scion of a traditional British military family, what won the war for the Manchus against the Taipings was not his presence so much as that of a British officer. That was all that was required to ensure victory for the Imperialists. And when he penned his self-congratulatory letters to his family and to Bruce, he probably had little thought or desire to attract to himself the kind of limelight that followed. For, while in many respects a rebel against British military regulations and customs, Gordon fully subscribed to the tradition which frowned on personal publicity for serving soldiers and required that any officer whose name appeared in the Press should pay a forfeit to his regimental fund.

Yet for all his 'national' conceit, Gordon felt suffocated by British military and social traditions. Detesting the system of regimental soldiering in England, he had written to his sister, Augusta, from Tientsin: 'I do not feel at all inclined to return to Great Britain. . . . I like the country, work and independence here; in England we are nondescripts, but in China we hold a good position.' Again, he wrote home on taking over the Ever Victorious Army: 'In England . . . you are under twenty masters and trammelled by regulations and orders and on meagre pay. . . . I could never remain in England for any length of time.'

When the civil war ended, Gordon was therefore willing enough to stay in China. There was still a job to be done for someone of his talents and experience. The Chinese, never a martial race, did not take kindly to soldiering and their armies needed instruction and training in modern methods and equipment. It was obviously in Britain's interest to supply the necessary instructors from the British garrisons at Shanghai, Canton, and Hong Kong, if only to protect British interests against another rebellion or, to use Gordon's own euphemistic phrase, 'to open China to civilization'. And in his own view there was no one better qualified to instruct Chinese soldiers than himself. 'The Chinese,' he said a few weeks after taking on the Ever Victorious Army, 'have in great measure changed their ideas of us during the short time I have been in command.'

Certainly Gordon had acquired a deep insight and understanding of the Chinese mind, which was altogether rare in a professional soldier. Nobody knew this better than Bruce, who in his despatches to the Foreign Office spoke of his 'tact in dealing with ... the jealousy and suspicion of the Chinese authorities'. And directly the civil war was over, Gordon was busily engaged in suggesting ways of reforming the Emperor's armies. This must be done through the governors in each province, he decided, and not through the Peking authorities which he considered 'a very helpless lot'. And it must be done gently and with tact. 'If we drive the Chinese into sudden reforms,' he said, 'they will strike and resist with the greatest obstinacy ... but if we lead them we shall find them willing to a degree and most easy to manage. They like to have an option and hate having a course struck out for them as if they were of no account.' Gordon even excused Chinese xenophobia on the gounds that these proud people had been greatly put upon by foreign powers. 'The Chinese have no reason to love us even for the assistance we have given them, for the rebellion was our own work indirectly,' he concluded.

Thus it was with every sympathy for the Chinese that Gordon embarked on the task of helping to train the Manchu armies. He stayed for five months; and then in November 1864 he remembered that he had promised his mother to be home by Christmas if humanly possible. He had not seen his family for over four years; and nine months earlier his younger brother, William, had died. He had been especially fond of William and had spent much time and some of his Army pay to help in setting him up as a farmer in New Zealand. The sudden tragedy only made it the more imperative that he should return home for a while to comfort his parents. But the thought that this might involve having to face the spotlight of publicity bothered him greatly. Somehow, he decided, he must slip into England unobserved. This meant, among other things, stopping any former British officers of the Ever Victorious Army coming to meet his ship. And so in his last letter from China he wrote on November 17 to his mother: 'The individual is coming home, but does not wish it known, for it would be a signal for the disbanded to come to Southampton....' Then he boarded the famous *Hyson* and steamed down the Grand Canal to Shanghai past rows of cheering Chinese soldiers waving flags, banging gongs, and exploding crackers—the traditional salute to celestial triumph—in honour of their departing friend and ally. A final touch of farce was provided by a curious bundle attached to the stern of the steamer and bobbing in its wake. Gordon hated new clothes, but, having no respectable civilian dress for his homecoming, he had had to order a new suit and bowler hat, and to ensure that they were properly seasoned before he put them on he had decided to wrap them in a bundle and tow them down to Shanghai!

Gordon's journey home was undertaken with mixed feelings. He dreaded publicity and he hated the idea of returning to England, yet he knew that he must do his duty by his parents. For, although a confirmed bachelor, he was also very much a family man. He was deeply devoted to his mother, had a typically Victorian respect for his father and was very attached to his brothers and sisters, especially to Augusta, who took over first place in his affections after his mother died. Throughout his stay in China he wrote to his mother by every mail, except during his interval of shame after Soochow, to reassure her about his health and happiness, the excellence of the climate and his relations with his superiors. He also sent home his diary of events and copies of the local English newspapers, together with maps and diagrams so that his parents could follow minutely the various reports of the fighting. And he would ask Robert Hart from time to time to send his brother copies of Bruce's despatches in which he was mentioned. In particular, when he decided to take the field again after the murders of the Soochow Wangs, he asked for Bruce's report to go to Henry Gordon, 'as it would comfort my people to see that I am not so universally condemned'.

Although parsimonious in some ways—his letters home were always written on both sides of the thinnest rice-paper sheets and he would often make four pages out of one sheet by writing from west to east and north to south on the same page—he was generous and thoughtful to his family and regularly sent home boxes of treasures and souvenirs—pieces of jade, bronzes, and enamel and porcelain vases by the dozen—together with detailed instructions as to their distribution: 'A to my father, B, C, and D for general and fair distribution among the "tribe" of Gordons, E and F to my father, G to Aunt Amy ... P, Q, and R to my mother ... Y to Henry....' Sometimes he would ask for a vase or a bit of jade to be sent to someone who had befriended him in China and had returned home. But he never kept a thing for himself and, in his own words, left China 'as poor as I entered it'.

This was not entirely due to altruism on his part. For Gordon was something of a Philistine about works of art. He could rave about the gaudily sumptuous *décor* and ornamentation of the Summer Palace in Peking, but he had no appreciation for the exquisitely delicate simplicity of the best jade, which he regarded as dull, but possibly worth something 'at the curio shops of London'. As for Peking itself, he could see little beyond its dirtiness. 'We are all of us getting sick of Peking,' he wrote; 'a dirtier town does not exist. I am sure one ride thru' its filthy streets ought to content any enthusiast.' Likewise with Cairo, which he visited *en route* from England to China and which he dismissed as being 'greatly inferior to Constantinople and twice as dirty'. The ancient glories of the Forbidden City, the spacious serenity of the mosque of Ibn Tulun, even the natural majesty of the Nile were all lost on this unaesthetic soldier of fortune.

Although he liked to live in the wilds of Asia or Africa and hated serving in his own country, Gordon was never able completely to escape from the thinking and attitudes of a British professional soldier. Eccentric though he was, his eccentricity was always limited by that unbreakable bond and those intransplantable roots that bound him to the conventions on which he was reared and schooled and to the family that was virtually his whole social circle. And, while he rebelled against those traditions and disciplines in adolescence and spent his whole life trying to avoid being 'trammelled' by them in Engand, paradoxically he spent most of his service abroad—in China and later in the Sudan —trying by one means or another to inculcate these same traditions into those foreign armies and administrations which he was appointed to lead. Consequently, he spent most of his life in a

78

kind of social hiatus between two worlds, never belonging to either, never able to adapt his ways to his environment. And in this unhappy no-man's-land of the spirit, he turned for comfort to religion and the Holy Bible as the only immutable rock of probity among the shifting quicksands of turpitude.

CHAPTER 7

FAITH AND CHARITY

By the time that Gordon reached England in January 1865 much of the Press publicity about him had died down, and he had little difficulty in avoiding the lionizing that he seemed to dread so much. He kept well clear of London society and official galas, and spent most of his time with his family at Southampton. Now and then an invitation to some social function would arrive and he would decline. If the invitation was for a function in Southampton, he would plead that he must be in London that day and, to avoid being caught out with a lie, he would promptly and at whatever inconvenience make tracks for the capital; and, conversely, if the function was in London he would hasten to Southampton. When he discovered that his mother had not only circulated his China diaries among her friends, but had shown them to a member of the Government, who suggested that they be printed for private circulation, he became greatly enraged and destroyed the only personal day-by-day account that existed of this curious piece of history. (A manuscript report by Gordon of the Ever Victorious Army's part in the Taiping rebellion has survived for posterity, but it is a dry, impersonal and largely factual document which tells us less than his letters to his family and contains none of those revealing personal asides which, if the journal he later kept at Khartoum is any guide, no doubt illumined the Chinese diaries which he so impetuously destroyed.)

Refusing to be lionized by society or to capitalize in public print his adventures in China left Gordon with little to occupy his restless energies. The War Office left him to his own devices, partly because he was due a spell of leave amounting to about two years, but still more because the Army authorities really did not know what to do with this strange military misfit. Not that there was any shortage of employment for officers who preferred services overseas. At this period British troops were engaged in a dozen different far-flung theatres of war consolidating the frontiers of the Second British Empire—in India, Afghanistan, West Africa, and Abyssinia. But neither now nor in the years to come was Gordon asked to take part in these engagements.

The reason for this has never been fully explained. Perhaps he was simply overlooked by the Establishment; more likely he was thought to be a little too unorthodox in his tactics and administration, a man who might too easily 'go native' or forget that his duty was to uphold British interests, not to reform foreign governments and peoples, and a man who would attract more public limelight than was healthy in a British serving officer. Thus the defence of those distant British interests was entrusted to other men more reliable, more stable and amenable to orders.

Inevitably, after a few months of unemployment Gordon became restive and eager to return to military duty. And although he yearned to be posted overseas, he accepted without protest or demur the only job that the War Office had to offer him—that of Commander, Royal Engineers at Gravesend, where he was to direct the construction of some new forts for the defence of the Thames estuary. It was a job which might have held great interest for a man with experience both of river warfare and of constructing forts. But Gordon came very soon to regard it as a mere chore. After his first inspection, he told the War Office that the forts were wrongly sited and would be useless if ever put to the test of defending London against a sea-borne invasion. But the War Office took no notice of his arguments and told him to get on with the job on the basis of the existing plans. So he obeyed his orders and carried on with his allotted task without further protest and with no interest in it, except to complete the job as rapidly as possible. Every morning he would start his rounds at eight o'clock, after a cold bath, a frugal breakfast and a brief spell of Bible-reading. For the next six hours he would work at the double, striding from place to place and making his shorter-legged subordinates run to keep up with him. When he travelled by water, he forced his boatmen to row as if their lives depended on it; and likewise those engaged in building the forts found him an equally exacting taskmaster. Then promptly at two o'clock every afternoon he would stop, and the rest of the day would be devoted to reading, mostly the Bible and religious works, meditation and pouring his thoughts on religion into long letters to his sister Augusta.

A few days after he took up his appointment at Gravesend, Gordon's father died on September 19, 1865. This was to prove a decisive climacteric in his life. The religious seed that had been sown at Pembroke eleven years earlier now started to bear fruit. And as he began to evolve a faith and a creed of his own, he turned to Augusta as the only member of his family to whom the Christian religion meant more than a social discipline, and started a correspondence with her on religious issues which was to continue for the rest of his life. There is something infinitely touching about these letters, which tell perhaps more of the man who wrote them than any other evidence. And the one sensation that emerges most clearly from all this voluminous correspondence is loneliness—the loneliness of the man who is not quite as other men are, who longs for liberation from the captivity of his fleshly body, and who sees death, not as the descent of eternal darkness, but as the opening of the gate to a new and glorious life, where the body is left behind and the spirit reigns triumphant.

'The world,' he wrote to Augusta soon after taking up his Gravesend command, 'is a vast prison house under hard keepers with hard rules; we are in cells solitary and lonely looking for release.' Christ, he went on, was also 'weary, sad, and lonely ... a man of sorrows and acquainted with grief and tears'. But at the end of the long and lonely road 'the wayfarer may be in that glorious home ... where there is no more curse, neither sorrow or crying, at rest forever with that kind and well-known friend'. And at Christmas time he wrote to her: 'I must write and wish you a happy Xmas. I will not say "many of them", for our joy is in our Lord, and we cannot wish many years will pass away before He comes to deliver us from our corruptible bodies and infirmities.' At the same time he counselled her not to be impatient for deliverance or for the realization of the true faith and, when seeking the manifestation of God's presence and power to answer prayers, to look for the smaller proofs and not to demand great miracles. 'Faith does not come like an avalanche upon one,' he wrote; 'it is simple trust and consequently the more we know God the more we will have trust (faith in Him).... But if we must have to see signs and wonders before we will believe, we cannot often see our prayers answered.'

Regularly once a fortnight he would bombard his sister with

long commentaries on the Holy Gospels and the parables or with religious tracts which he suggested were 'good for opening conversations with'. Again and again he reverted to the theme that all that which is of the flesh is evil and corrupt. He rewrote the parable of the sower and the seed so that the fruitful soil was the faith and the stony ground was the flesh, faith being able to withstand the weathering of tribulation and persecution, whereas the flesh withered away under such afflictions. 'All that the flesh admires is doomed.... The flesh as a substance is as useless as the dust is and to which it must return.... The flesh worships idols of silver and gold, its praise is the praise of men, its fears are for what man may say of it. Cursed is the man who makes flesh his arm.... As crucifixion was a slow process, so is our slow death for the flesh. It makes us yearn for complete deliverance.' At the same time he conceded that sin had its spiritual uses. 'We are born corrupt and if the devil had his way, we should be kept in ignorance of it; our permitted transgressions show us our state.'

The combination of boredom with his military duties and ever-increasing intoxication with his new-found faith made Gordon withdraw more and more from all conventional human associations. 'It is difficult,' he wrote to Augusta, 'to talk to people on worldly subjects who do not trace everything to God.' But as his sense of separation from the world increased, he would draw comfort from the belief that he was improving his soul. 'I own it is dull when we do not feel much in common with those we pray for. But after a time it will grow into love, and at any rate it ... keeps me from thinking of things of no import. It also tends to make us less selfish.' And he became, too, increasingly impervious to other people's critical opinions. 'I do many things that are wrong ... and if I own it in my heart that I am culpable, I have such comfort that I do not care what my fellow-man says.'

At the same time he cared about what his fellow-men did to the point of ferocious criticism and denunciation. The inadequacy of the established Church and the hypocrisy of its members particularly agitated him. And in a long indictment of their sanctimony he thundered: 'Explain oh! preachers how it is that we ask and do not get comfort, that your cold services cheer not.... You preach death as an enemy instead of a friend and liberator.... Be as uncharitable as you like but attend my church regularly. Does your vast system of ceremonies, meetings, and services tend to lessen sin in the world? It may make men conceal it. Where would you find more hardness to a fallen one than you would in a congregation of worshippers in the church of this day? Surely this hardness is of the devil and those who show it know not God.... Oh! Pharisees of this day, ye are ten-fold more self-righteous than the Pharisees of old.... Happy is it that there is a shepherd who does know and care for His sheep, for we would be in poor case if we fell in your hands. Fall down oh! ye mighty of the earth, ye kings and warriors and priests and hide yourselves from the face of Him who comes with all His people. He was hungry and thirsty and ye passed Him by. Little did you, in the days of your pride, think you turned the Royal Race from your doors and, by treading them down, trod down the King of Kings. Inasmuch as ye despised them, ye despised Him.' Leprosy, he proclaimed, was leprosy, whether it be covered by garments of silk or by rags. 'The self-righteous preachers and religious authorities of the outward church do all their works to be seen of men, they preach great sanctity and love and do not practise it themselves, they like a special dress and the place of honour at dinners and always take the chief seat in their church or chapel. Woe unto you hypocrites, for you shut up the Kingdom of God by preaching that man cannot be saved except by good works or by belonging to this or that community.'

It was a splendid sermon in the true tradition of the noncon-formist rebel, and it explained why so devout a Christian as he never joined any church or sect, but drew his own particular creed straight from the Bible. And it must be admitted that in most of his life he tried to live up to this high standard of sincerity and selflessness. But there were equally moments when he gave way to that same self-righteousness which he held against the established Church. 'I cannot agree,' he once wrote to Augusta, 'to the fact of a man who has led an ungodly life all his life having the same position as myself, who for forty years have been at great inconvenience to every prayer-meeting and service. I glorify God by this, and that man has dishonoured Him by not attending His services. I have not resisted God; he has. I ought to be saved, for I am better than him.'

Gordon was soon to have much more to weigh in the balance than his regularity as a church-goer. Not long after he came to Gravesend, he embarked on a personal mission to help the poorer people of the town, and especially orphaned boys, that was to become a living memorial to his Christian practice and to show that the religious fervour which inspired his letters to Augusta was no mere psalm-singing pretence. His sensitive nature had always been full of compassion for human suffering. Whether it were the poverty-stricken populace of Cairo, whom he observed on his voyage to China, or the degradation and misery of countless thousands of Chinese peasantry, starving because the tide of a cruel civil war had washed away their only means of subsistence, or the joyless faces of British working men and women, sullenly trudging their way to a long day's labour in a cold, grey dawn, he would cry out, 'How any of us can think this world a happy one is a wonder with so much sorrow.' And soon after he came to Gravesend he found the opportunity to occupy his considerable hours of leisure and to channel his new religious passion into helping to make at least this minute microcosm of the world a happier one for some of its inhabitants.

The opportunity sprang from a meeting with a highly religious and somewhat unworldly couple by the name of Freese, who heard that an officer called Charles Gordon often visited the local branch of the Religious Tract Society—which Mr. Freese had helped to establish—to buy religious works. Gordon was invited to tea at the Freeses' house on the outskirts of Gravesend, and greatly intrigued his hosts with his mixture of youthfulness and maturity. Immured in their life of good works in Gravesend, the Freeses however knew nothing of their strange visitor's background beyond his interest in religion; and when Gordon happened to mention China during the conversation across the teacups, Mr. Freese innocently enquired whether he had ever been there. On being told that he had, the unfortunate host went on to ask, 'Did you see anything of the Taiping rebellion when you were there?' To which his now exasperated guest replied, 'I should think I did. Why, it was I who put an end to it.'

Notwithstanding this embarrassing introduction, Gordon's acquaintance with the Freeses soon ripened into a friendship more intimate than any other relationship in his life outside his family. Irresistibly, he was drawn to this good Christian couple, not only through a mutual interest in religion, but also because, unlike most other professing Christians in the locality, the Freeses cared about the sick and the poor and the hungry and thought it their Christian duty to help to alleviate such suffering. Gordon had already given over his large garden to his poorer neighbours so that they might grow fruit and vegetables, which they could not afford to buy at market prices. Now inspired to fresh efforts by the Freeses, he began to help the young street urchins of Gravesend, taking them into his large official residence at Fort House, feeding and clothing them, teaching them the rudiments of education, and then finding jobs for them in the Merchant Navy. To start with, he was able to house all his boys, or, as he termed them, 'scuttlers', in his own residence. But soon the numbers grew to such proportions that he could not pack in any more. Still he insisted on feeding, clothing, and teaching all who came his way. Every room at Fort House, except for his own small private apartment, was taken over as a dormitory or class-room. Those who came in rags—and they were the majority—he clothed at his own expense, and he was soon buying suits by the score and boots by the gross and distributing them among the 'scuttlers'. In the way of education he taught them to read and write and do simple arithmetic—compulsory free education being then only a pipe-dream of the reformists—and, naturally enough, he read them the Bible and tried to pass on to them some of his own faith in God. On a lighter plane his curriculum also included community singing, usually at the end of the evening's classes, and the telling of adventure stories to stir the imagination of his listeners and to stimulate their interest in those distant places to which their journeyings in the Merchant Navy would later take them, and where their comings and goings would be plotted by flags stuck into a map that hung above his mantelpiece.

In the beginning Gordon did all the teaching himself, as well as buying and distributing and even mending the boys' clothes. But when the 'scuttlers' grew in numbers to several hundreds, he was forced to employ a young teacher to help him. Yet although it cost him more than he could really afford, he paid his assistant out of his own pocket and asked not a penny piece of any local charitable foundation. Added to this, he took on more teaching work, visited almost every school and Sunday school in Gravesend to preach his gospel, and often presented the boys with some mementoes of his Chinese campaign, such as captured Taiping banners or Imperialist standards.

Nor did his spending of money and energy for charitable purposes end with the 'scuttlers'. He also paid regular visits to the local workhouse, where he distributed tobacco and tea to the elderly inhabitants and read them prayers and passages from the Bible. He visited the old and the sick in their homes, to bring them such material and spiritual comfort as he had to offer. And he spent a small fortune on the distribution of religious tracts, which he either bought from the Religious Tract Society or had printed from compositions written by himself and Mrs. Freese. Wherever he went, he would scatter these tracts in the hope of converting his fellow-men to the true faith, sometimes pressing them upon complete strangers, other times scattering them at random in field or street. If he went for a walk he would take a package of tracts and strew them about as a sower dispenses seed in a freshly ploughed field; and when he went to London, he would scatter them out of the train window wherever he saw a group of men standing at a station or working on the railway line.

Before long Gordon had exhausted his slender resources on these various charitable and evangelical enterprises. And he was forced to sell many of his possessions, even including his Chinese medal, to keep going. But nothing could quench his ardour. Neither shortage of funds nor, as sometimes happened, failure to reform the habits and thinking of one of the less virtuous 'scuttlers' could turn him away from his mission. Gordon had found not only a spiritual compensation for the dreary round of soldiering in England. Far more important, he had found an outlet for his missionary zeal and an escape from the loneliness of being a misfit in human society. Probably at no period of his life did he come nearer to a state of happiness than at Gravesend. Gone, for the moment, were the petulance over minor reverses, the arrogance and posturing, the sense of superiority that he had shown in China. Thoroughly dedicated and totally absorbed in dispensing faith, hope, and charity, Gordon was for once serene, contented, at peace with the world and with his own soul. 'I have seen a little lately of rejoicing in trials,' he wrote to Augusta, 'and trust I may see more. I mean really feeling glad at annoyances, inasmuch as they work patience and experience and hope.'

Yet for all this new-found serenity and gratification of purpose, that curious longing for death which had started when he went to the Crimea never left him. On the contrary, if anything, his discovery of what he believed to be the true faith only seemed to make him the more anxious to know the glories of the next world. When on an inspection of his Thames forts his boat was holed and sank near the shore, he expressed his regret that the accident had not occurred in midstream. 'If it had been in the middle,' he said, 'I should be at home tonight in a very bright and happy land.' And when Mrs. Freese protested that he was being foolishly melancholic, he retorted that, since life was like being at school, 'Is it very strange if we long for the holidays?' Death, he claimed, 'is the glorious gate of eternity, of glory and of joy, un-mixed with a taint of sorrow.'

This was no mere passive fatalism that he was expressing, no ordinarily morbid curiosity to see what lay beyond this earthly life. Here was an active, even impatient, yearning for release from this sinful world, wherein lies the explanation of so much of Gordon's life and actions, from his reckless heroism in the Crimea and China to his last stubborn and suicidal stand at Khartoum.

CHAPTER 8

APPOINTMENT TO EQUATORIA

GORDON'S contented and insulated life of good works at Gravesend lasted for more than five years. Then early in 1871 the Government offered him the post of British representative on the Danubian Commission. It was a wrench to leave his 'scuttlers'; but Gordon nevertheless accepted the post, gave away his furniture to the Freeses and other deserving friends and neighbours, and a few weeks later left for Galatz, the Danubian Commission's headquarters on the Black Sea coast of Rumania.

It was a curious assignment to offer to a soldier of Gordon's stubborn and irascible temperament. True, his predecessor on the Commission had also been an Army colonel, but the work involved more diplomacy than soldiering and a lot of ceremonial and social functions which Gordon detested. 'There is a good deal of ceremony and glory which I shall not imitate,' he wrote. 'I cannot see much to do out here for an officer, but shall make myself acquainted with the country.' Nevertheless, it was familiar ground for a former member of the Bessarabian frontier commission, and to almost any other man would have been full of interest. Rumania was something of a shuttlecock in the long-standing conflict between Russia and the Ottoman Empire. Originally known as the Danubian Principalities of Moldavia and Wallachia, the area had formed part of the Ottoman Empire for more than 300 years, but at the start of the Crimean War had been invaded and occupied by Russia as far as the mouths of the Danube. In 1856 the Treaty of Paris placed the two principalities under the collective guarantee of the contracting powers—Great Britain, France, Russia, Prussia, Turkey, Austria, and Sardinia—with Turkey continuing to hold nominal sovereignty. A European Commission, established under the Paris Treaty, then proposed the union of Moldavia and Wallachia, and the principality of Rumania formally came into being in 1858.

Although the Ottoman Sultan still retained the outward

trappings of sovereignty, Rumania enjoyed a wide measure of internal autonomy and even boasted a relatively advanced system of democracy and constitutional government under a Hohenzollern ruler, Prince Charles, who had been elected by a national referendum and later became King Charles I when Rumania gained her full independence in 1881. But to ensure freedom of navigation of the Danube, the Danubian Commission—also established by the Treaty of Paris and consisting of representatives of all the signatory powers—continued to administer the river delta. Nor was such international vigilance unnecessary to ensure the neutrality of this much-disputed territory. Rumania was currently a hotbed of conspiracy, with Russia and Turkey bidding furiously for her support in preparation for the next round of their continuing struggle. Agents of the Tsar and of the Sultan abounded in Bucharest, offering a mixture of tempting bribes and menacing pressures to the ruling prince and his Government. Added to this, just prior to Gordon's arrival at Galatz, the Franco-Prussian War had torn the country apart and caused a deep cleavage between the pro-French majority of this Latin land and its German ruler.

For a man with any taste for diplomatic and political intrigue, the Galatz assignment could scarcely have failed to be of consuming fascination. But Gordon had no such tastes, and, as one who could only find contentment in either contemplation or combat, he hated every moment of his job on the Danubian Commission. He had little use for Prince Charles, who he thought a 'weak man' and 'little more than a puppet', although he liked his pro-British wife, who kept four English servants, ran her house 'after our ideas' and hated Rumania. In fact, his only real interest there seemed to be in a strange Russian sect, who he was told were 'made eunuchs after the begetting of a child'. For the first and only time in his life he yearned to be back in England, or, more specifically, at Gravesend, looking after his 'scuttlers'. So homesick for Gravesend did he become that he even tried, though without success, to persuade Mr. Freese to come out and act as his secretary, and bring 'a Gravesend laddie' with him. As in Peking and Cairo, he saw only the dirt of Galatz—'mud ankle-deep in all the streets'—and the misery of the populace, especially the Jews, who were treated as an alien race and forbidden to hold any property of their own. Needless to say, he also hated the diplomatic social round, and he refused to emulate his predecessor in seeking to dominate and dictate to his European colleagues on the Commission.

Added to these discontents and frustrations, the news from home was deeply distressing. Another of his brothers died early in 1872, and when he went to England for a spell of leave at the end of the year, he found his mother a dying woman. For the whole of his stay he scarcely left the family home at Southampton, and only managed to visit Gravesend and the Freeses once. And he returned to Rumania more depressed than ever, and not a little resentful that he was being put on the shelf by the Army authorities. Yet when the *Daily News* saw fit to condemn the War Office for allowing promotion to be purchased and for overlooking the claims of 'Chinese Gordon' to command the expedition that was sent against the Ashantis in Nigeria because he 'happened to be an Engineer' and from one of the scientific services, he promptly wrote to the Inspector-General of the Army to disclaim any association with the article.

But before the end of the year 1873 Destiny stepped in and transferred Gordon to an altogether different kind of service in an altogether different part of the world. Some months earlier, while visiting Constantinople, he had happened to meet the Prime Minister of Egypt, Nubar Pasha, who had been commissioned by his ruler, the Khedive Ismail, to find an English successor to Sir Samuel Baker, the well-known explorer, as Governor of Equatoria in the south of the Sudan.

Although still part of the Ottoman Sultan's empire, Egypt employed a number of British officers and officials to help in the running of the Army and the State. This system had been started by Ismail's grandfather, Mohammed Ali, the first autonomous ruler of Egypt under the Ottoman Empire and the conqueror of the Sudan in 1819, who borrowed heavily from European skills and ideas throughout his reign. This far-sighted founder of modern Egypt imported Western scientists, craftsmen, technicians, naval and Army officers, picked their brains and set them to work to build schools of engineering and medicine, develop new methods in agriculture and create a modern army. Mohammed Ali's successors not only continued this practice within Egypt, but extended it to their Sudanese domains: hence the appointment of Baker to Equatoria.

For Gordon, the combination of seclusion and challenge in Equatoria was an opportunity not on any account to be missed. And when Nubar asked if he would be willing to take it, he accepted without hesitation, subject to the British Government's approval. Nevertheless, while waiting for official permission, Gordon affected an attitude of fatalism. Writing to his sister, he said: 'As a man driving a horse turns him right and left without consideration whether the horse cares about that way or not, so God with some wise designs turns events one way or another ... so it is with men; events will go on as He likes. To be happy is to be like a well-broken horse, ready for any event.... Once possess this blessing of accepting God's ruling and a man will have little need of others; he suffices for himself.'

Perhaps he had his dying mother in mind as he penned these words. The old lady had recently suffered a stroke and the end was merely a matter of time. As it happened, she died at the end of 1873, at the same time that Lord Granville, Gladstone's Foreign Secretary, gave his official sanction to Gordon's appointment to Equatoria. And with her death the only fetter preventing his freedom of movement was cast off. God had ruled and the 'well-broken horse' was pawing the ground, impatiently 'ready for any event'.

Still, Gordon did not approach his new tasks without trepidation. For one thing, he was somewhat in awe of his predecessor, the bushy-bearded, swashbuckling 'Baker of the Nile', who looked and acted like a Turkish sultan and who had gained great notoriety—as well as a knighthood and the Royal Geographical Society's gold medal—for his explorations of the sources of the Nile and for his claims to have checked the slave trade in the southern Sudan. 'Against me,' he wrote, 'will be Baker and his adherents, Pce of W [Prince of Wales], etc., Geographical Society, the Anti-slavery Society, and all those men who think they ought to be chosen for the post and those who think it rather hard for the Khedive to invade and conquer independent tribes.'

Besides, Gordon's instructions from the Khedive included an order to continue the effort to suppress the slave trade which, despite Baker's claims, was still being carried on by Egyptian and other Arab dealers. Preying on the populations of Equatoria, Uganda, and the neighbouring African territories, these men had amassed large fortunes in the slave-markets of Zanzibar, Arabia and Persia. The Egyptian authorities, although officially opposed to such trafficking, did nothing effective to put a stop to it. Slaving had been for centuries a traditional part of Arab and Turkish commercial life. It had been condoned by the Prophet Mohammed on condition that slaves were treated as members of their owner's family. And the fact that this essential proviso had come to be observed solely in the breach was of little more concern to Egyptian officialdom than it was to the slave-dealers themselves. Still, the Khedive, who was one of the most prodigious spenders of his day, was living on borrowed money. And the money that he had borrowed, like the foreign officials and technicians whom he employed, came from Britain and other European countries, where slavery was strongly condemned and the anti-slavery societies had a powerful influence on policy. He could not afford, therefore, to appear to be conniving at the continuation of this traffic within his domains. Hence his orders to his new Governor to intensify the efforts begun by Baker to break up the slave-gangs of Equatoria.

Gordon did not take long to size up this situation. After seeing Ismail and Nubar in Cairo, he wrote to Augusta in February 1874: 'I think I can see the true motive now of the expedition, and I believe it to be a sham, to catch the attention of the English people, as Baker said. I think the Khedive is quite innocent (or nearly so) of it, but Nubar is the chief mover.' Nevertheless, he was by no means dispirited. Let Nubar intrigue and manoeuvre as he pleased. Once in Equatoria, he would be largely his own master and would govern as he pleased, whether the pashas in Cairo or the slave-dealers in the Sudan liked it or not.

Much as he relished the prospect of his new employment, Gordon had little use for most of his Egyptian employers, whom he dismissed as corrupt and incompetent. He described Nubar as a 'low-born Armenian', and distrusted him profoundly. And when some British consular official warned him against antagonizing the Khedive's Prime Minister, he became very irritated and asserted that no threat or intrigue from Nubar or anyone else in the Egyptian Government would divert him from 'acting loyally'. The sole exception was the Khedive Ismail, who used his considerable powers of charm and fascination on his new Governor to such effect that a strong personal link was established at their very first encounter. Gordon was later to make frequent and

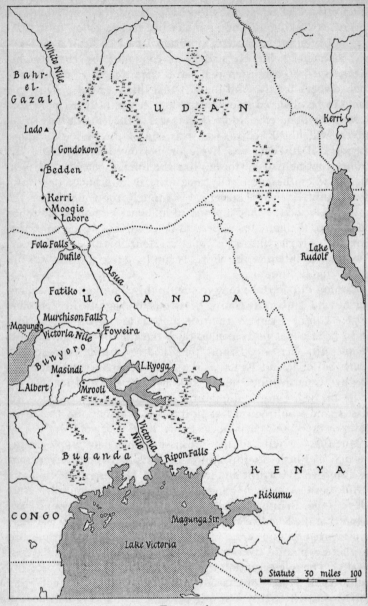

Equatoria

powerful use of this mutual bond of trust when it became necessary to by-pass his immediate superior, the Governor-General of the Sudan, and to put his case direct to the Khedive. But notwithstanding his personal liking for Ismail, he was determined to impress upon his new master that he was not a man who could be 'humbugged' or bribed into acting against his conscience or his judgement. Accordingly, his first act on receiving his commission from the Khedive's hands was to reduce his own salary from the proffered £10,000 a year to £2,000. Unlike Baker, who pocketed the full amount and, according to Gordon, 'drew £75,000 when he left, £40,000 for losses and expenses', he had to show the Khedive and his ministers that not every man worshipped 'gold and silver idols'.

This startling demonstration of incorruptible independence had, it seems, the opposite effect on the Khedive to that which Gordon intended. For instead of giving him credit for his gesture, Ismail felt certain that there must be some ulterior motive in Gordon's self-denial, and insisted on appointing an American officer serving with the Egyptian Army, named Colonel Chaille-Long, to serve with him as a watchdog over the Khedival interests.

The rest of the staff Gordon was free to choose for himself and consisted of three Englishmen (including a nephew of his, William Anson), another American, three Germans, an Italian, a Frenchman, and an Egyptian. It was an unhappy selection. Few of this polyglot group were to prove capable of enduring the Central African climate—five died within a few months and two were invalided home. As for the Khedive's watchdog, Gordon was to discover that Chaille-Long was about as untrustworthy and even more disloyal than Burgevine; and the Egyptian—a notorious slave-trader named Abu Saud, who was serving a prison sentence on charges laid against him by Baker—was in due course sent back to Cairo for plotting mutiny and for lining his pockets from selling Government property. Only one proved to be a success—the Italian, Romolo Gessi, a veteran of Garibaldi's liberation war in Italy, whom Gordon had first met serving as an interpreter in the Crimea and had later found living in Rumania. Gordon described Gessi as a cool, determined man with a genius for practical science and mechanics and the disposition of a Sir Francis Drake. But even with Gessi he was wont to quarrel violently for some act of forgetfulness or procrastination, which wrung from his enraged superior the bitter reproach, 'What a pity you are not an Englishman!'

Once the staff had been appointed, Gordon became his impatient self again and, refusing to stay in Cairo a day longer than was necessary, he set off on February 18, 1874, with Chaille-Long, leaving the rest of his retinue to follow on when they had collected the necessary stores and provisions. The first stage of his journey was by special train to Suez, on which he was accompanied from Ismailia onwards by Ferdinand de Lesseps, who, to Gordon's surprise, had only a few months earlier fathered a child at the age of seventy, and whom he found to be 'A nice, bright, strong old man'. From Suez he was to travel by special steamer to Suakim on the Red Sea whence he would journey overland to Berber on the Nile. The rest of the trip would be by river steamer to Khartoum, where he would stop off for a few days to make contact with the Egyptian Governor-General of the Sudan, Ismail Ayoub Pasha, and thence to Gondokoro, the capital of Equatoria. In all the journey was well over 2,000 miles; yet Gordon tackled it as if it were a 100-yard sprint, making every post a winning-post. Although he had never ridden a camel before, he made the 250-mile journey from Suakim to Berber in three days less than the fastest caravan, and completely exhausted his Egyptian mounted escort in the process. Then, as he sailed up the Nile, he kept exhorting the stokers to put on more steam until they were blowing as hard as their own boilers. And when the steamer ran aground, he took off his trousers and leaped into the river to lend a personal hand in helping to push her back into the deep channel. As at Gravesend, when he made his junior officers run to keep up with him on his rounds of inspection, so throughout his time in the Sudan Gordon delighted in outpacing and outriding his escort on every journey. And few things pleased him more than the astonishment of a tribe that he was visiting when he rode his camel into the camp entirely alone, an hour or more ahead of his panting bodyguard.

In these remarkable feats of endurance he was no doubt greatly helped by an immensely strong constitution and robust health. Whether in the bitter winter cold of the Crimea, the torrid humidity of a Chinese summer, or the hair-drier heat of the Sudan, he was very seldom ill, except with a liver complaint which he had had since he returned from China. And he could keep going long after the natives, let alone his fellow Europeans, were dropping from fatigue or fever. While in China he caught smallpox, but he threw it off as if it were no more than a mild attack of influenza. And in the Sudan, equipped only with a bottle of brandy and some quinine, he warded off or survived all manner of sickness, while members of his staff and the Egyptian garrison troops went down like flies.

But Gordon needed more than just an iron constitution to succeed in the task which he had taken on. He also needed co-operation and support from the Egyptian authorities, preferably from those nearest to the spot, i.e. the Governor-General and his staff in Khartoum. And, though Ayoub Pasha greeted him with all due ceremonial when he alighted from his steamer at Khartoum, Gordon did not take long to decide that the Governor-General was neither able nor willing to give him the help he wanted. Ayoub might receive him in full dress and with a brass band and a guard of honour of Egyptian infantry, but it was idle to expect more from him than these courtesies. For one thing, there was not enough money in the Treasury at Khartoum to pay for the proper administration of the neighbouring province of Kordofan, let alone Equatoria—and under the prevailing system Equatoria's budget was governed by Khartoum. For another, the Pasha was clearly too indolent and pleasure-seeking to be interested in what went on in his southernmost province 1,000 miles away.

Moreover, Gordon's instructions from Ismail included a specific direction to continue Baker's work of opening up the higher reaches of the Nile and to link up Equatoria with the Great Lakes, Albert and Victoria in Buganda—now part of the state of Uganda. In other words, Gordon was to extend the Khedive's frontiers still further to the south. Ismail had a prodigious appetite for territory and had expanded Egypt's dominions by taking over most of the Red Sea coast as far as Cape Guardafui on the Indian Ocean and by seizing the Abyssinian province of Harar. And most recently Baker, in 1872, had added the Kingdom of Bunyoro, to the east of Lake Albert, to the Khedive's growing empire. The struggle for control of the Nile between Britain and France which culminated in the clash at Fashoda in 1898 had not yet begun. But Britain had already got a toe-hold in East Africa at Zanzibar and was casting a covetous eye on the territories of the interior. Ismail was therefore anxious to stake his claim in Buganda before the British established themselves there.

Such grandiose plans required far more help and co-operation than could conceivably be forthcoming from Khartoum; and Gordon realized before he left for Gondokoro that he would soon have to draw heavily on his personal credit with the Khedive if he was to make a success of his mission. Confident that he would have no difficulty in gaining direct access to Ismail, he made little effort to come to terms with Ayoub Pasha. In fact, during his brief stay in the Governor-General's palace, he gratuitously insulted his host by stalking out of an entertainment at which some semi-naked girls were joined in the middle of their performance by the over-excited and probably intoxicated Austrian Consul, Martin Hansal. And when he reflected on his behaviour after the event he unrepentantly insisted that he had done the right thing in the circumstances and that his protest would teach Ayoub a lesson in how not to divert an English guest.

Gordon seems to have spent a lot of his time teaching his host lessons in this or that. When he returned the Governor-General's lavish hospitality, he taught him a lesson in simplicity by feeding him tapioca pudding on cheap local plates, although his staff had discovered a huge treasure-chest of French wines, Sèvres china, and the finest glass and linen, which Baker had left behind for his successor. And there were lessons in how not 'to cajole a member of the Gordon family' which were administered by the simple, blunt method of telling the Governor-General, and anyone else who tried to argue with him, to shut up and go away. Ayoub must have been thankful to see the back of Gordon when he left to continue his journey to Gondokoro. But his joy was short-lived; for within little more than two months Gordon was back full of complaints about mismanagement of affairs in Equatoria by the authorities in Khartoum, and demanding a free hand to govern his province as he saw fit.

Certainly there was ample justification for these complaints. The Egyptian garrisons were negligible in numbers and were being paid by Khartoum in gin and slave-girls rather than in cash. To supplement their meagre rations, the soldiers had taken to cattle-stealing, which had enraged the local tribes and driven them together to resist all authority and to withhold payment of their taxes. The chaos and corruption that Gordon found in Equatoria was well summed up in a marginal commentary that he wrote on the printed text of a lecture given by Baker to Cambridge University on his 'achievements' in the Sudan. Where Baker claimed that under his régime 'the slave-hunters were driven from the country at the point of the bayonet', Gordon commented that, while the slavers were cleared out of the district immediately to the north of Gondokoro, all the eight slave stations to the east, west, and south were left unmolested, 'though they were on his route and easy of access from the Nile'. Gordon continued: 'His government when I came up was 400 men at Gondokoro, 300 men at Fatiko and you could not go out of either place half a mile.' On Baker's statement that he promoted agriculture among the tribes by distributing vegetable seeds, Gordon tersely remarked: 'Never one seed given.' And where Baker said that 'a slight tax in corn was cheerfully paid for the support of the troops', he asserted that 'not a grain of corn was paid or obtained except by expeditions to take it'.

Gordon was not always very fair in his criticisms of Baker's record in Equatoria. But there is, nevertheless, little doubt that these comments gave a substantially accurate picture of the situation as he found it, and that Baker had spent a good deal more of his time and energy in exploring and opening up the frontier with Bunyoro than in administering Equatoria and suppressing the slave trade. Certainly there was good reason for Gordon to return, as he did, post-haste to Khartoum to extract from the Sudan Treasury enough hard cash to settle his garrisons' backpay, and to demand direct from the Khedive full autonomy for his province, especially in matters of finance.

Ismail promptly conceded these demands, and Gordon was off up the Nile again within a matter of hours, although this time without any ceremony or salutes being offered to him by the Governor-General, whose authority he had overridden. He had got what he wanted; he had an independent command and was answerable to no one but the Khedive himself. But he was facing a challenge that was to tax to the limit his resources of physical endurance and spiritual faith.

CHAPTER 9

EXPLORATIONS

IN being ordered to suppress the slave trade, Gordon had been set an almost impossible task. For one thing, most of the mudirs, or headmen, of the towns and villages of Equatoria and elsewhere were hand in glove with the slavers, and there was scarcely an Egyptian official in Khartoum who could be relied on to enforce the anti-slavery laws. Every one of them was involved in some aspect or other of slave-dealing, and at one point Gordon suspected his own Egyptian A.D.C. of being in league with the slavers. Added to this, the slave trade was encouraged and protected by Kabba Rega, the King of Bunyoro and Mutesa's refractory neighbour, who had held out against Baker's annexation of his domains and was continuing to resist all attempts to impose the Khedive's sovereignty upon his kingdom. Most important of all, the greatest slaver in the whole of the Sudan, a distinguished-looking pasha of the old school named Zubair, had carved out a kingdom for himself in the Sudan's western province of Darfur, where, according to the eye-witness account of at least one explorer who visited him, he 'surrounded himself with a court that was little short of princely in its details'. Zubair had not only refused to pay tribute to the Khedive, but had defeated an Egyptian army which had been sent to bring him to book. Gordon's seven river steamers might patrol the Nile night and day in Equatoria but, with Darfur in the hands of the prince of slavers, the traffic could continue unimpeded along the caravan routes to the west of the river.

On top of all this lay the problems that arose from the un-homogeneous character of the Sudan's population. For here in this vast territory, as large as western Europe including Scandinavia, was—and still is—the frontier between Arabia and Africa. The north from the Egyptian border at Wadi Halfa to Khartoum—comprising Nubia, Kassala, and parts of Darfur and Kordofan—was Arab by race and, since its conquest by

Mohammed Ali, Moslem by religion. This area enjoyed at least a rudimentary civilization dating from the sixth century A.D., when it was encompassed by the evangelizing efforts of the Byzantine Empire to create an outpost of Christianity in neighbouring Abyssinia. But the southern Sudan was a different story. Racially African and Negro, it had been untouched by any form of civilization, apart from a Hammite incursion from the north about 1,000 years before Christ. Rival missions of Catholics from Europe and Moslems from Zanzibar had recently tried to proselytize the pagan population, but with little success. Human life meant little in these parts, where, as Gordon was soon to discover, a family would willingly exchange a child for a cow. Thus, however much the tribes of Equatoria might suffer from the depredations of the slavers, they had lived for so long with this traffic in human beings that they had come to accept it as an inevitable part of their lives, and they could scarcely be expected to recognize Gordon and his Egyptian garrisons as their liberators and to do their bidding without question or qualification.

Baker had realized these daunting truths soon enough and, despite his claims to have suppressed the slave trade, had given up the unequal struggle. But Gordon, having criticized Baker for his shortcomings, was committed at least to try to improve on his predecessor's negative performance. And to this end, before leaving Khartoum, he issued in March 1874 a decree which, as he described it, 'in fact put the district under martial law'. The people were reminded that slave-trading was illegal; the import into Equatoria of arms or powder, except by the Government's agents, was prohibited; passports were required to enter the province; and a Government monopoly of the ivory trade was declared. At the same time Gordon decided to make contact with King Mutesa of Buganda, whose support was essential to pave the way for linking Equatoria with the Great Lakes. There was much to be said for lining up with Mutesa against the friend and protector of the slavers, Kabba Rega. He had lately been visited by H. M. Stanley and had affected a strong interest in that journalist-explorer's dissertations on the subject of Christianity. He might therefore well prove a man after Gordon's own heart. But Mutesa could also be most difficult and unpredictable. At one time it was said that he contemplated diverting the Victoria Nile to irrigate his kingdom by blocking off the Ripon Falls, where Lake Victoria

Nyanza debouched into the river—a feat which Staneley claimed was not as difficult as it might seem, since the lake lay 'on a plateau like an inverted basin and could be made to trickle over at any point'.

As his emissary to this curious monarch, Gordon chose Chaille-Long. He had by this time tumbled to the fact that the American had been sent to spy and report on him to the Khedive, and in his irritation had begun to find fault with nearly everything that Chaille-Long did. 'He is not worth anything,' he wrote to his sister; 'always going to do something or other and never does it ... a regular failure who lives on what he *has* done.' Nevertheless, there was no other suitable member of his staff to send to Buganda; and, besides, he could think of no better way of getting rid of this cuckoo from the nest. So Chaille-Long was packed off to Mutesa's court, while Gordon himself collected the rest of his staff who had come up from Cairo with his stores, and set off up the Nile.

A few days later he arrived at the junction of the Saubat River, which flows into the Nile from the east a few miles downstream from the Sudd—a vast, fetid swamp of papyrus ferns and other aquatic vegetation with roots up to five feet long, in which the river loses itself for nearly 200 miles of its length. For centuries past the Sudd had formed an impassable barrier for any vessel until a navigable channel was cut through it shortly before Gordon arrived in the Sudan. And since it had been hitherto impossible to navigate the Nile to the south, the Saubat had become established as the main river route for the slave convoys proceeding from Equatoria into Zubair's domains in Darfur. But nobody had thought of stationing a garrison there to intercept the slave traffic. Gordon therefore decided on the spot to remedy this deficiency and, acting on his principle that 'self is the best officer to do anything for you', he put himself in charge of the Saubat garrison, with a small detachment of troops and a bodyguard bequeathed to him by his predecessor and nicknamed 'Baker's Forty Thieves'. Gessi was sent, with his nephew William Anson, to set up a similar garrison at Rabatchambe at the southern end of the Sudd. And the rest of the staff were despatched with a small escort to Gondokoro, where Abu Saud, acting as Deputy Governor, was to take over the central administration, such as it was.

Gordon stayed at Saubat until September, personally directing operations against the slavers, helping to protect the tribes against the prevalent local pastime of cattle-stealing and trying to teach them the rudiments of agriculture. With so many local officials in league with the slave-traders and cattle-thieves it was an uphill task. But he thrived on his work and, at least to begin with, he met with considerable success. In the very first month, thanks to the interception of messages from a slave-trader and cattle-thief to the Mudir of Fashoda, he caught a caravan of 300 slaves and 200 cattle, and induced the slave-trader to work with him under the threat of a long term of imprisonment. Further successes followed, with batches of several hundred slaves being liberated from river boats, often hidden under piles of wood or contraband ivory.

Gordon was greatly encouraged by these achievements, which he proudly reported in the letter-journal that he wrote to Augusta by every mail. As always when things were going well, he made light of his afflictions, such as mosquitoes, sandflies, ants, rats, and scorpions; and although the heat and humidity often made the ink run so that he had to write in pencil, he said of the climate: 'if God wills, it is as healthy as the Isle of Wight!' In fact, to judge from his letters at this point, he might have been in a semi-paradise inhabited by such exotic wild life as hippopotami, crocodiles, antelopes, cameleopards, storks, pelicans, and birds of every breed and colour.

But his mood was soon to change when he left Saubat to return to Gondokoro. A few weeks before leaving, he had heard from Gessi that William Anson had died, probably of blackwater fever; and when he arrived at Gondokoro, he found 'a complete hospital' with almost all his staff ill and obviously unable to endure the climate and conditions of Equatoria any longer. Added to this, a number of his Egyptian soldiers were sick and some had died of fever. Gordon made up his mind at once. All the sick were to be invalided home and 'no more fellows [i.e. Europeans] to be sent up here', and his headquarters would be moved forthwith from the low-lying and unhealthy 'collection of straw huts' that was Gondokoro. For his new headquarters he first chose a place called Rageef in the hills that lay to the south, and when Rageef proved difficult of access for the steamers he moved to Lado, a few miles downstream and again on high ground.

Both moves were accomplished without great difficulty and, with his staff reduced to Chaille-Long (away in Buganda), Gessi, Abu Saud, and an English engineer named Kemp, Gordon began once again to count his blessings. At least Abu Saud's report on his stewardship was highly encouraging. Due to his 'great influence ... all the chiefs have given in their submission and are most peaceably inclined', he wrote. But Gordon's relief did not last long. By the end of September he had become disenchanted with Abu Saud. He had been warned in Cairo and again in Khartoum not to try to turn his notorious 'poacher', who had made war against Baker, into a gamekeeper. But he had stubbornly refused to listen, describing Abu Saud as the only member of his team with any 'kick in him', and promoting him to be his deputy over the head of the Egyptian garrison commander at Gondokoro, Raouf Bey, whose protests brought about his instant dismissal and return to Khartoum. Now, after a week or two back at his headquarters, he discovered that Abu Saud was stealing and selling ivory in defiance of the Government decree. As for his claim to have influenced the submission of the local chiefs, Gordon had come to the conclusion that any submissions had been obtained by brute force and that Abu Saud had adopted a 'bumptious and bullying' attitude towards them and had 'usurped all my functions'. Nettled by the discovery that his confidence in his deputy had been so sadly misplaced, he dismissed him on the spot, and packed him off back to Egypt.

With such frustrations at headquarters, Gordon's temper began to fray badly. 'I am cruel, revengeful, vicious to those under me,' he confessed to his sister; 'a perfect tyrant, I am. But you want to be a tyrant among these people ... they take advantage of your kindness.' He was also particularly short-tempered with his Egyptian soldiers. 'I look on the Chinese as far superior to them in every way,' he wrote in a letter bitterly complaining about their slowness and incompetence. 'One's work is really more the reform of the Egyptians than civilization of the natives.'

Still, for all the difficulties at Gondokoro, the news from Saubat continued to be good. There the garrison was carrying on their good work against the slavers, and early in October were able to report the capture of a convoy of no less than 1,600 slaves. Gordon also took pride in a successful experiment designed to break the power of the tribal rulers by paying for casual labour direct to the workers themselves and not to their chiefs. He was also making some progress in teaching the tribal leaders the rudiments of civilized life, including the use of coins as a means of exchange rather than the traditional beads or calico—not exactly an easy task with wild Dinka chieftans, who walked about stark naked, save for a necklace, and whose ceremonial greeting of friendship to their newly appointed Governor consisted of licking the backs of his hands and spitting on each of his cheeks.

Then in mid-October Chaille-Long returned from his mission, bringing news that Gordon wanted to hear from Buganda. Mutesa had received his American visitor with warm friendship, and, to gladden Gordon's heart still further, Chaille-Long had found the route to Buganda a lot easier than anyone had anticipated. Cutting across country via Fatiko, he had by-passed Lake Albert and, fourteen days out of Gondokoro, had struck the Nile again at Foweira, after which there were no cataracts to navigate as far as the falls at the northern end of Lake Victoria, so that the river had taken him to within three days' march of Mutesa's palace.

As part of his scheme to link Equatoria with the Great Lakes and to annex Buganda to Ismail's growing empire, Gordon planned to sail a couple of twin-screw steamers—the *Khedive* of 108 tons and 20 h.p. and the *Nyanza* of 38 tons and 10 h.p.— together with two smaller steel boats, up the Nile. Now, as always, in a hurry to reach his next objective, he conceived a short-cut, based on Chaille-Long's reconnaissances, which involved dismantling the steamers at Dufile (on the present Uganda–Sudan border) and conveying them overland via Fatiko to Foweira. Mutesa's palace was only a short haul from Lake Victoria; and if Chaille-Long had been able to get by river from Foweira to within three days' march of it, presumably there would be only one more obstacle—the Ripon Falls—to surmount before the steamers could be launched on to the lake.

This was thrilling news and he was delighted with its bearer. Forgotten were his previous disparaging comments about Chaille-Long. Now Gordon found him 'greatly improved and worth a great deal to me if he will stay'. Three months later the American was sent down to Khartoum to obtain reinforcements for the fever-stricken garrisons. But even though he failed to satisfy Gordon's demand for black troops and brought back 400 Egyptians, with

Raouf Bey at their head, Gordon would not condemn him. 'Oh! my dear Augusta,' he commented, 'for two days I dared not ask Long ... whether these troops were Arab or black troops. At last I asked. They were Arabs! ! ! Now, out of 250 Arabs I brought here, I should say half were dead and 100 were invalided; so you may imagine my horror. He did his best, poor Long, but it was killing for me.... This reinforcement was worse than useless—much worse. Out of 150, eighty-four were sick the day after arrival, and now is comparatively the healthy season.' But within a few weeks the brief honeymoon was over. Chaille-Long had 'tumbled back into procrastination and forgetfulness', and Gordon decided to get rid of him at the first opportunity.

In fact, by this stage, Gordon had fallen out with every member of his staff, except Gessi, who had escaped to Khartoum to get the steamers ready for the expedition to Lake Victoria. Even the reliable Kemp was now 'always ill ... and utterly forgetful ... an ill-bred fellow [who] has often taken impertinent liberties, taking without by your leave my stores'. The letter-journal was now becoming one long complaint about his dwindling group of officers, who he felt were putting on him and using him for their own ends. 'What with the soldiers and the officers I am heartily sickened of the whole work.' He was also bothered by a regular traffic of travellers, including botanists, naturalists, and geologists who, hearing that Equatoria was being opened up, were swarming up the Nile like bees after a new queen. Least welcome of all these visitors was Martin Hansal, the Austrian Consul, who came to visit his old haunts at Gondokoro, where he had been a missionary for two years, without, so Gordon tartly asserted, making any visible converts. Since it appears that Hansal spent most of his stay in bed, due to over-indulgence with the brandy-bottle, Gordon was perhaps justified in his criticisms.

The mood of benign optimism had changed to inspissated gloom. Gordon now began to question the whole purpose of his mission in Equatoria. Was he right, for instance, to persuade the tribes to sell their ivory to the Government? Might this not put them in a position where they would be 'a prey to my Arab successor'? 'Not a single tusk came during Baker's time' because the tribes then had no faith in the Government. But, since they trusted him, they had conformed to the law. Yet their new-found confidence might prove to be a noose around their necks, when some corrupt Egyptian official should take over as Governor and cheat them for his own ends. 'What right,' he said, 'have I to coax the natives to be quiet for them to fall into the hands of a rapacious pasha after my departure ... [or] to upset Kabba Rega, or delude Mutesa into security to be eventually swallowed up?' Likewise, he wondered whether he was really doing the best thing for the slaves, whose convoys he intercepted, by turning them loose? Not a few of the slaves he had liberated in the Saubat district seemed to be more afraid of being set upon and killed by the local tribes than they were of being kept and sold as slaves.

So depressed did he become with these anxieties that he wrote to his sister that, if the Khedive were suddenly to decide to dismiss him, he would deem it a blessed release. His only consolation was his religion. 'What comfort one gets in all worries by looking to higher things! ... Imagine the intricacy of the government of the world, the detail required for each person, each work, each rag of humanity, and judge of His wisdom who can never make the least mistake and is still and tranquil in the turmoil of it all.' Summing up his feelings in the spring of 1875, he wrote to his sister: 'I hope to get the Nile communications open to the lakes ... to put boats on Victoria Nyanza, to settle Kabba Rega and say good-bye ... 18 months will finish it for me.' And he finally resolved his doubts about his mission with the comforting reflection that he would 'trust to the Higher than Highest to look to the welfare of these heathen after I go'.

In this mood of alternating resignation and despair, he then set about planning the expedition that was to open up 'the Nile comunications' with the Great Lakes. This required a wide measure of delegated authority, never Gordon's strongest administrative quality. Someone had to look after the northern part of Equatoria while he was away in the south struggling up the Nile cataracts. Someone had to go to Buganda and keep Mutesa sweet. And someone had to be his backstop in Khartoum to ensure the regular flow of supplies, which was being threatened by Ayoub Pasha's deliberate refusal to co-operate, out of pique at having Equatoria removed from his jurisdiction. Gessi, already in Khartoum preparing the steamers for the lakes expedition, was the obvious choice for supply agent. But, since Gordon had finally fallen out with Chaille-Long and had sent him back to Khartoum, he was now without his original ambassador to

Mutesa. However, at this point three new Europeans arrived fortuitously at Lado, notwithstanding Gordon's pronouncement that 'no more fellows' should join him. These were two Englishmen, Lieutenants Watson and Chippindall of the Royal Engineers, and a Frenchman, Ernest Linant, whose brother, a member of Gordon's original staff, had died at Gondokoro. Linant, being an accomplished linguist, was quickly sent off as envoy to Mutesa, while Watson and Chippindall were detailed to organize the expedition to the lakes; and to look after the north of the province Gordon, for want of any desirable alternative, nominated Raouf Bey.

Having settled his administrative problems, Gordon now fell to pondering the physical difficulties of getting his steamers up the Nile—the *Khedive* on to Lake Albert and the smaller *Nyanza* on to Lake Victoria. He discarded his plan for transporting them in sections overland via Fatiko—a journey too long and too fraught with the risk of attack from Kabba Rega's hostile tribesmen to be a practical proposition. But the alternative was not without its problems. From Bedden, thirty miles upstream from Lado, there were rapids at intervals all the way to Labore, which would mean carrying the steamers at least this far. After this the Nile was an unknown quantity, although reported to be fairly easily navigable as far as Dufile, half-way to Lake Albert. At great length and in the minutest detail, he debated in his letter-journal the pros and cons of this route. Could the dismantled steamers be carried in carts? he wondered. Could the native porters draw the carts? Would they endure the miseries and privations of the journey or would they 'pitch the carts on purpose into ravines'? What about the effects of the rainy season on the operation? Yet, if he had to abandon all ideas of overland transport, how could his ships negotiate the Bedden rapids? What about digging a canal to circumvent this rocky barrier?

Augusta, understandably enough, seems to have found all this technical argument somewhat tedious. 'Judging from your letters,' Gordon complained in his replies, 'you do not take much interest in the course of events up in these parts.' Her replies, he said, were 'very poor things', which contained nothing but chit-chat about people in England who did not interest him at all. But Augusta was not the only person whom he contrived to madden by his constant fussing and fretting about routes. Chippindall, although to begin with one of Gordon's sincerest admirers, was soon driven to distraction by his insistence on doing his own staff work and by his constant distrust and cross-examination of his officers. 'He seems always to think that nobody but his blessed self can even screw a box-lid on,' he wrote in exasperation to a friend. 'He is a fearful egotist ... and how he bores me night after night about the levels and distances ... whether Baker's levels are right, whether the distance is this or that, what you think; then if you give an opinion [you are] nailed at once, and your reasons asked and worried at, till out of sheer fag you agree to any proposition he likes to put forward.'

In the event he decided to take a chance with the river route and to abandon the plan for overland porterage. But first it was necessary to reconnoitre the Nile and to establish a chain of river stations between Lado and Dufile. Chippindall was detailed for this duty while Gordon occupied his time 'coaxing the natives', pacifying the local sheikhs, and entertaining his troops with 'magic lantern' shows. He also did a personal reconnaissance as far as Kerri, some sixty miles upstream, where he was relieved to find no rapids for a stretch of twenty-five miles south of Bedden. His relief was even greater when, in the middle of April, Chippindall returned from Dufile with encouraging reports of the possibilities of navigating the Nile from there to Lake Albert. And with river stations now established at Rageef, Bedden, Kerri, Labore, and Dufile, the stage was almost set for the steamer expedition to start. All that lacked were the steamers, and here an unexpected hitch had occurred. This was the rainy season and, due to an abnormally high rise in the river's level, the steamers were unable to make their way south of Khartoum. First May, then June went by with no sign of a steamer, and Gordon began to think that the Sudd must have closed in again and cut him off completely from the outside world.

Ruefully he wrote that the Khedive should have adopted his suggestion for opening up communications between Equatoria and East Africa. In January 1875 he had suggested to the Khedive that, in view of the hazards of navigating the Nile, the base for communications with his Equatorian domains should be established at Mombasa Bay on the Indian Ocean, some 250 miles north of Zanzibar. There was no great difference in distance between the two routes, each being about 3,000 miles long. But the sea-route to the lakes via Mombasa Bay presented, so he claimed, none of the obstacles—cataracts, rapids, sudds, etc.—of the Nile route. And he proposed that the Khedive should send an expedition forthwith to establish the necessary links for this new eastern detour. But it seemed that Ismail had been forced under British pressure to deny his proposal. And Gordon was left to reflect somewhat bitterly that 'Great Britain does not want Egypt to debouch on the sea', for fear of a threat to Zanzibar.

By the first week of July he could wait no longer for his steamers and he decided to try to force a passage up the Nile with a small flotilla of locally built *nuggars*, broad, well-constructed native boats about thirty feet in length. The lessons which he and his men would learn from getting these smaller boats upstream would come in very useful when the steamers eventually got through to Lado. By superhuman efforts, three *nuggars* had earlier been passed through the rapids from Bedden up to Kerri, and it seemed unlikely that they would encounter any worse obstacles before Lake Albert. So the decision to start without the steamers was made; and with its making Gordon's mood briefly switched again from gloom to optimism. Now he reckoned that the powerful *Khedive* would be able to make the trip to Dufile in as little as thirty-one days. And no sooner had he come to this conclusion than the *Khedive* arrived at Lado and began cautiously to thread her way upstream.

Meanwhile Gordon pioneered onwards from Kerri with his *nuggars*. It was a back-breaking, heartrending task hauling these ungainly boats against a current so powerful that if one of them broke loose—as frequently happened with the inferior tackle and rotten ropes—it would be swept four miles downstream before it could be recovered and secured. Sixty to eighty natives from the tribes around Lado and Rageef were needed to haul each boat through river gorges narrowed in places to a mere forty yards, down which poured a hostile torrent of water. 'Your brother prays the *nuggars* up,' Gordon wrote to Augusta, 'as he used to do the troops when they wavered in the breaches in China, but often and often the ropes break and it has all to be done over again. I do not feel that I ever could do any more work after this command.' And as always, he was full of complaints against his men. 'Oh! dear what a people to slave for!! They never have a knife or a hammer nor a bit of yarn nor anything of the sort; they have

110

not the least idea of preventing a rope running out too rap-idly....'

Nor did he always know exactly where he was and how long it would take to reach Dufile, since it was 'impossible to get any information from the natives, who cannot count'. And although nine days out from Kerri he received the welcome news that the *Khedive* had successfully negotiated the Bedden rapids, he now began to abandon hope of getting the steamer up that year. 'I have four things to contend with,' he wrote in his letter-journal. '1st, the natural difficulties of the river, 2nd, the march through shy and unknown tribes who have never seen a foreigner, 3rd, a useless and unreliable set of soldiers and officers encumbered with women and children—there are 120 women and children to 108 soldiers—4th, want of good ropes to haul the *nuggars*.' And he concluded by saying that 'the anxiety has killed any enthusiasm in me; I never had a more anxious time'.

Two days later disaster struck in the Yerborah rapids below the village of Moogie, where two *nuggars* and a smaller boat drifted on to the rocks and stuck fast in midstream, taking their own tow-ropes with them. Only by using other boats could they be freed. And, rather than risk losing yet more of his small flotilla in the raging torrent, Gordon elected to wait until the flood subsided and to establish yet another river station at Moogie.

This decision was to bring further trouble to his expedition. For the riparian tribes, observing that these strangers, numbering no less than 500, appeared to be digging themselves into a forti-fied position within their territory, soon switched from shyness to hostility and began a series of attacks on their camp. During his stay at Lado, Gordon had had time and opportunity to pacify the natives and to enlist their co-operation for his journey south. He had forbidden his soldiers to maraud and plunder native villages and had invited the tribal sheikhs to report any offenders to the officer in charge of the nearest station, who would carry out the necessary punishment. As a result, Gordon had met with no hos-tility near Lado. 'One has no fear of every bit of high grass as before,' he had gladly recorded of his journey as far as Kerri. But by the time he reached Moogie, his patience was running out and he was no longer prepared to spend weary hours reasoning with riparian sheikhs, the more so as he was only going to stay there until he could refloat his *nuggars*. He therefore ordered his soldiers to shoot any natives approaching the station who appeared to be hostile, and to teach the tribes a lesson by 'taxing their cattle'. At this point Ernest Linant returned from his mission to Mutesa and, finding his chief under constant attack, suggested taking a party of soldiers to burn the huts of the nearest hostile tribe. Gordon agreed and Linant set off. But he failed to allow for the cunning and capacity for concealment of these tribesmen and walked into an ambush in which he and all save one of his escort were speared to death.

This tragedy all but destroyed what remained of Gordon's confidence. At night he could not sleep, and took to prowling round the camp to see if the sentries were on the alert. Inevitably he found them often asleep at their posts, which led to renewed outbursts about these 'cowardly, lying, effeminate brutes, these Arabs and Sudanese without any good point about them that I have seen; it is degrading to call their leaders and their men officers and soldiers; I wish they had one neck and someone would squeeze it'. He had already weeded out a number of Baker's 'old soldiers' and sent them back to Khartoum—apart from those sent home for health reasons—because, he said, they had become 'pampered and spoiled'. Now he found that the unhappy residue were no match for the savage tribesmen, who used the tall grass that grew to a height of six feet along the river banks, to ambush his expedition and to make themselves an almost invisible target for his riflemen. The night attacks were particularly wearing and often created a state of panic in the camp, the natives enjoying the advantage of being able to shoot their arrows and hurl their spears at the tell-tale flashes of rifle-fire, which gave away the positions of the defenders.

The more indignant Gordon became about his own soldiers, the more he seemed to admire the native tribesmen, despite the trouble that they were causing him. And once again he fell to questioning whether he was really doing the right thing by these tall, magnificent specimens of black humanity in trying to open up their lands to the world outside. 'Poor people,' he wrote; 'they are happy in their way, perhaps more happy than those who have much more of the things of this world.' His object was to stop slavery by promoting trade in goods, such as ivory, as a lucrative alternative. But would this make the people any happier? For he had little doubt that the liberated slaves who were serving in the

Khedive's army were more unhappy as soldiers than they had been as slaves; and, in any case, service in the army did not necessarily protect them from being sold as slaves again. Gordon had only recently lost an efficient officer who was caught selling six of his soldiers to a slave-trader and had committed suicide rather than face trial and possibly execution in Egypt.

Besides, what lay in store for him if he did reach the Great Lakes and bring Mutesa politically and commercially within the area of the Khedive's writ? Linant had returned with a confused and somewhat less encouraging report of the King of Buganda than that brought by Chaille-Long. Mutesa had once more professed to be a friend of Egypt and an implacable enemy of Kabba Rega, against whom he suggested that he and Gordon should align themselves. 'Take west and north,' he said in a pencil scrawl brought by Linant, 'and I will take east and south, and let us put Bunyoro in the middle and fight against them.... I want to be a friend of the English. I am Mutesa, son of Suna, King of Buganda. Let God be with Your Majesty, even with you all. Amen.' Yet for all these protestations of friendship, he had tipped off his so-called enemy when Linant left, so that Kabba Rega could attack him on his return journey, as indeed he did. Mutesa had also affected a strong interest in Christianity—H. M. Stanley was paying him yet another visit when Linant arrived—and he had agreed to forbid slavery and to open up trade with Egypt. Still, according to Linant, the King was a complete savage who revelled in cruelty and frequently carried out ten to twenty executions in a day. All in all, it seemed that the King of Buganda was merely trying to use his new contacts with Egypt to serve his own ends. As Gordon had observed earlier in the year, 'Mutesa continues to send courtesies and sent also 10 elephants tusks; but this does not pay, for he sends a lot of men down and they eat the *dhorra* [maize], which is scarce; in fact he sends down to hear the news and get presents.' (With Linant he sent a couple of watches to be repaired!)

Unable to move from Moogie and under constant attack from the natives, Gordon reverted to black despair and began to think every man's hand was against him. He had heard that Hansal and the German explorer, Schweinfurth, had complained to the Geographical Societies in Vienna and Cairo that he made various Austrian and German botanists and geologists feel thoroughly

113

unwelcome when they visited Gondokoro. He had received no word of commendation or sympathy from the Khedive—though, to be fair, Gordon had done little but complain in his despatches to Cairo about the quality of Ismail's troops and the improbity of his Governor-General in Khartoum. Now, immured in his camp and under constant attack by the local tribes, it seemed that even God was against him and was answering not his prayers, but the incantations of the black magicians beyond the stockades, who cried to Heaven to halt his expedition and send them back whence they came. Everything had gone wrong and everybody was either sabotaging or exploiting him. He even complained bitterly that H. M. Stanley had sent down with Linant a batch of letters for posting without any money or stamps, and that he had had to pay £1 for the postage out of his own pocket!

For a brief moment the gloom was to lift when the *Khedive* managed to force her way upriver to join Gordon at Moogie. But on September 13, when all seemed set for the long-delayed move south, the steamer broke loose in the same Yerborah rapids where the *nuggars* had got adrift and, caught by the current, was carried broadside on to the rocks. For five days Gordon's men laboured to free her, but their tackle kept breaking under the strain and their efforts were unavailing. And in the end Gordon, who was now without any European helper—Chippindall having been invalided home—sent in desperation for Gessi to come up from Khartoum with proper equipment and skilled men. At the same time, rather than stay any longer in this hostile area, he decided to press on with his remaining *nuggars* to Dufile, and from there to reconnoitre the possibilities of getting the *Khedive* up to Lake Albert in the following year.

A few days later the river succeeded where all human effort had failed and lifted the *Khedive* off the rocks at Moogie. But although Gordon received the news when he was encamped at Labore, only a few days' march away to the south, rather than risk another immediate holdup with the *Khedive* in the next set of rapids south of Moogie, he decided to continue his reconnaissance and started off along the 'inland' road for Dufile three days later.

It was a miserable march. At night his tent leaked and, with the rain soaking his bedding, he could not sleep. During the day he was pestered by flies—'harvest bugs' he called them—and his clothes were permanently wet through with sweat from the effort of goading his men along in the damp, oppressive heat. Only an insatiable curiosity to discover what uncharted hazards lay between Labore and Lake Albert forced him to go on, plus a determination to prove whether or not Chippindall's optimistic report was justified. Three recent explorers of this region, including Grant and Speke, had spoken of a series of cataracts or rapids above the point where the Asua River joins the Nile. Yet if these cataracts really were above the Asua junction, might they not be relatively easy to pass? The Nile certainly should be a much smaller river beyond this point. And from the information he had, the cataracts were by no means precipitous—a fall of just over 200 feet in fifteen miles. Turning these possibilities over and over in his mind as he pressed on to Dufile, his confidence began to return, and he began to feel certain that he would have the *Khedive* on Lake Albert by the following spring.

But within a few days all his hopes were dashed. And in one of the most downcast of all the entries in his letter-journal he recorded: 'October 17; IT IS ALL OVER! I started from Dufile this morning and, keeping on the higher level to avoid the wet edges of the river, came on it about five miles from here. I fancied for some time I heard a voice like thunder, which increased as we approached the river. At last we stood above it on a rocky bank covered with vegetation, which descended abruptly to the stream; and there it was, appalling to look at, far less to think of getting anything up or down, except in splinters. It was more a rush down a slope or one-in-six than a fall. Above it the water was smooth, and 80 to 150 yards wide; and here it was suddenly contracted to two passages of 15 and 20 yards wide; for a rocky isle stood in the centre. It boiled down, twisting into all sorts of eddies, while the banks, steep and precipitous, prevented a great length of view. These shoots last for two miles.... Of course it is all over, the idea of taking up the screw steamer or the *nuggars*, or indeed anything.'

Gordon had discovered the Fola Falls, the tenth and by far the most formidable obstacle to navigation between Lado and Lake Albert, a truly savage stretch of surging water and jagged rocks where the river seems to hurl itself from almost every angle in an unending series of angry rushes, foaming and fuming forward as if bent on destroying everything in its path. Now all his plans had to be revised. For although the *Khedive* only drew six to eight inches of water and the *Nyanza* even less, there could be no question of either steamer negotiating this barrier. They would have to be carried overland to Dufile after all. And as he sat pondering his next move and wondering whether to set off for Fatiko and Foweira to reconnoitre the Nile between the Great Lakes, the postbag arrived with a letter from the Khedive, which complained that he had drawn for his supplies too heavily upon the resources of the Khartoum Government and had made too little use of the native tribes.

For the calmest and most equable of men, it was a disheartening letter to receive at such a time. But for Gordon, who was neither calm nor equable, it was too much to stomach at such a crisis in his fortunes. For months, while he had been going through a living hell, he had heard nothing from his employer. And now, instead of understanding his problems, the Khedive was clearly listening to the nefarious complaints of people like Ayoub Pasha. Ordering his men to pack everything up, he decided to leave Equatoria for good, and drafted telegrams to the Khedive telling him to 'send up my successor'.

EMPIRE-BUILDING FOR THE KHEDIVE

IN deciding to tell the Khedive to send someone to take his place because of a chance complaint of his administration, Gordon was running true to form. There can scarcely have ever been a serving soldier who accepted jobs more readily and who resigned more regularly—often out of pique—only to withdraw his resignation when the moment of pique had passed. And, sure enough, within twenty-four hours of his decision to leave the Khedive's service, he had recanted and elected to stay. For on the very next day, delving deeper into the postbag, he came across an earlier letter from Ismail which spoke of his efforts in Equatoria with 'fulsome civility', and told him that, in response to his proposal for circumventing the Nile route, an Egyptian force had been despatched to the mouth of the Juba River, on the coast of what is now Somalia, to link up with his expedition. Immediately Gordon stopped the telegrams and told his thoroughly bemused soldiers to unpack. 'The man had gone to all this expense under the impression that I would stick to him,' he wrote. 'I could not therefore leave him.' Then, deciding to leave the *Khedive* at Moogie and to bring the smaller steamer, *Nyanza*, overland to Dufile, he hurried off to meet Gessi, who, in response to his SOS, was now on his way up from Lado.

At Kerri the two men planned together the new assault on Lake Albert, in a mood of renewed hope and confidence. Gordon had mapped the Nile and the inland routes so that the journey to the lake no longer held any unknown hazards. And Gessi had brought up with him a group of skilled workmen and a contingent of troops. With upwards of 1,000 men to help him, the business of carrying the sections of the *Nyanza* presented no great problems. There were plenty of porters and iron hand-carts at every station on the journey. And before the end of December, thanks to these minute preparations, the convoy arrived at Dufile, triumphantly pulling the *Nyanza* and two steel boats section by section in the iron carts.

At this point Gordon decided not to explore Lake Albert himself, and instead to survey the Victoria Nile between the two lakes. He admitted that the Khedive and the Royal Geographical Society would probably be 'very much angered' by this decision, but he contended that he was an administrator and not an explorer, and that a trip round Lake Albert in the tiny *Nyanza* held no attractions for him. 'A fifty-foot steamer with a hot boiler close to you, with no accommodation, would do for me,' he wrote. Gessi was, therefore, chosen for the 'pinchbeck honours' of exploring the lake. The only member of the expedition who had remained in Gordon's good books, he was 'a smart fellow ... better than many a Royal Engineer!'

So, after a brief respite, which he spent shooting quail and guinea-fowl, Gordon left Gessi and his skilled work team at Dufile to put the *Nyanza* and the steel boats together, and headed south for Kabba Rega's kingdom of Bunyoro with a small escort of troops. It was a strange march through what appeared, to his surprise, to be almost uninhabited country. For Kabba Rega, having heard exaggerated accounts of the strength of Gordon's expedition, had withdrawn well to the south of the Victoria Nile. But the absence of native resistance was almost countervailed by the heat and humidity and by the ferocity of the mosquitoes and other insects, which stung like 'a bayonet' and attacked in such numbers that Gordon gave up carrying any weapons so as to free his hands to protect his neck. Nevertheless, he managed to maintain the cracking pace of sixteen miles a day and, after a week's stay at Fatiko, he reached the Victoria Nile at Foweira on January 14, 1876. Here he divided his force into three sections. One was sent downriver to establish a station at Magungo, where the Nile flowed into Lake Albert; another was despatched to Masindi, the capital of Bunyoro, thirty miles east of Lake Albert, which Kabba Rega was reported to have abandoned; and with the remaining section he moved on south to Mrooli, travelling even faster than before and marching as many as thirty miles in one day.

Here, eschewing once again the opportunity to 'go on the lake', he despatched a Sudanese Arab officer, Nuehr Agha, with 160 men and orders to visit Mutesa and seek his agreement to the establishment of an Egyptian garrison on the northern border of Buganda and on the north shore of Lake Victoria. Then taking the residue of his force back down the Nile in canoes, he covered the seventy-three miles from Mrooli to Foweira in thirty-six hours. But the pace had been too hard even for Gordon's wiry frame to withstand, and at Foweira he succumbed to malaria and was forced to pause for a few days. Dosing himself with his stand-by medicines, 'Warburg's Tincture' and chlorodyne, he managed to resume the march and, as if bent on breaking all records, headed back to Dufile at an average speed of twenty miles a day. He reached his destination on February 8, less than six weeks after he had left it, having covered 400 miles in twenty marching days.

At Dufile he found that Gessi had been joined by another Italian explorer, Carlo Piaggia, and had completed the preparation of the steel boats. Piaggia's arrival was a windfall, for he had considerable experience of Central Africa and of its native inhabitants, and was clearly cut out for the job of taking one of the boats up to Lake Victoria through Mutesa's territory. So it was arranged that the two Italians would set off without delay—Gessi to explore Lake Albert and Piaggia to establish the Khedive's flag on Lake Victoria. On March 7 the expeditions left Dufile, and Gordon returned to his headquarters at Lado to attend to the accumulation of administrative business. But he could not stay for long so far from the centre of activity, and after three weeks he was back at Kerri to await news from the lakes.

Yet even amidst Kerri's 'glorious glades of forest' he found a host of bothersome problems. Among other things, a drought had set in and the magician of the local tribe had refused to 'give one drop of rain unless the Government gives him cows'. So irritated did he become with these petty problems that he railed at almost everything and everybody. A particular cause of complaint was the way the natives would stand and watch him at work, silently staring, but never coming near enough to converse. And as always happened when he became irritated by his surroundings, he fell back into indecision about his future plans. 'Never was a man more tossed in his mind than I am,' he wrote to his sister. 'One day I say to myself, let the things go to the dogs and leave them to their fate; and on another day I feel I will work it through, in spite of them all ... but then again I think for what use should I expend myself and expose myself to disputes.'

The old cycle of inconsistency had returned. One moment when things were going well, he was brim-full of unwarranted optimism and happy to stay on the job; the next day he would be cast down by some mishap into an equally exaggerated defeatism and an overwhelming desire to be quit of his responsibilities. In February, frustrated by a delay in Gessi's and Piaggia's departure for the lakes, he had been in the depths of depression and wanted to leave Equatoria for good not later than May. And writing in his letter-journal, he reverted to his desire for death: 'Let me be called at this second; I fear nothing, for the world to come has better pleasures than this world.' But after they had finally got away, he remembered that he could not bear the idea of 'R.E. work or the afternoon and sunset of life in England'. And, as he sat at Kerri wondering what his two Italian lieutenants would bring back in the way of new discoveries, he decided to consult his Bible for the answer as to whether he should stay or not. Reading the words of St. Peter's First Epistle, 'Humble yourselves therefore under the mighty hand of God, that He may exalt you in due time; casting all your care upon Him, for He careth for you', he concluded that here was his answer or, as he put it, 'the pearl'. With a deep sense of relief, he wrote: 'Since I had the "pearl"—He careth for thee, etc.—and as it were resigned the rule of the province [to God] I have had much comfort and peace and ... I can say "Nunc Dimittis".'

Needless to say the 'pearl' did not suffice for long, and after a few months he was thinking, and writing to Augusta, the same inconsistent thoughts as before and explaining to his bewildered sister that 'my letters are my journal and impressions of the moment. I cannot be bound by them.... (To say) "You ought to know your own mind" is to me as if you said, "You ought to have red hair." ... I wish I was more decided but alas I cannot be so and I envy Gessi who knows his own mind.'

The immediate cause of this remark was the report brought by Gessi and Piaggia on their return from the lakes. Gessi had sailed all round Lake Albert and had established that there was only one river that flowed into the lake of sufficient size to be the Nile and that was the river that flowed from Lake Victoria. Thus the controversy between Richard Burton, who claimed that the Nile rose in Lake Tanganyika and flowed through Lake Albert from south to north, and John Speke, who insisted that the true source was Lake Victoria, was now resolved. But while Gessi had proved that the Nile could not rise in Lake Tanganyika, he had raised another problem by claiming to have found a large river branching out of the Nile in a north-westerly direction thirty miles downstream from Lake Albert. And to add to the confusion Piaggia returned six weeks later with the news that another river flowed out of the Victoria Nile thirty miles upstream from Mrooli.

This was a 'terrible affair', for it raised doubts as to whether the river that they had ascended was the real Nile or merely an off-shoot. For a man of Gordon's training as a Royal Engineer, there was only one thing to do: to go and see for himself and to survey the Nile from Dufile to Lake Albert and from Mrooli onwards. Casting aside his dislike of 'going on the lakes', Gordon resolved to go right through to Lake Victoria himself and to hoist the Khedive's flag at the northern end of the lake. Gessi was sent back with Piaggia to Khartoum to resume his duties as agent in charge of supplies. The *Khedive* was dismantled at Moogie and the sections were packed so that they would be ready for transporting overland to Lake Victoria in the following year. And on July 20 Gordon set off from Dufile with the *Nyanza*, now at last ready, and two steel boats.

At first all went well. To his great relief, he could find no trace of Gessi's river. And after leaving the *Nyanza* on Lake Albert, just as he started his journey up the Victoria Nile, he received a further welcome report from Nuehr Agha that King Mutesa had accepted an Egyptian garrison and had been annexed to the Khedive's empire. Gordon immediately telegraphed the good news to Cairo and pushed on up to the Murchison Falls with his steel boats. From there began a long and painful march along the river bank through dense jungle, with 'a heavy damp dew penetrating everywhere', and, of course, voracious insects to add to the misery of the march. 'The silence and solitude of this country ... is simply killing,' Gordon remarked of this eerie and inhospitable land. Yet somehow he found the energy to keep going and to map the seventy miles of uncharted and unnavigable river between Magungo and Foweira, where, after six days' tramping, he arrived on August 11.

Here a bombshell greeted him. Nuehr Agha had returned from Buganda and, as Gordon was about to congratulate him on his achievement, the Sudanese captain shamefacedly confessed that Mutesa had turned the tables on him and made his Egyptian garrison virtual prisoners. 'Mutesa,' Gordon recorded dejectedly in his letter-journal, 'has annexed my soldiers, not been annexed himself.' What was he to do now? His first thought was to march on Buganda and force Mutesa to release his troops and accept annexation. But on reconsideration he decided that he did not have enough troops, and that those which he had were 'idle, selfish, deceitful and cowardly', with officers incapable of even organizing a ration issue, let alone of leading their men in battle against Mutesa's warriors. Diplomacy was the only method in the circumstances, and here by a stroke of luck he had recently acquired the perfect emissary.

While he was at Kerri he had been joined by a German doctor, Edouard Schnitzer, who, after living for many years in the Middle East, had become a Moslem and had taken the Islamic name of Emin. Gordon had at once taken Emin on his strength, appointing him medical officer for Equatoria. Emin was already known to Mutesa and was actually in Buganda at that moment. Gordon therefore decided to send Nuehr Agha to make contact with Emin and through him to secure the release of the Egyptian garrison, in exchange for a treaty formally recognizing Mutesa's independence. At the same time he would make a deal with Kabba Rega, offering to leave him in peace—although he was supposed to take him prisoner and send him to Egypt as a rebel against the Khedive's rule. He would also negotiate with Buganda's eastern neighbour state, Usoga, which controlled the opposite bank of the Nile to Buganda, for the right of access to Lake Victoria. According to Speke's book, *Sources of the Nile*, Usoga had been 'only partially subjected' by Mutesa and might well respond to such an approach made on behalf of the Khedive of Egypt. Thus by neutralizing Kabba Rega and circumventing Mutesa through Usoga, Gordon hoped to win through to Lake Victoria and to force the King of Buganda 'to loyalty to Egypt without touching his country'.

It was a cunning plan and he was delighted with it. But, typically, he discarded it within twenty-four hours without even attempting to get in touch either with Kabba Rega or the ruler of Usoga. Moreover, from a suddenly renewed 'desire to be out of this country' by the end of the year, he also abandoned his plan to hoist the Khedive's flag on Lake Victoria, contending that it was a great mistake for him to have any dealings with Mutesa, beyond offering him a treaty of independence and requesting the release of the troops. Stanley had been quite wrong to urge the despatch of an English Christian mission to Buganda, no matter what interest in Christianity its King may have shown to him. If the Khedive wanted to annex Buganda, let him do his own dirty work without involving an English agent or intermediary. 'Egypt is water,' he wrote, 'Uganda is water; the English are oil. Water will mix with water, but never with oil.' All he would now do would be to survey the Nile as far as Mutesa's borders—sixty miles from Lake Victoria—and then, having collected his troops, leave Equatoria for good.

With the threat to his independence removed, Mutesa was only too happy to comply with Gordon's request. And a week later Emin, accompanied by Nuehr Agha and the released Egyptian soldiers, joined Gordon at Foweira. A quick reconnaissance was then conducted up the Nile to complete the survey. Here Gordon was harassed by spear attacks from some of Kabba Rega's warriors, which wrung from him the acid comment: 'Baker, I thank you for all this; a little wisdom with Kabba Rega and we should have all these men friends.' But he managed to complete his task without any fatal injuries and, equally to his relief, without finding any trace of Piaggia's river upstream from Mrooli. Returning from Mutesa's border he struck inland to the west and headed for Masindi to visit the garrison which he had sent there eight months earlier. Not altogether to his surprise, he soon discovered that Masindi had not after all been abandoned by Kabba Rega and that his troops, while pretending to be in the Bunyoro capital, had in fact established themselves forty miles away to the north.

A year before Gordon had railed about his soldiers, saying: 'How cordially glad I shall be when the whole relations between us cease. I cannot help it, but I have taken such a dislike to these blacks that I cannot bear their sight.... No one but those who have been in these countries can appreciate the immense blessing that discipline is.... As reasoning is out of the question with them it is no use using it (you would not reason with a cow, you would drive it).... Natives have generally some regenerating qualities, either a commercial, military, religious, or patriotic spirit. These people lack each one of these motive influences.' But now Gordon's face was set towards the north, with its promise of release from his burden of governorship, and he could afford to be more charitable. And although he blundered deep into hostile territory and had a most uncomfortable march back to Magungo, his only comment on his troops' latest indiscipline and incompetence was: 'Poor creatures! you cannot expect better.'

At Magungo an embarrassing problem awaited him. Ismail had replied to Gordon's telegram informing him of the 'annexation' of Buganda with his warmest congratulations and a decoration—the Order of the Medjidieh, First class. 'This is dreadful,' he wrote in his journal. However he added: 'I am glad His Highness is pleased, though it is for an event which has not taken place.' And he left the Khedive still thinking that Buganda had been added to his dominions, preferring to explain what had happened when he returned to Cairo. Then, bidding farewell to Emin, he hurried off to Lado, where he embarked in one of his steamers for Khartoum.

His work was done. Or was it? He had, it is true, opened up communications with Lake Albert and put the *Nyanza* on the lake to promote legitimate trade between the natives and the Government in such indigenous products as ivory, and he had personally sent about £100,000 worth of ivory down to Khartoum. His lieutenant, Gessi, had circumnavigated Lake Albert, and it was now proved that the Nile must emanate from Lake Victoria; and he had personally mapped the Nile to within sixty miles of its source. But he had not annexed Mutesa; he had not put the Egyptian flag or a steamer on Lake Victoria; he had not subdued, still less captured, Kabba Rega; and, although he had harassed the slave-traders and freed many hundreds of slaves, he had not suppressed the slave trade. In fact, the slavers had been dealt their severest blow by the much-maligned Ayoub Pasha, who, while Gordon was in Equatoria, had lured Zubair to Cairo, where he was put under lock and key, and had then succeeded in penning Zubair's son, Suleiman, together with his rebel army, into the south-eastern corner of Darfur. Thus, for all practical purposes, apart from getting the *Nyanza* on to Lake Albert and mapping the Nile, he had left the situation largely as he found it.

Perhaps Gordon had come to this same assessment of his errors and omissions by the time that he arrived at Khartoum. For, once there, he began to have doubts about quitting the Khedive's service. 'Reason says strongly, do not stay and aid such a government,' he wrote, 'but I do not like to be beaten, which I am if I retire.' And in Khartoum he resolved that, if he was still wanted, he would return to his province after a short spell of home leave. ('I want OYSTERS when I come home,' he wrote to Augusta, 'and lots of them, not a dozen, but 4 dozen.') Yet before he reached Cairo he had decided to leave, apparently as a reaction to seeing the Khedive's former Minister of Finance, Ismail Sadik, hitherto the most powerful man in Egypt, being taken up the Nile in chains, having been senetenced to exile in the Sudan for graft. And, on November 29 as he journeyed north from Khartoum, he wrote: 'I have D.V. made up my mind to serve His Highness no longer.'

Soon after his arrival in Cairo, Gordon went to see the Khedive and told him that he was 'determined' to leave the Sudan for ever. Among the reasons that he gave was that he could not do his job in Equatoria with Ayoub Pasha in Khartoum putting every possible spoke in his wheel. He could not, he claimed, stop the slave trade in the south while the Governor-General was conniving at its continuance from the centre. But he reckoned without the power of Ismail's charm and subtle flattery. And by the end of the interview he had relented and undertaken to return to the Sudan after a short respite in England, on the Khedive's promise that 'these irregularities would cease'—a promise, which, as he subsequently confided to a friend, he did not for a moment believe would, or could, be kept.

Needless to say, he was to change his mind yet again during his stay in England. Soon after his return, an article in the London *Times* suggested that he be sent to Bulgaria to help in protecting the Christian population against persecution by their Moslem Turkish overlords. Flattered by such recognition from the Press, Gordon went to discuss the idea with the Foreign Secretary, Lord Derby, and on the strength of this interview wrote to Cairo to inform the Khedive that he would not be returning to the Sudan after all. Then when the Bulgarian project came to nothing, he toyed with the idea of taking Gessi on an expedition to open up Central Africa from Zanzibar. But a few days later, on January 17, 1877, a telegram arrived from the Khedive, expressing surprise that, after they 'parted with the words *Au revoir*' Gordon should have decided not to return. Ismail went on to say: 'I can only attribute your message to the pleasure that you very naturally felt when you found yourself back again in your own country ... but I refuse to believe that, when Gordon has once given his word as a gentleman, anything will ever induce him to go back on it. I cannot, therefore, my dear Gordon, accept what you have said in your letter and I shall expect you back according to your promise. Your affectionate, Ismail.'

Gordon's immediate reaction was typically stubborn. Writing on the back of Ismail's telegram, he drafted the following reply, 'I have considered H.H.'s letter [*sic*]; convinced that my place can be filled with facility, I have decided not to return. In not returning I trust H.H. will not judge me harshly.' But the reply was never sent. On reflection, he knew that he was hooked and, as his flippant postcard to Augusta clearly suggests, he was by no means sorry. 'On return from Woolwich, tossed,' he wrote, 'Head to go, Tail to stay; it fell Head!!!' A few days later he met a former fellow-subaltern from the Crimean War, General Graham, to whom he told his story, no doubt well larded with complaints about Ayoub. Graham had no hesitation in advising him to insist with the Khedive that he be appointed Governor-General of the whole Sudan and not just sent back to look after Equatoria. If Ayoub was frustrating his endeavours, the answer was for him to replace Ayoub. The logic of the argument, no less than the prospects it held forth, appealed irresistibly to Gordon, who wrote to Augusta on the eve of his departure: 'The Khedive ought to give me Khartoum and I have promised Graham not to go up unless he does so.'

On his way to Egypt he met Nubar Pasha, who was temporarily out of favour and living in Paris, and who warned him that in the unlikely event that the Khedive would be willing to give him the Sudan, Ismail would do his best to sabotage him at every turn. But Gordon suspected that there was probably a strong element of sour grapes in this advice and, on arriving in Cairo, sent for the new Prime Minister's secretary and gave him his 'ultimatum'. So as not to appear too demanding, he suggested as an alternative that the Khedive might send his own Oxford-educated son to take Ayoub's place, in which case he would himself settle for Equatoria once again.

The trick worked well enough. Seeing that he must either comply with the 'ultimatum' or lose Gordon and not wishing to send his son to such outlandish parts, Ismail informed Vivian, the British Consul-General, the next day that he would in all probability meet Gordon's wishes. But to make sure that this changeable Englishman did not try to back out again, he cleverly made no move to confirm this statement to Gordon himself. After waiting two days for the Khedival summons, Gordon could finally bear it no longer and asked to see his employer, upon which Ismail, satisfied that his fish was now on the bank, conceded his demand. So Gordon became Governor-General of the Sudan and of the Red Sea provinces of Harar and Berbera, recently seized from Abyssinia—in sum, an area the size of western Europe. And to mark his promotion he was granted the rank of Marshal in the Khedive's army and presented with a resplendent uniform trimmed with gold lace.

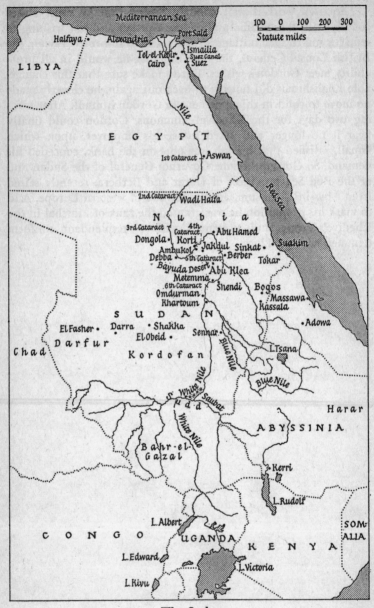

The Sudan

CHAPTER 11

GOVERNOR-GENERAL OF THE SUDAN

GORDON was to leave Cairo immediately. But on his way to Khartoum he was to make contact with King Johannes of Abyssinia, a former tribal chieftain who had seized the throne on the death of the Emperor Theodore and with whom the Khedive had been at war since the conquest of the Red Sea coast, and to try to reach a peaceful settlement with him. This was an important matter for several reasons. For one thing, Britain, as a friend and ally of Johannes, was bringing pressure on Ismail to make peace with Abyssinia as soon as possible. For another, the Egyptians had lately had the worst of the argument with Johannes and had lost the district of Bogos, which lay across the road and telegraph lines linking the port of Massawa, then in Egyptian hands, with Khartoum. To secure the return of this territory was a difficult enough assignment at the best of times. And, to add to Gordon's difficulties, the Egyptian Army was deeply demoralized by cunning propaganda spread by Abyssinian agents, to the effect that the Prophet Mohammed had laid a curse on any Moslem who made war against the God-fearing Christian Abyssinians, who once gave asylum to his Moslem followers, when they were being persecuted by the rulers of Mecca.

The situation was still further complicated by the fact that a former governor of one of Johannes' provinces, an ambitious tribal chieftain named Walad el-Michael, had rebelled against the King. In the hope of carving out a principality of his own, he had made common cause with the Khedive's armies when, on Theodore's death, they had moved in to grab their slice of Abyssinian territory. After Johannes had defeated the Egyptians in Bogos, Walad el-Michael continued to resist his authority by armed raids. And at the same time he made it clear that he would defy any attempt by the Khedive to place him under restraint. Yet unless some guarantee were forthcoming on behalf of the

Egyptians that these attacks on Abyssinia would cease, Johannes would conclude that they and Walad el-Michael were in collusion and would refuse to make any concessions over Bogos or any other area.

On February 18, 1877, three years to the day after he had left for Equatoria, Gordon set off from Cairo to try to square this vicious circle. He was in a confident, though somewhat reflective, mood. Writing home, he said: 'To give your life to be taken at once is one thing; to live a life such as is before me is another and more trying ordeal. I have set my face to this work and will give my life to it.... I am only very very slightly elated by the honours and powers given me and this elation arises from a feeling of satisfaction that His Highness has confidence in me. I think of how many would be weighed down by this immense charge.... But to me I never give the question a thought. I feel sure of success, for I do not lean on my own understanding and He directs my path.'

From Massawa, where he arrived on February 26, Gordon sent messages to Johannes informing the King of the purpose of his mission. And when almost three weeks later no reply had come, he marched off inland to look for the trouble-maker, Walad el-Michael. Eight days later he found Walad el-Michael's camp and there proposed to the rebel chieftain that he should cease hostilities against the Abyssinians forthwith. In return he offered to ask Johannes to give him the governership of a province or, if this were impossible, himself to give him a governorate in the Sudan. Walad el-Michael demurred at first; but after two days of intensive argument, he agreed to accept three territories under the Sudan Government lying to the north of Bogos. However, when Gordon suggested that he go with him to Johannes as a living witness of the truce, the rebel chieftain stubbornly refused, saying, 'God forbid!'

Gordon, who was under no illusions about Walad el-Michael, knew only too well that such a truce must necessarily be an uneasy arrangement. But he had been forced to settle for the lesser of two evils. As he put it in his own picturesque report on these negotiations: 'There were two courses open to me.... The one to stay at Massawa and negotiate peace with Johannes and to ignore Walad el-M. and, if afterwards Walad el-M. turned nasty, to arrange with Johannes to come in and catch him. This certainly would have been easiest for me. Johannes would have been delighted and we should be rid of Walad; but it would first of all be very poor encouragement to any future secessions and would debase Egyptian repute. The process of turning in the Polecat (Johannes) to work out the Weasel (Walad el-Michael) would play havoc with the farmyard (the country) ... and it might be that the Polecat having caught the Weasel might choose to turn on the Hens (which we are) and, killing us, stay in the farmyard. For to tell the truth, we, the Hens, in the days of our prosperity stole the farmyard from the Polecats when they were fighting among themselves before they knew we were Hens. The other course open to me was to give Walad el-M. a govt. separated from Johannes which I have done and I think this was the best [and] most honest course.'

However, Gordon was unable to take his negotiations any further. For as he went in search of Johannes, word came that an attack had been launched on Abyssinian territory in the region of Lake Tsana, the source of the Blue Nile, by King Menelik of Shoa, Johannes' southern neighbour and a traditional enemy of Abyssinia, and that Johannes had gone to deal with this new threat to his kingdom. Unable to make any personal contact, Gordon promptly drew up a treaty embodying Egypt's terms and the assurances he had obtained from Walad el-Michael, signed it himself and sent it to Johannes with a message, saying that he had been unable to delay his journey to Khartoum any longer and that, unless he heard to the contrary, he would consider the treaty's terms as having been agreed. Then, turning his back on Abyssinia, he set off at breakneck speed for Khartoum, which he reached after a series of forced marches of up to forty-five miles in a day and innumerable complaints about the miseries of the climate, the laziness of his soldiers, and the wayward nature of his camel. After this journey he vowed that, when he had finished his work in the Sudan, which he foresaw as involving annually some 5,000 miles of travelling, he would come home, lie in bed until noon every day and 'never walk more than a mile'.

On May 5 Gordon was 'enthroned' with great ceremony as Governor-General, and when the Chief Magistrate had read out the Khedive's firman of appointment he replied to the cheers of the populace with a speech of only nine words: 'With God's help, I will hold the balance level.' As often happens in Arab countries at the outset of a new régime, he immediately became the object of great popular adulation. (The only dissentient gesture came from the sister of Ayoub Pasha, who, on hearing of her brother's dismissal, lost her temper, broke nearly all the windows and ripped the cushions in the Governor-General's palace.) And within less than a week of assuming office he introduced a series of reforms that was to endear him still further to his subjects. Torture in the prisons was abolished, as was public flogging with the *kourbash*, a buffalo-hide whip usually applied to the soles of the victim's feet as a means of extracting a confession of guilt or payment of taxes. The poor were helped by distributions from the privy purse, petitions were invited from all those who laboured under a grievance against the previous Government. Water was to be pumped from the Nile as a service to house-holders who lived a long way from the river. And the Ulema, the local high priests of Islam, were given back the privileges of which Ayoub Pasha had stripped them.

But after three weeks he had had enough of Khartoum, and before the end of May he was off again on his camel to deal with yet another outbreak of trouble in Darfur, where the Governor, Hassan Pasha, who had been installed by Ayoub after Zubair's detention, had lost control and was faced with an uprising of the tribes, led by Haroun, the late Sultan's twenty-one-year-old nephew. Principally to blame in this situation were the bashi-bazooks, troops from Egypt who were spread across Darfur, as elsewhere, in small pockets without adequate supplies and often without pay for months on end, and who had enraged the local Bedouin by marauding and pillaging their flocks, sometimes for profit, but often out of dire necessity for food. Unused to the ways of the desert, the bashi-bazooks also frequently threatened to destroy the water supply of a whole tribe. For in these parched desert areas, where scarcely a well existed, the only means of collecting and conserving water was to use the hollow trunks of the tabaldi trees, a custom which survives to this day; but instead of taking water from the inside of these makeshift reservoirs the soldiers, partly from laziness and sometimes out of sheer mischief, shot holes in the tree trunks so that, when they had drunk their fill, the water drained away entirely.

Such provocative behaviour could have only one result, and when Gordon left Khartoum the tribes were in open revolt and were reported to have invested the two key centres of Darfur—Darra and Fasher. It was a dangerous and difficult situation, and one cannot help but admire Gordon's courage in setting out, with an escort of 500 'nondescript' troops, to bring the tribes to heel. Not only did he march straight into rebel-held territory, where he could have been assailed at any moment by overwhelmingly superior forces; he was also inviting attack from Suleiman, Zubair's son, who had at least 3,000 armed warriors—Gordon believed at the time that he had 10,000—within striking distance at his headquarters at Shakka, in the south of Darfur. But, having confided his Government as well as his immortal soul to God, he pressed on fearlessly to relieve the beleaguered garrisons. 'I sincerely hope,' he wrote, 'not to have to fire a shot in this revolt. The poor people have been driven into it and Haroun has only taken advantage of the discontent.'

Surprisingly enough, his wish was almost granted and three months later the revolt was put down with hardly any bloodshed and without Gordon having to use much more force than that of his own will-power and personality. Arrayed in his Marshal's uniform and 'flying along like a madman' on his camel, he went from one station to another, relieving the astonished garrison and adding them to his strength before charging off to relieve the next. By so doing he mustered a sizeable enough force to impress the rebellious tribes, and at the same time removed from each place the cause of the discontent which had brought about the revolt.

By July he had got as far west as Darra and had pacified all the tribes *en route*. At Darra the Leopard tribe proved more difficult to handle, and for the first and only time on this expedition Gordon had to use force to bring them to heel. Then, after the briefest pause, he was off again to Fasher to relieve its garrison. The revolt was now over and, to prevent another outbreak, he decided to withdraw all the troops from Darfur and to leave the security of the province in the hands of the tribes, subject to a tributary payment of £10,000 a year, thus eliminating the risk of friction between the garrisons and the population and, as he put it, creating 'a far more effectual frontier than my venial [*sic*] governors'.

It was a bold plan, particularly since the leader of the revolt had evaded capture by fleeing westwards into the mountains near the borders of Chad. But before Gordon could put it into effect, reports reached him that Suleiman was marching up from Shakka, intent on regaining his father's former domains, and that Walad el-Michael was threatening to break his truce with Johannes.

This was a bad blow for Gordon. He had recently heard that Zubair, to secure his release from detention, had ordered his son to co-operate with the Sudan Government. And he was therefore toying with the idea of appointing Suleiman as Governor of Darfur in place of Hassan, whom he considered 'mad'. Now, not only was he unable to employ Suleiman, but he must go and do battle with him. This meant that he would have to rely on Hassan to hunt down Haroun and leave Walad el-Michael free to stir up more trouble in Abyssinia.

Still, whether Suleiman was co-operative or hostile, he was now the arch-slaver in the Sudan, and his headquarters at Shakka was, as Gordon put it, the 'main nest' or the 'Rome' of the slave trade. Sooner or later he would have to tackle the connected problems of Suleiman and slavery. His mission was after all to suppress the slave trade; and Egypt and Britain had just signed a convention under which slave-hunting was stigmatized as 'robbery and murder', and the sale of slaves was to be forbidden after the lapse of seven years in Egypt and twelve years in the Sudan. Moreover, the Khedive had decided to give immediate effect to his agreement by decreeing that all slave convoys were to be seized, the slaves to be freed and the leaders shot. Thus there was nothing for it but to march against Suleiman and 'put him to death'.

Yet, as he pondered his next move, Gordon's mind kept coming back to the problem which had baffled him in Equatoria—the disposal of freed slaves. Some of the slaves whom he had seized from captured convoys during his recent journeyings in Darfur had been conscripted into his small expeditionary force. But he could not make them all into soldiers and, besides, there was the problem of the women and children. Yet if he turned them loose they would either band together and become vagabonds, and hence a menace to the local population, or they would be picked up and be enslaved again by the nearest tribe. 'An escaped slave,' he commented, 'is like an escaped sheep, the property of those who find him or her. One must consider what is best for the individual, not what may seem best to the judgement of Europe. It is the slave who suffers, not Europe. There is not the slightest doubt but that if I let the slaves be taken by my soldiers, by the tribes, or by the Gallabat merchants, instead of there being a cessation of slave caravans, there will be a great increase of them ... and a corresponding outcry against me.... Some [of the slaves] would sooner go with the Gallabat merchants or with the soldiers or with the tribes.... Even if they could, they would not go back to their now desolate homes to be attacked by more powerful tribes and again be slaves to them.... How on earth are slaves to be freed in twelve years?'

Worrying about this perplexing problem, Gordon fell back into his plaintive mood and grumbled incessantly about his soldiers, his servants, the climate, the flies (of which he drew minute sketches, illustrating their bayonet-like sting!) and the discomfort of travel for weary hours and distances on camel-back. He had to do everything and see to everything himself, he complained; he had no trustworthy aide, no European to help him or take some of the burden off his shoulders. He had presumably forgotten that, when he had a European aide in Equatoria, he had written: 'If ever you go to Africa on exploration business, go alone, for it is only possible to exist when you are alone. The worries of a companion only make your own greater.' Now when he discovered that his secretary and an Egyptian colonel on his strength had been taking bribes, he burst out: '*I Hate* (and there is no other word for it) these Arabs and I like the blacks, patient, enduring and friendly as much as the Arab is cowardly, cruel, and effeminate. All the misery is due to these Arab and Circassian (Turkish) Pashas and authorities. I would not stay a day here for these wretched creatures; but I would give my life for these poor blacks.' Yet not many months earlier, when he encountered the Fola Falls, in Equatoria, he had described his black troops as 'cows' and 'oafs' and declaimed: 'I cannot help it but I have taken such a dislike to these blacks that I cannot bear their sight.'

But then Gordon's nature was nothing if not kaleidoscopic, as was shown by a story related by Sir Ronald Storrs about an Egyptian Bey whom Gordon wanted to promote to the rank of Pasha. The Khedive refused his permission, whereupon Gordon threatened to resign as Governor-General. The Khedive then gave in, only to receive a telegram from Gordon a few weeks later saying that he had decided to hang the man. The precise engineer with a passion for detail and accuracy could under stress give way to the wildest exaggerations and contradictions, lashing out with his whip, as well as with his tongue or his pen, in furious remonstrance against some unfortunate officer whose training and discipline fell too far short of Woolwich standards. Like the wind in the Sudan, his mood could change from a cool, soft northerly breeze to a harsh, grit-laden blast out of the hot south that stung everybody within reach. True, he had to suffer many exasperating annoyances, as, for instance, when an officer carrying his despatches to the Khedive in the saddlebags of his camel failed to tether the beast properly, so that it broke away in the night and careered off into the desert with the despatches still on board. But all too often when things went wrong, Gordon would read into some act of incompetence a conscious desire to frustrate and sabotage his policies, inspired by corrupt and venal motives. And then again in his more rational moments, usually when things were going his way, he would disarmingly admit to having been 'egotistical' and to making over-harsh judgements.

Such a moment occurred as he was fulminating at Fasher against the entire Arab race. First came the news that Hassan Pasha, in an unexpected master-stroke, had caught up with Haroun and destroyed what remained of his rebel army. Then came reports that several Bedouin tribes had turned against Suleiman, whose henchmen had treated them even worse than the Egyptian garrisons had done, and that he could now count on reinforcements of up to 30,000 tribesmen if Suleiman should fight. And as he digested these glad tidings, Gordon's thinking became at once more rational and more charitable. He had been wrong to accuse the Khedive of having his tongue in his cheek when ordering him to abolish slavery. Likewise, he had misjudged Ayoub Pasha in saying that he wanted to perpetuate the slave trade. For any profit they might gain from its continued existence was more than outweighed by the encouragement it gave to men like Zubair and Suleiman to raise large private armies and so to threaten Egyptian sovereignty in the Sudan. Of course, he and the Khedive must be at one over the abolition of slavery and the suppression of Suleiman.

But the Khedive's enthusiasm for shooting the leading slave-traders raised a new problem. If, under the Anglo-Egyptian Convention, slavery was not to be finally abolished before twelve years in the Sudan, would not such punishment in the interval be against the law? And if so, how was he to deal with Suleiman if and when he caught him? His Egyptian staff had no such qualms, and strongly advised him to lure Suleiman to his camp and then kill him, a suggestion which Gordon rejected out of hand, saying, 'If I used treachery to him, how could *you* ever trust *me*?' There was only one answer to the problem. That was to send Zubair's son down to Cairo to swear fidelity to the Khedive and to let Ismail deal with him as he had dealt with his father, or however else he wished.

So deciding, Gordon set off to encounter Suleiman, who was reported to be marching on Darra. And on September 2, their two forces met a few miles south-east of the town. Greatly daring, Gordon, dressed in his gold-encrusted Marshal's uniform, rode into the rebel's camp with an escort of only fifty horsemen and, coming straight to the point, delivered his terms to the 'dumbfounded' Suleiman. Gordon told him that he knew he was preparing a revolt and that he had decided to disarm his gang and 'break them up'. Suleiman decided to play for time and the following day sent his submission. But the arrogance and hostility of his demeanour, together with his rigid refusal to swear fidelity to the Khedive, suggested to Gordon that this 'nice-looking boy of 20 or 22 who looks a spoilt child that a good shaking would do good to' was in fact contemplating treachery.

He had guessed right for, at the same time as he sent in his submission, Suleiman had told his chiefs to prepare for war. But by no means all of his officers were so keen as he to try conclusions with this Englishman, whose soldierly repute had spread throughout Darfur, and when heads were counted Suleiman found that he could rely on only about half his force. Immediately his attitude changed towards Gordon, whom he now obsequiously addressed as his 'father'. But when he asked for a governorship, Gordon sternly refused him, unless he either went to Cairo to salute the Khedive or showed some other proof of his loyalty. Gordon had been informed of the split in Suleiman's camp and was gambling on the ultimate defection of all his adversary's forces. No doubt Suleiman feared the same thing; for, having failed to wheedle Gordon, he promptly gathered up the loyal half of his force and marched back to Shakka.

Gordon followed him, determined to 'thaw' him into a co-operative frame of mind. Despite his superiority of numbers, he hesitated to use force for fear of reuniting against him Suleiman's 'smart dapper troops ... the terror of Central Africa'. And when he arrived at Shakka, it seemed that the thaw had begun. 'The cub is now very friendly,' he wrote. So friendly was he that Gordon, apparently forgetting his vow to send him down to Cairo, tried instead to win his co-operation by offering him the post of Deputy Governor in the neighbouring province of Bahr-el-Ghazal. Suleiman protested indignantly at being given so lowly a position and demanded the governorship. But Gordon was not prepared to yield an inch beyond his proffered compromise and Suleiman retired to his veranda, sulkily refusing to engage in any further discussions.

Unable to coax his adversary into a more co-operative frame of mind, Gordon had to make the best of an inconclusive encounter. There were other problems demanding his attention in his vast territory and, as he was still disinclined to risk using force, there was no point in his staying any longer in Darfur. Leaving Suleiman to sulk in his camp, he therefore left Shakka on September 17 to begin the 700-mile trek back to Khartoum, reflecting as he went upon the results of his mission so far. Perhaps from a desire to justify his lenient treatment of Suleiman, he indulged some dangerously wishful thinking about the prospects for peace in Darfur. 'I am glad to say,' he wrote, 'I see no disposition now on the part of the slavers to resist the Government; and I therefore hope the slave *razzias* are at an end or will be by the end of the year.' But he was under no illusions about the difficulty of putting an end to slavery. 'The holding of slaves,' he said 'will never cease under any government, let it be as strong and uncorruptible as you like.... When you get the ink out of the ink-stained blotting-paper, then slave-holding will cease in these lands.... No government, either British or Khedival, could enforce its abolition without militarily occupying the whole country.'

As he rode his camel back to Khartoum, turning these thoughts over and over in his mind, Gordon became increasingly defeatist in his attitude to slavery and worked himself into a rage against the uncompromising attitudes struck by the anti-slavery societies and the Churches, Protestant and Catholic, on the subject. How could these high-minded churchmen and reformists know anything of the problems he had to face? Little did they realize that for released slaves the only alternative to starvation was to become 'slaves of the government'. And whatever they might sanctimoniously proclaim from their ivory towers, he believed 'it would be better to legitimize the transport of slaves, and were it not that I do not wish to unnecessarily raise opposition, I would order it'. But the opposition of the abolitionists in Europe, however unworldly and impractical their thinking, was something that Gordon could not afford to ignore. Were he to have done so, the Khedive would have been obliged to dismiss him. So, bottling up his indignation, he resolved to close down the three principal slave-markets at Shakka, Gallabat and Katarif and to try to stop the *razzias* at least across the Bahr-el-Ghazal border, where the black tribes from Central Africa offered the best hunting-ground for the slavers.

Gordon returned to Khartoum on October 14, thoroughly worn out and, as he put it, 'a shadow'. And small wonder, for he had logged the astonishing total of over 2,500 miles of camel-riding since he landed at Massawa in February. Nevertheless, the Khedive had shown his appreciation of his work in a telegram congratulating him on his success in pacifying the tribes of Darfur and in scotching Suleiman's plans for revolt. And, reinforced by this royal approbation, he immediately started to plan his next tour of inspection, which was to start in nine days' time. Walad el-Michael's threat had not matured. So on this occasion he intended to go north down the Nile to Berber, Dongola, and Wadi Halfa, where he planned to make drastic economies in the costs of the railway that was being built to link Khartoum with Egypt, and where he had been told that the railway engineers were living in luxury at the expense of the Sudan Government. Then he would go to Aswan and across to the Red Sea, then down to Massawa, from where he would try again to contact Johannes, returning via Massawa to visit Berbera and Harar and then back to Khartoum. Strangely enough, he did not include Equatoria in this, or any subsequent expeditions during the whole of his service as Governor-General. True, he had received on his return to Khartoum the welcome news that Kabba Rega had decided against further resistance and wished for peaceful relations with Egypt. But Kabba Rega was by no means the only unfinished business that he had left behind him in the south. For at this point the Government of the province was in the hands of Ibrahim Fawzi, a junior officer who had served under him in Equatoria, who turned out to be deeply implicated in slave-trading and who later had to be dismissed.

Perhaps he thought that it was sufficient to have left Emin to report any abuses by Fawzi; or possibly he did not want a second dose of this insalubrious area to mar the mood of contentment which he was enjoying as a result of his successes in Darfur and the Khedive's congratulations. For although he moaned that he was constantly being pestered by petitioners and by men who 'telegraph me from hundreds of miles off to say that their slave has escaped and will I see to it', he was happy enough as he steamed down the Nile to Berber. He had achieved what he regarded as the perfect relationship with his Sudanese subjects and, as he told his sister, was 'much feared and I think respected, but not over much liked'. And he felt he had 'culminated' and wished for no other and no higher post than the one that he had.

Not surprisingly, his peace of mind was short-lived. Before he reached Wadi Halfa, word came that the district of Sennar on the Blue Nile in the eastern Sudan was threatened with attack by Johannes' forces. Having earlier heard sinister reports that Russian agents in Abyssinia were trying to goad Johannes to resume hostilities against Egypt—no doubt as a means of drawing some of the fire of the Ottoman Sultan's forces from the Russian front in the recently renewed Russo-Turkish War—Gordon took the news seriously enough to cancel the rest of his tour and returned post-haste to Khartoum. The report had in fact been somewhat exaggerated and the attack on the Sennar district was no more than a raid to obtain grain. But when he came back to Khartoum, he heard that Walad el-Michael was up to his old tricks again. And, fearing lest the uneasy truce with Abyssinia might be shattered by this rebellious chieftain and mindful of the fact that Johannes had still not vouchsafed any reply to his treaty project, he felt that he should make another attempt to reach a definitive settlement with these two warring parties.

On November 26 Gordon mounted his camel and rode eastwards to Walad el-Michael's camp high in the hills of the disputed Bogos territory. It was an agonizing march, the last stage being over precipitous mountain tracks more suitable for goats than camels. And, to make matters worse, he was warned by the people of Bogos that he was walking into a trap, that Walad el-Michael was not in a mood to be reasoned with and that he might never leave the rebel's camp alive. But this kind of advice only made Gordon the more determined to see the thing through. 'People may say you tempt God in putting yourself in positions like my present one,' he wrote, 'yet I do not care.' And three weeks after starting from Khartoum, he walked into the rebel's mountain hide-out with an escort of only ten soldiers.

Immediately he and his men were conducted to a small compound, where he felt he was 'in the lion's den ... boxed up in a little space with a ten-foot fence around it'. Furiously, Gordon protested to Walad el-Michael that he was being kept as a prisoner and warned him that he would suffer in the end for so treating his Governor-General. Profuse apologies and strenuous denials greeted his remonstrance; but in the ensuing talks Walad el-Michael showed that he had lost none of his brashness by seriously suggesting that Gordon should give tacit approval to his attacking and seizing the Abyssinian border town of Adowa. He pointed out that Johannes would not rest until he had recovered all the territory which Ismail had pilfered from him and that, when he had dealt with Menelik's aggression in the south, he would return to the charge against Egypt. This might happen sooner rather than later, since he had heard that Menelik's Queen had turned against her husband for taking another wife and had caused a large number of his troops to defect. Thus if Egypt were to keep one jump ahead of Johannes, Adowa must be taken as soon as possible.

Gordon adamantly refused to have anything to do with this preposterous project. His job was to make peace with Johannes, and the last way to do this would be to loose Walad el-Michael against Abyssinian territory, no matter what threats Johannes might be contemplating for the future. Besides, he felt that the territories which Ismail had pilfered from Abyssinia, while Johannes was busy putting down rebel chieftains like Walad el-Michael, were worse than useless additions to the Khedive's domains. They could not be defeated against a determined Abyssinian attack, and the only sensible course was for him to seek a settlement with Johannes which would guarantee Egypt's communications between Massawa and Khartoum. Having made his views clear to Walad el-Michael, he therefore went off in search of

Johannes to clinch the deal. But try as he might, he could not even discover where Johannes was, let alone reach him. And so, as the year 1877 drew to a close, Gordon was forced once again to leave the Abyssinian question unresolved and to return to his duties at Khartoum.

CHAPTER 12

FINANCIAL CRISIS IN EGYPT

DURING all the seven years that Gordon was to spend in the Sudan there were very few occasions when he could sit down and apply himself to the day-to-day business of administration from the centre. In fact, since the Egyptian conquest the Sudan never had a ruler who spent so little time in his capital city. Hence the almost total lack of documentation on his system of government and on the reforms which he introduced. Not that the routine work of Governor-Generalship appealed to a man of Gordon's temperament. For he infinitely preferred the open desert to his stuffy palace among the drab and depressing collection of mud houses and dust roads that was Khartoum. And notwithstanding the discomforts of camel-riding, he was infinitely more at home careering about the vast wastes of his realm, adjudicating disputes and settling grievances on the spot, than he was amid the hordes of servants and soldiers and the primitive pomp that surrounded and, for him, suffocated the Khedive's viceroy in his capital city. For the first time since Mohammed Ali annexed the Sudan, the Governor-Generalship was really brought to the people by Gordon. He was the first of the Khedive's viceroys ever to visit Dongola, although it was no distance off the direct route from Cairo to Khartoum. And if his administration was sometimes slack at the centre because he was so often absent from his capital, Gordon's constant journeying among the outlying towns and villages of this vast territory earned him the plaudits of many thousands who had never seen his predecessors.

He was therefore eagerly looking forward to resuming his interrupted tour in the north when, on February 5, 1878, he received a telegram from the Khedive urgently requesting him to come to Cairo and alleging that Egypt's creditors were trying to interfere with his 'sovereign prerogatives'. Ismail at this point was approaching a crisis with his British and French creditors, who were putting pressure on him, not merely to settle his debts, but also to submit to Anglo-French control over Egypt's finances. Ever since he had become Khedive in 1863 he had spent money like water, and by 1876 he had increased Egypt's public debt from £3¼ million to £94 million. Much of this money was frittered away on prestige projects to make Egypt appear to be in the forefront of civilized nations. '*Mon pays*,' he would say, '*n'est plus en Afrique; nous faisons partie de l'Europe actuellement.*' In token of this claim, military equipment was bought from Europe in totally unnecessary quantities. At the other end of the scale, an Egyptian princess is said to have run up an account of £150,000 with a French dressmaker. Even useful projects, such as the harbour works at Alexandria, cost almost double what they should have done. And to pay for all these extravagances money was borrowed and credit received, often at usurious rates of interest from unscrupulous European moneylenders and contractors.

Nevertheless, not all of this borrowed money was squandered or misspent. Ismail did much to develop railways and telegraphs; he also established a Post Office, reorganized the Customs with the aid of British officials and remodelled the military schools founded by Mohammed Ali. And, of course, his greatest monument was the Suez Canal, opened in 1869. Today he would probably be hailed as a dedicated developer of his country; but in an age when there was no World Bank and no sympathy without security, he was branded by his creditors as a spendthrift recklessly bent on inflating his country's debt for self-aggrandizement. And by 1875, when he could raise no more loans in Europe, he was forced to sell Egypt's holding of 176,602 shares in the Suez Canal Company for just under £4,000,000.

But even this sell-out could not balance the books. Nor did it serve to reduce the onerous rates of interest which Egypt was being forced to pay on her borrowings—up to 36 per cent. in some cases. And Ismail was therefore compelled to seek foreign advice, and hence to accept the thin end of the wedge of European control over Egypt's finances. On May 2, 1876, he issued a decree setting up a Commission of the Public Debt with three commissioners on it, representing France, Italy, and Austria, with whom it was agreed that Egypt's debt should be consolidated at the figure of £91 million. Britain, although one of Egypt's largest creditors, at first refused to take part in the Commission, since the then Foreign Secretary, Lord Derby, considered it to be an un-

Charles George Gordon

Li-Hung Chang, Governor of Kiang-su

The Mahdi

Sir Evelyn Baring, British Consul
General in Egypt

'Chinese Gordon'

Bible in hand—Gordon's statue in Trafalgar Square, London

Statue erected to Gordon's memory in Khartoum

Gordon's head being shown to Slatin Pasha

warrantable interference in Egypt's internal affairs. And she further objected that the figure of £91 million was too high and would impose too heavy a strain on Egypt's resources. France was in due course persuaded of this view, and in October 1876 Mr. (later Lord) Goschen, representing Britain, and M. Joubert, for France, were sent to Cairo to negotiate an arrangement which resulted in the 'Unified Debt', as it was now called, being written down to £59 million. As part of the bargain the Khedive accepted that two Controllers-General be appointed to supervise the revenue and expenditure of his Government. An Englishman, Mr. Romaine, was nominated as Controller-General for the revenue and a Frenchman, Baron de Malairet, dealt with the Egyptian Government's expenditure. And, having thus overcome its objections to interfering in Egypt's internal affairs, the British Government now decided to appoint Major Evelyn Baring—a former officer in the Royal Artillery—then Private Secretary to the Viceroy of India, and later to become Lord Cromer and *de facto* British ruler of Egypt—as their representative on the Commission of the Debt.

From the beginning this arrangement proved to be both unhappy and unworkable, as some of the less venal European contractors in Egypt had foretold. Not only did Ismail resent having to defer to people who wanted to curb his lavish spending, but he had also become profoundly suspicious of all Europeans, and was inclined to lump them all together indiscriminately as a lot of usurers and adventurers out to line their pockets at Egypt's expense. Inevitably, therefore, he soon fell out with the newly established commissioners and controllers, who demanded that his expenditures should be cut back to pay the interest on his debts. And over the next twelve months the situation deteriorated rapidly, as the Khedive found himself pressed for repayment both by the creditors of the Unified Debt and by contractors and other suppliers of goods and services to the Egyptian Government. In a desperate effort to scrape together enough money to meet Egypt's obligations, taxes were collected from the *fellahin* by the most brutal methods some nine to twelve months in advance, and Government employees went unpaid for months at a time.

Then, to add to the misery and misfortune of the peasantry, in 1877 an abnormally low rainfall reduced the Nile to a fraction of its life-giving powers and brought famine in Upper Egypt. With the people starving and forced to eat refuse and garbage, Ismail asked to be let off paying the next instalment of the Unified Debt interest. But the French insisted on their pound of flesh and Britain fell into line rather than upset her French ally on the eve of the Berlin Congress, which was to settle the situation arising out of the recent Russo-Turkish War.

Egypt was forced to pay up, but at the cost of such suffering and injustice that, by the end of 1877, even the French representative on the Commission of the Debt, M. de Blignières, was convinced that a major crisis, and possibly even a revolution, were threatening, and that before the next instalment was paid a searching enquiry must be held into Egypt's financial position. Baring and his Italian and Austrian colleagues agreed, and the suggestion was duly put to the Minister of Finance. But Ismail, suspecting that the proposition would lead to still greater foreign control over Egypt, quickly countered with a proposal for a more limited enquiry to ascertain the true amount of the Egyptian revenue. The four commissioners replied that such an investigation would be worse than useless. But Ismail was determined to limit their powers to pry into his affairs. And on January 27, 1878, he issued a decree setting up his own enquiry and invited Gordon to come to Cairo to preside over it, as the only Englishman on whom he felt he could rely to give him sound and unbiased advice.

How he should have thought that Gordon, with no knowledge or experience of financial matters, could help him is not clear. But when his Governor-General reached Cairo on March 7, 1878, he was in such a hurry to see him that Gordon was not even allowed to bathe and change out of his travel-worn clothes before being ushered into the Khedive's presence. As the two men sat and dined together, Ismail poured out his troubles and asked, or rather insisted, that Gordon should accept this commission. He could summon de Lesseps to help him, for this Frenchman had shown himself to be a friend of Egypt. But Ismail adamantly insisted that the Commission of the Debt must be kept out of the enquiry. They were only out to further the bond-holders' interests and to this end to get control of the Egyptian economy.

Unable to refuse any job and even more unwilling to deny 'Pharaoh'—as he had nicknamed the Khedive—Gordon accepted Ismail's request and, although the Consuls-General of all the creditor nations tried to put pressure on him to include the Commissioners in his enquiry, he stubbornly refused to override the Khedive's instructions. They reminded him that he was a European and an Englishman by birth and that his first duty was therefore to his own country's interests. But he retorted haughtily that 'when a man enters the service of a foreign state, he should entirely enter into consideration of that state, he should act for that state as for his own country'. Besides, the Commissioners had, he observed, been very hard on Ismail and deserved no consideration from him. The utmost he would do was to pass on to the Khedive a warning from the four Consuls-General that he would be risking his throne if he kept up his boycott of the Commissioners. But when he did so, Ismail dismissed the message as an idle threat. The only one of the creditor countries that he worried about was Britain; and he felt sure that, with Gordon on his side, the British would not proceed against him.

At this point Baring entered the lists in an attempt to get Gordon to reverse the Khedive's ruling. But Gordon contemptuously brushed him aside. Commenting on this early encounter with the man who, as his immediate superior during the final tragic stand against the Mahdi at Khartoum, was to become the butt of his savage and sarcastic criticism, he wrote: 'Baring is R.A. and I am R.E. Baring was in the nursery when I was in the Crimea. He has a pretentious, grand, patronizing way about him.... When oil mixes with water, we will mix together.' As for Vivian, the British Consul-General, he dismissed him as 'a pretty black-eyed boy' who had found Woolwich too tough a school when they were there together.

But while Gordon was inveighing against his compatriots for being pretentious or effete, the pressure was building up against him. And, sad to say, it was an intrigue involving Egypt's 'good friend' de Lesseps and the Khedive's own entourage, which helped in the end to defeat him and Ismail. De Lesseps told Gordon straight away that he should accept the Commissioners' demands and, after the opening meeting of the enquiry, he sent a message to Ismail implying that he would only serve with the Commissioners. Infuriated by this further attempt to put pressure on him, the Khedive charged Gordon with the sole responsibility and told him to prosecute his enquiry with all speed. But at this point the Khedive's private secretary paid a secret visit to de

Lesseps and begged him to hold firm and to refuse any co-operation unless the Commissioners were brought in. Unlike his royal master, the secretary took the threat of the European representatives to dethrone Ismail very seriously and feared for the consequences of the Khedive's defiant attitude.

De Lesseps agreed not to yield and Gordon carried on alone and in complete ignorance of the intrigues that were being conducted against him and Ismail. And after several weeks of intensive work, he recommended to the Khedive that, as a first step, he should suspend payment of the next instalment of interest on the Unified Debt and should use this money to pay the salaries of a large number of Government employees who had not been paid for many months. The telegraph clerks at Aswan, for instance, had been without any salaries for almost a year, as he discovered on his recent journey down the Nile from Khartoum. But when he informed Goschen of his proposal, there was an immediate explosion. Goschen informed Vivian, and Vivian was promptly instructed by London to warn Ismail against taking any action or advice without the full agreement of his creditors' representatives. At the same time the British Government suggested that Baring at least should be associated with Gordon's enquiry.

Already weakened by de Lesseps' stand against him, Ismail now knew that the game was up. But Gordon made one final effort to stiffen his resistance. Writing to Cherif Pasha, the Finance Minister and a son-in-law of Mohammed Ali's French military adviser, Colonel Seves, he said that if the Khedive was 'troubled', he was prepared to compromise to the extent of having a British official sent out from London to assist his enquiry. But, he added, he would not under any circumstances act with any of the four Commissioners, 'for I had begun to see with Pharaoh wavering it was necessary for me to look to my retreat ... [and] this also gave His Highness a reason for refusing H.M. Govt.'s recommendation that Baring should be on the Commission of Enquiry because he could quote my objection'.

His efforts were in vain, and four days later he discovered that Ismail had given in and agreed to the Commissioners of the Debt taking part in the enquiry. Yet the Khedive could not bring himself to send for his friend and tell him to his face that he had capitulated, and Gordon had to drag it out of him at an interview that was as awkward as it was unhappy. 'His Highness was bored with me,' Gordon wrote, 'and could not bear the sight of me.... I have no doubt it is better as it is. I have no doubt that His Highness and I would have fallen out about the composition of the Commission of Enquiry, for I feel sure that it was meant to be packed and that I was only to be a figurehead.'

Gordon duly resigned and returned to Khartoum. And Ismail was forced to accept a full-scale enquiry, with de Lesseps presiding and including Baring and a Mr. Rivers Wilson—a senior British Treasury official and the British Government's representative on the Council of the Suez Canal Company.

The days were now numbered for that autonomy which Mohammed Ali had won for Egypt by his defiance of the Ottoman Sultan seventy years before. True, Baring was soon to be persuaded by hard facts that some respite should be allowed in the interest payments on the Unified Debt and that for Egypt's creditors to insist on their pound of flesh would be 'oppressive to the peasantry and also contrary to the true interests of the bondholders'. But Baring was overruled by the Commissioners of the Debt, and the land of the Pharaohs was duly mortgaged to pay its creditors in full, regardless of the hardships inflicted on the peasantry, who had to pay, and on the Army and the Government employees, who had to go without their salaries.

More humiliating still, the de Lesseps enquiry recommended, and the Khedive was compelled to accept, that the tasks of the Controllers-General should be performed by British and French representatives acting as Ministers in his own Cabinet. Thus, five months after Gordon had left Cairo, Rivers Wilson was appointed Minister of Finance and de Blignières became Minister of Public Works, which situation Gordon was prophetically to describe as destined inevitably to lead to 'a mixed occupation of the country by the European powers'.

CHAPTER 13

WAR AGAINST THE SLAVERS

GORDON left Cairo on March 30, 1878, saddened and disillusioned by Ismail's surrender and thankful to be out of the atmosphere of intrigue and pressure that brooded over Egypt's capital. Two years earlier he had written: 'Of all the countries of the earth I can imagine none so detestable to govern as Egypt; years of oppression have eradicated everything from their character which would make a nation.' And now he felt that these harsh words had been no exaggeration. In fact, at few stages of his service under the Khedive was he more deeply depressed than now. Every moment of his stay in Cairo had been a misery, and he had hated everything about the place, from the dinners which he could not eat, having completely lost his appetite for 'civilized food', to the political intrigues, which he could not keep up with or understand. And although he owned that 'I had my Koh-i-noor with me, i.e. the presence of God', he felt quite desperate as he wrote to his sister: 'My crop of troubles is never to be got under. Slave questions, finance, government, all seems at sixes and sevens. There is no peace or rest and were it not for His Highness I would come home next mail for good. H.H. appoints men to my government with pay, etc., and then if they do not fit into their places he says to me, "Settle with them." I was quiet enough in my lands, but even H.H. sends me firebrands as if there was not enough inflammatory matter. I see no one scarcely but remain in my sulks, wishing and wishing that my end had come.'

On his way down the Nile in answer to Ismail's recent summons he had only a few weeks earlier written to his sister: 'I wish, I wish the King would come again and put things right on earth; but ... there are very few who wish Him to come, for to wish Him to come is to wish for death and how few wish for this.' And now once again he was saying that he had no desire to live beyond the completion of his service in the Sudan. But Destiny was not going to offer any easy issue from his afflictions. And Gordon was driven to seek his release by telegraphing to the War Office to say that, if his services were required by the British Army, he was 'disponible'. His offer was, however, ignored and he was left to gather himself together and set off for Berbera and Harar, remarking bitterly as he went that he now felt 'very different about the Sudan and H.H.; it is only a sort of sense of one's duty that keeps one up to the work'.

Two months later he was back in Khartoum, having once again dismissed Rouf Pasha, this time from the Governorship of Harar, for murderous and venal conduct. Back in the capital a vast array of problems kept him busy with the central administration for the next six months. There was the question of penal reform still to be completely resolved. And there were the prisoners themselves in the local gaol, each one of whose cases Gordon studied minutely, weighing the evidence and the judgement and reviewing the sentence. But greatest of all his problems was finance. In the previous year, he had spent £250,000 more than he had collected in, and, in addition to a national debt of over £300,000, the Sudan Government was still overspending at an annual rate of £100,000.

The difficulty, as Gordon had been forced to realize, was that having abolished the use of the *kourbash* as a method of extracting the revenue from the populace, the people were simply not paying their taxes. At best, no more than two-thirds of the revenue was being collected—which led him to reflect rather ruefully, 'Why should I stay here to do what any Arab governor can do much better?' But the point of exasperation was reached when de Lesseps' Commission of Enquiry, in the mistaken belief that the Sudan had in the past contributed to the Khedive's revenues, asked that such contributions should be 'resumed'. This was too much for Gordon, who in the interests of economy had only recently cut his own salary from £6,000 to £3,000, and in a rage he telegraphed to the Foreign Office in London to ask that instructions be sent to Rivers Wilson and Baring to withdraw this unreasonable demand.

The Foreign Office did as he asked, and Gordon heard no more from Cairo. But the dropping of this demand did nothing to placate his feelings towards those European ministers and officials who now held the Khedive's purse-strings in their close-fisted grasp. On the contrary, his indignation waxed stronger every time he thought about them, and especially about Baring and Rivers Wilson. When the Khedive invited him to come to Cairo to discuss the financial problems of the Sudan, he declined on the grounds that he did not want to 'be put in antagonism with the Minister of Finance'. And in telling his sister of his exchange with Ismail, he added the comment, 'the Gordons are a combative tribe'.

Just how combative were his feelings towards Rivers Wilson was shown when the Minister of Finance wrote to ask for an explanation of an Egyptian officer's complaint that he had been mistreated while serving in the Sudan. To this innocent, though perhaps tactless, enquiry Gordon retorted with unusual sarcasm that, although the Khedive, out of gratitude for his services, had no doubt appointed Rivers Wilson Commander-in-Chief, pending official confirmation of the fact, he could not recognize the Minister of Finance as having anything to do with military matters. Gordon, of course, held Rivers Wilson principally responsible for the attempt by the Commission of Enquiry to force the Sudan to pay revenue to Egypt. And he also charged him with not only refusing financial help to the Sudan, but actually taking money rightly due to the Khartoum Treasury by charging Customs dues at Suez on goods in transit for the Sudan. He further held, and with some justification, that it was highly improper for Rivers Wilson to keep his job with the Suez Canal Company while serving as a Minister in the Khedive's Cabinet. In fact, to Gordon everything about the man seemed somehow false. 'The position of the present Finance Minister is an impossible one,' he wrote, 'engaged as he is towards the creditors of the Great Debt by whose mediation he became what he is now, and occupied as he is in the Ministry of H.H. to insure the welfare of the country. These two engagements are diametrically opposed.'

But regardless of whether Rivers Wilson abused his position as the Khedive's Minister of Finance and cheated the Khartoum Treasury out of some of its revenues, the financial situation in the Sudan was rapidly approaching crisis point. Several major economies had to be made. First on Gordon's list came those useless liabilities, Ismail's Red Sea provinces. If the Khedive wanted to keep them, he would have to pay for them out of the Egyptian revenue. Berbera, Zeyla and Harar were of no possible advantage to the Sudan and required a heavy financial outlay to maintain them. The most sensible solution, Gordon suggested to Ismail, would be to sell them to the Italian Government, which was eager to establish a colonial foothold in the Somali corner of Africa. Then there was the question of communications with Lake Victoria. Gordon had earlier sent Emin to visit Kabba Rega and Mutesa to discuss once again the possibilities of getting steamers up to Lake Victoria, and he had ordered four steamers to be built in England for this purpose. Now he gave orders to abandon this costly venture and to consolidate the Khedive's frontiers at Mrooli.

Finally, there was the railway that was being built from Wadi Halfa to Khartoum, which Gordon regarded as quite unnecessary and far too expensive. Rather than build a railway all the way to Khartoum, Gordon felt that it would be sufficient to construct a by-pass at each main cataract on the river, as had been done at Aswan in Egypt, and a short-cut across the big S-bend in the Nile in the region of Dongola-Berber. The contract for the railway, which included the supply of some £600,000 worth of equipment and involved another £300,000 of labour costs, had been negotiated by the Khedive's ministers in 1875, but had been handed over to the Sudan Government in 1877. And the depleted Treasury in Khartoum just did not have enough money to build a railway from the frontier all the way to the capital. The Khedive would not be at all pleased at the cancellation of a project which he felt would help to stimulate the incipient tourist trade—Thos. Cook had recently acquired a monopoly of the passenger traffic on the Nile. But Gordon, nevertheless, took the plunge and ordered that all work on the railway be abandoned.

He could hardly be blamed for making these drastic economies at this time. Not only was his Treasury in deficit, there was also a prospect of having to fight two serious campaigns simultaneously and at opposite ends of the Sudan. Far away to the south-west the egregious Suleiman had followed his father's bad example and taken possession of the Bahr-el-Ghazal Province, overthrowing Gordon's Governor, Idris, and massacring the Sudanese garrison; while to the north-east, Walad el-Michael had gone for Adowa after all and decisively defeated one of Johannes' generals. Only a few days earlier Gordon had received word that Menelik had finally laid down his arms. And it now seemed more than likely that Johannes would come scurrying north to avenge Walad el-

Michael's aggression, with incalculable consequences to his efforts to make peace with Abyssinia. Happily, the danger was averted by a curious stroke of good fortune. Gordon had recently written to Johannes' defeated general to assure him that, if Walad el-Michael should break the truce and attack Abyssinian territory, Khartoum would wash its hands of the renegade chieftain and leave him to fend for himself against any counter-attack which Johannes might launch. This letter happened to be among the documents which Walad el-Michael seized from his defeated enemy. And its effect when read by the renegade was more salutary than Gordon could ever have hoped. Without further ado, Walad el-Michael sent in his submission to Johannes. And a few days later Gordon received a letter from the Abyssinian King informing him that an envoy was on his way to the Sudan to discuss the frontier problem, and adding that, while he was not disposed to make peace with his enemy of long standing, the Khedive, he would do so with Gordon.

Delighted to have an excuse to get out of his capital, which had suffered an autumn of malaria epidemics due to an abnormal rise in the Nile bringing a plague of mosquitoes, Gordon dashed off to meet Johannes' envoy at Katarif, halfway between Khartoum and the Abyssinian frontier. After treating the envoy to a nine-gun salute, he told him to inform Johannes that the Khedive was not prepared to hand back the territories he had conquered and that these territories were anyway of no use to Abyssinia. However, if Johannes accepted the situation, he would try to meet him on two points that he wanted settled: the return of the Emperor Theodore's crown, which had been looted by British troops during Napier's expedition, and official Coptic recognition of a link between the Abyssinian and the Coptic Archbishopric in Alexandria. Having thus bluntly stated his terms—which could scarcely be termed a 'discussion' of the frontier problem—Gordon ordered a further nine-gun salute, dismissed the envoy and returned to Khartoum to inform the Khedive that he now had settled the Abyssinian question!

Meanwhile, the news from the south-west allowed of no such wishful thinking. The 'cub' had clearly grown into a savage wolf, and Gordon was greatly concerned about this new threat from Suleiman. Besides, he believed that the revolt had been masterminded by Zubair, who had been intriguing for several months in

Cairo to be allowed back to the Sudan. Since Nubar Pasha had won his way back into the Khedive's favour and been appointed Prime Minister again, Zubair had redoubled his efforts. For Nubar was to say the least a lukewarm opponent of the slave trade, and when Zubair offered, as the price of his return to the Sudan, to contribute £25,000 a year to the Khartoum Treasury, plus a Negro battalion to reinforce the Sudanese Army, he telegraphed to Gordon suggesting that the offer be accepted.

Gordon had blown hot and cold about Zubair. In 1876, when Zubair was lord of all Darfur, he had written that no doubt he 'has some idea of government, for these natives would never have been faithful to him if he had not known how to conciliate them'. But he had recently discovered from correspondence seized in Khartoum that Zubair had been goading his son to rebellion, and he now vowed that he would hang him if he ever came back. In the unlikely event that the 'arch-slaver' would ever pay £25,000 to the Sudanese revenue, such a sum would be certain to come out of the profits of slave-trading. Besides, if Zubair were allowed to return a free man, 'there was nothing to prevent him overrunning all Africa', for there were no native chiefs powerful enough to stand against him. Therefore, in reply to Nubar's telegram, Gordon said that he did not need a Negro battalion and did not want Zubair in the Sudan. He also wrote to the Khedive asking him to put the 'prince of slavers' back under lock and key, and himself confiscated the considerable fortune belonging to his family, much of which had been stolen from the late Sultan of Darfur, together with all their property in Khartoum.

But with Nubar as Prime Minister, Gordon had little doubt that no action would be taken to place Zubair under restraint; and it was therefore all the more important and urgent to suppress Suleiman's revolt as quickly as possible. By a fortunate coincidence, his old partner from Equatoria, Romolo Gessi, who had left the Khedive's service when Gordon left Equatoria, happened to arrive at Khartoum on his way up the Nile to explore the Saubat River at the very moment when Suleiman struck at Bahr-el-Ghazal. And, loyal friend that he was, he agreed without hesitation to abandon his expedition and to take charge of operations against the rebels. Thus on July 15, 1878, Hessi, whose exploits had earned him the pseudonym of the 'Garibaldi of Africa', left Khartoum and marched on Suleiman with a force of 2,400 men. It took him five months to make contact with his adversary; but on Christmas Eve he contrived by a ruse to seize one of Suleiman's camps. And on the following day, when Suleiman attacked with a force of 10,000 men, Gessi beat him off and forced him to withdraw with the loss of about a quarter of his army. After a few more skirmishes, in which Gessi again managed to come off best, Suleiman called for help from his fellow slave-traders in the Shakka region and invited Haroun, the recently defeated leader of the Darfur rebellion, to join forces with him. And it was when Gordon heard of this call to arms by Suleiman, with its inherent threat to raise the tribes of Darfur once more against the Government, that he decided to go straight to Shakka to confer with Gessi and to put a stop to any reinforcements leaving to join the rebels.

He was in for another terrible march. By day the heat was unbearable and the nights were bitterly cold, and he suffered badly from his liver and from palpitations of the heart. After marching for five days in these conditions, he reckoned that it took at least two days' rest to cool down the human body. For days on end in the desert they would find no water, the usual wells and tree-trunk reservoirs having gone dry for want of rain. A typical entry in Gordon's letter-journal tells the story: 'We are in a fix. We expected to find water here sufficient for 40 camels; there is not enough for two! ! ! and the nearest wells are 1½ days off and the camels are exhausted. I must go all night and try to avoid the heat. What a country!' To start with, he managed to defeat the temperature problem by travelling at night across the desert and resting by day. But when he left the desert and reached the savannah jungle around Shakka, even the comparative comfort of night marching was denied to him. For here the expedition lost itself in the dark and was forced to hack its way through the forest by day under a remorseless sun.

Physical distress was not Gordon's only misery. Once beyond El Obeid, he soon began to realize how dismally he had failed to put down the slave trade. Almost every day of the 340-mile march to Shakka he encountered a slave convoy on its way to the north from Bahr-el-Ghazal, conveying hundreds of poor miserable creatures, men, women, and children, some only three years old. On such occasions he would conscript the men for service with his escorting troops, and the women to act as wives, and send the children to the nearest garrison to await their parents' return. He was sorely tempted to shoot the slave-dealers, but the maximum sentence under the law for dealing in, as opposed to hunting, slaves was five years' imprisonment. So he desisted and either turned them loose in the desert or sent them back to Khartoum in chains, after a severe flogging.

Meanwhile, Gessi, although desperately short of ammunition, had struck up an alliance with several ferocious cannibal tribes, and with their support was trying to hunt down Suleiman before he could obtain reinforcements. He succeeded in burning Suleiman's stronghold to the ground, but the rebel managed to escape with his life, and made for the hills away to the north-west. A few weeks later Gessi and Gordon met at a village north of Shakka to discuss the situation and to decide what should be done with Suleiman if and when he was captured. Clearly his next move would be to effect a union with Haroun and try to make common cause with the Darfur tribes. At all costs he must be caught before he could do so. As to what punishment he should then suffer, Gordon had personally made up his mind that he deserved to be executed for rebellion, whatever lighter penalties the law might provide for his slaving activities. But he refrained from giving Gessi any clear direction, and merely told his lieutenant that he would be supported in whatever decision he took at the time.

Gessi thereupon resumed the hunt with a small mobile force of 250 and, less than three weeks later, caught up with his quarry, thanks to information supplied by local tribes, who lived in deadly fear of the arch-slaver. Before dawn on the following morning his small force surrounded the village where Suleiman had halted for the night with his escort. A message was sent in via one of the villagers that the rebels were surrounded and, if they did not surrender within ten minutes, would be attacked from all sides. Suleiman had over three times as many men with him as Gessi, but the bluff worked and, as pandemonium broke out among the villagers, making resistance impossible, Suleiman and his chiefs came out and gave themselves up. At this point it seems that Gessi, in the absence of any direct order from Gordon, was uncertain whether or not to shoot his prisoners. But the next evening, when he halted for the night, he was informed that they were planning to escape and was forced to make a quick decision: whether to risk this dangerous rebel escaping or to make sure that he would never threaten law and order again. He decided to play safe and Suleiman and his chiefs were promptly taken out and summarily executed.

The 'son of Zubair', as Gordon called him, was dead, and a few weeks later Zubair himself was convicted by a Khartoum tribunal of complicity in Suleiman's rebellion and sentenced to death *in absentia*. A while later, Haroun was killed by Egyptian troops and his forces finally dispersed. Thereafter an uneasy peace descended on Bahr-el-Ghazal and Darfur. But the destruction of Suleiman and Haroun did not necessarily resolve the question which had been uppermost in Gordon's mind ever since he took office as Governor-General: Could the slave trade be bought to an end, as he had once hoped, or would it continue under any government, as he had now begun to fear?

Whatever the answer might be, Gordon knew one thing for certain: honest government would never be assured, let alone slavery suppressed, so long as Egyptian pashas continued to govern the provinces. Six months more of Arab government, he contended, 'would raise the heads of all the evils I have scotched, and the result would be catastrophe'. He had asked Sir Richard Burton and Sir Samuel Baker to come and help him, but both had refused. However, two likely-looking Europeans had recently presented themselves at Khartoum, offering to serve the Sudan Government. One was an Englishman called Frank Lupton, a former Merchant Navy officer serving in the Red Sea, who struck Gordon as a man of high quality. The other was a young Austrian army officer, Rudolf Carl von Slatin, who was recommended to Gordon by Emin, and who had shown great ability during the first few months of 1879 when serving as Inspector of Taxes at Khartoum. Gordon therefore lost no time in appointing Slatin to Darfur and enrolling Lupton in the Government at Khartoum. Meanwhile, Gessi was given the governorship of Bahr-el-Ghazal with the rank of Pasha and Emin was instructed to take over in Equatoria from the now-disgraced Fawzi (whose life Gordon claimed to have spared on the toss of a coin!).

But it was already too late to stop the rot which had set in throughout the Sudan. Gordon could destroy the Suleimans and the Harouns; and he could dismiss as many Egyptians as he liked and replace them with Europeans. Yet even as he was making his new appointments, he seems to have realized how powerless he was to institute reforms and, in particular, to suppress something so endemic in the life of the Sudan as the slave trade. In a long disquisition on the subject of slavery written at this juncture, he examined the issue from every angle. First, there was the economic problem to be considered. The economic consequences of abolishing slavery were not to be lightly dismissed. Gordon estimated that over three-quarters of the Sudan's population were slaves and that the country would suffer a loss of two-thirds of its revenue if the slave trade were abolished. Agricultural development depended almost entirely on slave labour, and would be brought to a standstill. The Army would also suffer, since many thousands of his troops were former slaves who had been bought and released from captured caravans.

Then there was the problem of intercepting the caravans with inadequate and unreliable Egyptian troops, whose sympathies often lay with the slave-traders. Gordon reckoned that for the sixty-three convoys which had been captured in the past eight months—of which nearly two-thirds had been seized by him during his march to Shakka—probably 500 had escaped detection and got through to the north. 'The Gordons are sharp,' he wrote, 'but I fear the Arabs are sharper.'

There was just a possibility that he might be able to strike a crippling blow at the slave-traders by throwing a cordon across the approaches to El Obeid from the south-west, whence all the 'feeder lines' ran from the slavers' main hunting-grounds in Bahr-el-Ghazal. But what would be the point of stopping all these convoys if, owing to the chaotic state of the law and the refusal of the authorities in Cairo to back him, he was unable to deal out exemplary punishment to the slave-traders who were caught by his cordon? Ismail might tell him to shoot these men, but the Khedival decree, which was the law of the land, provided a prison sentence of between five months and five years for such wrongdoers. The distinction drawn between slave-hunting, which was branded as 'robbery with murder', and slave-selling, which was considered a lesser crime, enabled any slave-hunter caught with a caravan to plead that he was merely a middle-man and even to demand compensation for the confiscation of his slaves.

To add to the confusion, Nubar Pasha had recently telegraphed to say, with all the authority of his office as Prime Minister, that 'the sale and purchase of slaves in Egypt is legal' until the expiry of the seven-year period of grace in 1884. And Gordon had retorted: 'I have no belief in the Cairo Government acting against slavery and I would ask if even the [Anglo-Egyptian] Convention and [the Khedival] Decree have ever been publicly posted on the wall of each town and village of the Cairo Government. Twice it has been posted in every town and village of the whole of the Sudan, and it will be continued to be posted annually. Surely some notice should be given to the people of the tremendous change which is to come over them in five years' time.' The Egyptian Government had appointed many highly paid officials with orders to stop slave-trading. Yet, he remarked, 'it is notorious that whenever a caravan escapes from the Sudan into Egypt it is perfectly safe. How many caravans have been captured in Egypt against the 63 caravans I have captured in the Sudan. I do not believe that one has.'

Gordon concluded his remonstrance with a dig at the British and French Ministers in Ismail's Government for condoning the official Egyptian attitude. 'At present we are under a responsible ministry; the act of one minister is the collective act of the whole, and in that ministry are two Europeans who share their acts.' Good constitutional doctrine no doubt for a well-established democracy such as Britain, yet scarcely applicable to nineteenth-century Egypt!

As he pondered on this long list of insurmountable obstacles to the fulfilment of his mission, Gordon became once more obsessed with a feeling of hopelessness. He had come to the conclusion that, as he put it, 'I could not govern the country to satisfy myself.' An Arab Governor-General, he now contended, could do no worse than he and might do a lot better, certainly when it came to gathering taxes from the people, who had come to regard his relatively kindly and civilized ways as weakness. Without using methods of extortion, he could never gather enough revenue to balance the Government's books. And without co-operation from Egypt he could not expect even a partial success for his efforts to stop the slave trade. All that he now wished for himself was to fall into 'a dreamless sleep'. He had lost all appetite for life. And from the depths of his depression he wrote to the Khedive to say that he could not remain any longer as Governor-General of the Sudan.

CHAPTER 14

RESIGNATION

ISMAIL'S reaction to his Governor-General's resignation was characteristic. Instead of bluntly refusing to let Gordon go, he invited him to Cairo to discuss his problems. Like an understanding father dealing with a temperamental son, he sought to humour and to calm him with suggestions that all his difficulties could be resolved by discussions with the Egyptian Government. But Gordon, knowing all too well the power of the Khedive's charm, stubbornly refused to be drawn. He had had a sickener of Cairo during his last visit, he remarked in his letter-journal, and the last thing he would do would be to expose himself to more pressures and intrigues by the Khedive and his ministers. He would only go there on his way home when he left the Sudan for good, and not to be talked into carrying on with a mission which had become futile. What possible good could he do in Cairo, either for himself or for the Sudan? Not only did he see no purpose in discussing his problems with the Khedive's ministers, but he now regarded Ismail himself as worse than useless.

Ismail, who had once been 'so very kind' and with whom Gordon had enjoyed a special relationship never before accorded to the Khedive's Governor-General, could now do nothing right. At best he was now too 'enfeebled' by foreign pressures and political intrigues to be of any help to the Sudan. 'I truly have nothing to thank His Highness for, except civil speeches,' was his tart summing-up of the man whom he had only a few months earlier been proud and pleased to call his friend. And now he even saw fit to record against him that he had sold to a 'wretched French museum' (the Louvre to be exact!) a collection of ancient armour which had been bought in Darfur 'at a cost of £100 of my own coin'. All that Gordon would concede to his former friendship was the denial of any suggestion that his decision to resign was due to his being 'vexed' with Ismail. And to this end he asked his brother, Henry, to put it about that his forthcoming return was due to 'liver! smoking! and cognac!'

For the time being, however, the question of Gordon's resignation lay in abeyance. Ismail had his hands full trying to fight off the ever-increasing encroachments of the representatives of his creditors. Not only had he been forced to appoint an Englishman and a Frenchman as Ministers in his Cabinet in control of his revenues and expenditures whose loyalties lay with his creditors and not with Egypt; worse still, he had been compelled to accept the position of a constitutional monarch with all the limitations of his powers which this entailed. And then on top of all this the European powers, not content with attacking his public position, had invaded his private domains and forced him to mortgage his landed properties, amounting to nearly 1 million acres, to raise a loan of £8,500,000 from Messrs. Rothschild to pay the next instalment of interest due to his creditors on the Unified Debt!

Ismail was an altogether more pliable character than his grandfather, Mohammed Ali. But these humiliations were altogether too much. He particularly resented the constitutional reforms which had been forced upon him and which meant that he was held responsible for decisions by European ministers over whom he had no control. To add to his problems, the abnormally high Nile of the previous autumn had caused as much havoc as the drought of two years before. Severe flooding had resulted, with damage to crops in Lower Egypt, and urgent relief measures were needed to help the large number of peasants who were homeless and starving. Yet to meet this further unforeseen charge upon the country's slender resources no relief was offered by the Commission of the Debt in respect of Egypt's repayment of her creditors. Then, when some confusion arose regarding the title to the Khedive's estates and Rothschilds withheld further payment of their loan, Nubar's Government decided to make the necessary economies at the expense of the Khedive's Army. Two thousand, five hundred Egyptian officers were promptly retired; but when they came to Cairo to collect their arrears of pay, there was not enough money to pay them. A furious demonstration followed, which resulted in Nubar and Rivers Wilson being seized by a group of some 400 officers, who held them prisoner until the Khedive personally pledged that their grievances would be met.

This was the kind of explosion which Ismail expected, and

secretly hoped, would follow the Shylock practices of his European overlords. Drawing much moral reinforcement from this demonstration, he decided to dare everything in a valiant attempt to assert his independence. First, he insisted that he must wield a proper share of power or he could not be responsible for public order. Then he demanded and obtained the resignation of Nubar, who was replaced by Cherif. A special advance was then obtained from Rothschilds to meet the officer's pay claims. And, finally, in April he divested himself of his Anglo-French overlords by dismissing Rivers Wilson and de Blignières from his Government and insisting that an all-Egyptian Cabinet be formed.

At first neither Britain nor France did more than complain rather ineffectually at Ismail's defiant gesture. But when a Khedival decree was issued modifying both the amounts of Egypt's interest payments and the timing of such payments, both powers began to sit up and take notice, especially after Germany had taken the lead in protesting against Ismail's decree in threatening terms. Germany was only a very minor creditor of Egypt, but Britain and France could not appear any less keen to safeguard their bondholders' interests. And in June, after consultations between London and Paris, the two powers presented protests to the Khedive, together with a strong hint that he should abdicate without delay if he did not want to be deposed. At the same time they served notice on the Ottoman Sultan in Constantinople, as the Khedive's constitutional sovereign, that, if he did not depose Ismail, they would take the law into their own hands and do so themselves. The unfortunate Ismail appealed to his Turkish sovereign; but in vain, for at this serious juncture of Ottoman affairs, when his empire was dwindling rapidly in almost every quarter, the Sultan could not afford to defy two such powerful friends as Britain and France. And on June 26, 1879, Ismail was informed of his own dismissal and of his replacement by his son Tewfik, in a telegram from the Sultan addressed to 'the Ex-Khedive', which said that it had become clear that his 'continuation in the office of Khedive could have no other result than to multiply and aggravate the present difficulties'.

Gordon heard the news of Ismail's April *coup* while on his travels in Darfur and Bahr-el-Ghazal. Needless to say, he was delighted. Rivers Wilson and his French colleague had got what they deserved. That 'mushroom lot', as he contemptuously described the European officials who had sprung up in every department of the Khedive's service, had driven Ismail too far. Instead of being 'fatherly' to him and treating him as an Asian, they had bullied and humiliated him and had expected him to fulfil his commitments as a European would have done! And, seen from the distance of the Sudan, the *coup* was a salutary 'warning against meddling' for Britain and France and a lucky 'escape' for their governments before they had become too deeply involved. Ismail had redeemed himself, and was now the 'splendid leopard' who had broken out of the cage in which the European powers had tried to imprison him. 'Li Hung-chang,' Gordon wrote, 'was just of the same ideas; he granted the advantage to the Europeans, but he counted the *moral* cost and found it too expensive.' The Europeans could have exercised the necessary controls to prevent waste in the Khedive's spending 'without the expensive, cumbrous and to the nation, unpopular machinery' which they had created and which, if Ismail had not rebelled, would have led irresistibly to the occupation of Egypt. 'As ships without ballast drift, so do governments and men without principle.' But Ismail had refused to drift and had saved himself and the European powers from an otherwise inevitable clash.

A few weeks later doubts began to set in as rumours reached him from Cairo that the Khedive had been forced to sign an agreement with Britain and France reinstituting European control over his finances. And with this news Gordon's attitude towards Ismail began to harden once again. 'There is no doubt,' he wrote, 'H.H. used me for his object and that I have used H.H. for my object. I owe him nothing and he owes me nothing. . . . H.H. says, "have I not trusted Gordon?" I say, "Yes, to the extent of not clashing with his own views." Whenever support did clash with his views, then H.H. did not support me. You may say, "But you cannot expect H.H. to accept all you propose. H.H. must have some voice in the government." That is true, but the points on which we differed were such as to admit of no doubt as to my own view being correct. . . . However, as I said, we are quits.'

Foreseeing that the Khedive might be driven off the throne now that the European powers had re-established their control, Gordon was getting ready to wash his hands of him. True, he hoped that Ismail would stand firm by his refusal to employ Europeans in his Government, since this would make it easier for him to bow out of the Sudan. Still, however many allowances one may make for his anxiety to be quit of so exacting and impossible a task, it is difficult not to feel a little shocked by his reaction when he read in a telegram from Cherif Pasha that Ismail was no longer Khedive. 'I do not see much to be regretted in the deposition of Ismail. . . . It does not affect me in the least,' was his only comment, apart from saying that the substitution of Tewfik was a foolish move and refusing to send the new Khedive any telegram of congratulations on his accession.

A legend has grown up that, so affected was Gordon on hearing of Ismail's downfall, that he upped and resigned from the Governor-Generalship in a spontaneous act of loyal protest. In fact, his letter-journal to Augusta devotes no more than a brief paragraph, less than 150 words, to the whole tragic and dramatic incident; whereas page after page thereafter is filled with the inevitable debate as to whether in these altered circumstances he should go or stay in the Sudan. One day he would stay, 'although were it not for the people of these lands I would not hesitate to resign'. Twenty-four hours later he had 'nearly' made up his mind to leave, as Tewfik was a 'miserable creature', and to serve him would be to submit to the rule of the British and French Consuls-General, plus Baring and the rest of the 'mushroom lot'. And this could only end in a row, especially with Baring, for whom he had by now conceived such an intense dislike that he regarded the 'pretty black-eyed boy', Vivian, by comparison as 'a thorough gentleman and a perfectly straightforward fellow'.

In the end Gordon decided to resign and to use the change of régime as his pretext for doing so. And after proclaiming Tewfik as the new ruler of Egypt and the Sudan, he left Khartoum 'for good and all', as he hopefully put it. On August 23 he reached Cairo, where he was promptly ushered in to see the new Khedive. Here once again Gordon was to change his opinion about a man whom he had condemned without adequate knowledge and to rend most ungraciously another whom he once never tired of describing as a true and loyal friend. 'A miracle had happened,' he remarked in his letter-journal. 'Here was a man with talent, energy, and manner of the "Incurable" [Gordon's newly coined epitaph for Ismail], with a quality the latter did not possess, i.e. honesty. It was really quite astounding; he was not profuse at all; in fact he paid me not one single compliment.' Tewfik was no longer the miserable creature of the British and French Consuls-General; now he was a splendid fellow who was 'scoffing' at the Europeans and making a resolute stand for Egyptian independence. As with Ismail, Gordon now felt that his only true friend and supporter in Cairo was the Khedive, whereas with every member of his Cabinet his relationship was one of bitter mutual hostility. He even thought of calling on the Ottoman Sultan on his return journey to England to tell him what a splendid appointment he had made, and what a blessing it was that the 'Incurable' had left the scene.

Undoubtedly the explanation of this volte-face was that Gordon was seeking to justify another abrupt change of course. On his arrival in Cairo he had told Tewfik that he was not going back to the Sudan. But when the new Khedive asked him as a parting favour to make one more attempt to conclude a peace settlement with Johannes, Gordon, as usual, could not refuse the assignment, and before the end of August he was on his way back to Massawa.

Once again he was in for a long and painful march into the mountainous hinterlands of Abyssinia. And although on this occasion he did make contact with Johannes, it was not until many weeks later that he finally caught up with the elusive monarch. The long-awaited encounter was both unpleasant and abortive. Johannes was 'a sour ill-favoured looking being [who] never looks you in the face, but when you look away he glares at you like a tiger.... He is of the strictest sect of the Pharisees—drunk overnight, at dawn he is up reading the Psalms.' Johannes' ploy was to try to wheedle Gordon away from his loyalty to Egypt with flattering remarks about his friends and co-religionists, the British. But, fulfilling his instructions to the letter, Gordon insisted on being treated as a representative of the Moslem Khedive and bluntly told him that 'Egypt would resist his demands as impossible and would arm his enemies', Such a blunt warning not to press his request for the evacuation of Egypt's conquests was something to which Johannes was unaccustomed 'in his own den and amid his own people'. And when he began to bluster, Gordon rubbed salt in the wound by telling him that he was not God and should not try to act as if he were and that, so far as any of his threats went, 'six feet would hold me and would hold him too'.

On this acid note the meeting ended; and without any attempt to reason, still less to negotiate, with Johannes, Gordon headed back to Egypt, thoroughly soured by the whole business. The rigours of the long march to and from Abyssinia, coming so soon after the privations of his recent expedition to Darfur and Bahr-el-Ghazal, had brought on his heart palpitations again and completely sapped his remaining energy; and when he got back to Massawa he was prostrated with exhaustion. As often happened at such moments of stress, his temper was exceedingly short, and he rounded on the man responsible for sending him on such a fruitless errand. Now he wrote to his brother Henry that he had from the start 'instinctively felt that Tewfik was false' and that his sole purpose in sending him to Abyssinia was to expose him to the possibility of some mishap in the hope of embroiling Britain in Egypt's dispute with Johannes! He would not serve Tewfik a moment longer, and on his return to Egypt in January 1880 he got the surgeon of the British Consulate at Alexandria to issue him with a certificate stating that he must retire from the Khedive's service, owing to total nervous exhaustion.

Armed with this conclusive medical opinion, Gordon went to Cairo to hand in his formal and final resignation. Tewfik, somewhat half-heartedly, sought to dissuade him, but backed down when he saw it was no good insisting. And a few days later Gordon set sail for England, taking with him a letter from the Khedive which expressed thanks for the loyalty with which he had always served the Government and which added, somewhat pointedly, that 'in view of your persistent tender of resignation I am obliged to accept it'. Egypt and the Sudan lay behind him, forgotten and unmourned, as he pretended to himself. And as he journeyed homewards he wrote to his brother to say 'I want to get a lodging [in London] with bedroom and sitting-room which is about halfway between your house and South Kensington Museum. I do not care how high it is; I want no curtains or things which hold tobacco smoke.'

CHAPTER 15

INTERLUDE

To judge from Gordon's letter-journal during the latter stages of his Governor-Generalship, there can be little doubt that he was not only tired of the Sudan, but of life itself. And in his further correspondence with his sister over the next two years this impression becomes still more evident. 'It is odd,' he wrote a few months after his return from Egypt, 'to have lived one's life out, ere it is finished.' The mystic side of his nature had clearly come to dominate his thinking. Hitherto his mysticism and religious contemplation had usually been relegated to the background during periods of intense activity. 'You can scarcely expect pearls just now, hunted as I am on all sides,' he had written to Augusta from Cairo in the middle of his abortive inquiry into Ismail's finances. But from now on, whether active or not, Gordon came to live more in the next world than in this one and to long increasingly for his 'release' from this earth. Only a month after he returned to England he wrote to his sister to say how he was *longing with great desire for death*.... This world is too small and one longs for a larger sphere in the future world ... a sphere where one can know one's fellow face to face without the hypo-Wylde is a pleasure to visit, for she is laid up with an incurable crisy of this earth.' And again, after visiting a sick friend, 'Miss disease. How willingly would I change places with her!'

Yet such was his God-fearing faith that he was able to discipline himself to wait upon the workings of Divine Providence and not, as he was later to put it in a significant passage in his Khartoum journal, to 'take things out of God's hands'. 'Really,' he told Augusta, 'life needs only a little patience to bear with the present. If we could only look on our lives as an affair of 24 hours, we could bear up in whatever position we were cast in, and how little it would signify if we were great or small. For the former would feel how ephemeral was their greatness and the latter would not care to be great.'

Certainly no one ever made more of a fetish of despising and avoiding the 'great' than Gordon. As invitations poured in upon him from London society, which was seeking once again to lionize this remarkable explorer and empire-builder, he refused them all. 'Men think dinners are conferring a favour on you,' he had written from the wilds of Equatoria, 'and that you are bound to them in return. I look on the constant invitations to dinner as a positive infliction. You cannot go and see a man without his pestering you with his tiresome dinners where you are sure to say something you regret.... Why do they not give their dinners to those who need them?' He made no distinctions in his refusals. High and low in society were lumped together as 'butterfly people' and turned down with equal firmness. The Prince of Wales received the same treatment as any social-climbing hostess. And when His Royal Highness's discomfited equerry came to tell Gordon that he could not refuse the invitation of the heir to the throne, he was met with the reply, 'Why not? I refused King Johannes when he invited me to go to his hot spring in the mountains and he might have cut off my head for refusing. I am sure His Royal Highness will not do that.'

'Then let me say you are ill,' pleaded the equerry.

'But I am not ill,' Gordon replied.

'Then give me some reason I can give to the Prince.'

'Very well, then,' said Gordon. 'Tell him I always go to bed at half-past nine.'

As an escape from the relentless pursuit of the English social world, Gordon took the first overseas job that was offered to him —that of Private Secretary to Lord Ripon, who had just been appointed Governor-General of India. Certainly it would be hard to imagine a post less suited to Gordon's peculiar qualities and character, requiring as it did extreme tact, a calm temper, and a subservient nature, not to speak of an ability to spend long hours being pleasant to stuffy people at even stuffier dinner-parties and receptions. And even before he landed in India, Gordon realized his mistake. Writing from Aden *en route* for Bombay, he told his sister, 'I cannot say I like the berth and I shall get away as soon as I can do so in a respectable manner.' Four days later he wrote again: 'I have made up my mind to leave either in Sept. or beginning of October. I think it will be no surprise to Lord Ripon who sees I am too truculent for the post.'

In fact, he did not last as long as September. Within a week of his arrival in India he resigned his post. 'Yes, I ratted,' he wrote to his brother Henry, 'but I ratted so as to hurt Lord Ripon very little and we parted the best of friends.' He added that what he saw of India 'sickened me'. It was in his sight 'the most wretched of countries. The way the people live is absurd in its luxury and they seem so utterly effeminate and not to have an idea beyond the rupee. I nearly burst with the trammels which are put on you. I declare I think we are not far off losing it and the sooner it went the better, I think. It is only the upper ten thousand in England who benefit by it. All the salaries are too high by half. It is a house of charity for a lot of idle useless fellows.... How truly glad I am to have broken with the whole lot.'

Yet he could not bear the thought of returning to England and regimental soldiering. 'Judging from what one sees of the Army,' he wrote, 'I have no wish ever to join it in any capacity.' He knew that he had become almost unemployable in his own country's service. 'Having the views I have I could not curb myself sufficiently ever to remain in H.M. Service. Not one in ten million can agree with one's motives and it is no use expecting to change their views.' If he could not get an extended leave of absence, there was nothing for it but to resign from the Army altogether. 'I mean to go whether they like it or not.... I will give them my commission,' he proclaimed.

However, as he wrote those words, a telegram was on its way to him from Robert Hart in Shanghai inviting him to come to China and try to restrain the Chinese government from going to war with Russia, with whom they were currently involved in a bitter disputation. Gordon accepted without hesitation and applied for leave to the War Office, who asked him to state more specifically the purpose of his China visit. Typically he replied, 'Am ignorant; will write from China before expiration of leave,' which the War Office did not think was an adequate explanation and refused to sanction the project. Possibly they suspected that Gordon intended to raise a Chinese Army for a preventive war against Russia, a scheme which Sir Samuel Baker was known to have discussed with him. But when it was found that Gordon had already left India, the military authorities bowed to the inevitable and granted him leave, subject to his engaging to take no military service in China.

With tongue well in cheek, Gordon replied: 'I will take no military service in China; I would never embarrass Her Majesty's Government.' And on arriving in China, he went straight to see his old Commander-in-Chief, Li Hung-chang. Li was all for a peaceful settlement with Russia. But both at Peking and outside it influential voices were advocating war, and petitions were being raised against Li for failing to take a sufficiently patriotic line. It was a difficult situation, and Gordon felt that he might well lose his head for interfering in China's affairs and make a 'quick exit'. But he decided none the less to go to Peking to strengthen Li's hand by warning the Chinese Government against doing anything rash.

In Peking he found that not all the Emperor's ministers shared the views of the belligerent faction and he was well enough received. In fact, he seems to have been more at loggerheads with the British Legation than with the Chinese Government. In a letter to his brother, he said that he deeply resented the mistrust shown to him by Britain's representatives in China, who tried to 'dictate my words' to the Chinese Government. He felt that the British Minister and Robert Hart were in some way conspiring against him, and complained bitterly about 'the way I am hunted and bothered by people trying to pump me'. For some unexplained reason, he had resented Hart ever since he left China in 1865. 'I am glad the government did not give him a C.B.,' he wrote to Augusta from Equatoria. 'Li Hung-chang always hated him.' (In fact, the Government was to confer far greater decorations on this distinguished public servant, for in 1882 he became K.C.M.G., in 1889 G.C.M.G. and in 1893 a baronet!)

When Gordon later returned to England he was to learn to his delight that the British Minister in Peking had paid him the handsome compliment of asserting that his efforts to mediate with the Emperor's Government had undoubtedly been 'the cause of China making peace'. But at the time he was so incensed by the Minister's apparent distrust that he decided to 'throw off the yoke' of a British serving officer, and telegraphed to the War Office that he could not desert China in her present crisis and, to be free to act as he thought fit, he would have to resign his commission in H.M. service. Then, less than a month later he changed his mind about staying in China. Li, he said, was too weak and unreliable, and 'I could not do him any good if I stayed.'

On his return home he received a telegram at Aden telling him that his resignation had not been accepted, his leave was cancelled, and that he was to return to England forthwith. To this curt rebuff, Gordon plaintively replied, 'You might have trusted me. My passage from China was taken before arrival of telegram which states "leave cancelled", etc.' But when he got back to England, he thought it prudent to write and explain his conduct to the Secretary of State for War. 'I was not insubordinate in going to China when I resigned at Bombay,' he avowed. 'I never meant to enter Chinese service. I may have been wanting in courtesy in not awaiting the Government's acceptance of my resignation and going to China, but it was not insubordination any more than your cook giving you warning and going away without your leave.... I looked on war as so detrimental to China and England that any effort that I could make would be cheaply bought at any personal sacrifice.'

No reply appears to have been sent to these protestations, apart from the granting of an extended period of home leave. This Gordon spent visiting friends and old haunts. First he went to Pembroke, where he had served his first assignment as an R.E. officer and where now memories of his early mysticism came flooding back to his mind. 'I can well remember,' he wrote to his sister, 'when ordered to the Crimea, my sincere hope was that I would be killed there. It is odd to think what one has gone through since then and still to retain the wish for the other world.'

From Pembroke he went to Ireland, where, true to form, he was to spend only a few weeks before bursting with indignation over the poverty and misery of the people. England, he affirmed, had neglected Ireland badly and there was a danger of civil war. The Irish were a law-abiding people, but there was a limit to what they would endure from their English rulers. Only in crimes 'against the person' were the Irish statistics worse than those of England, and these were crimes of vindictiveness and revenge for wrongs done to the people. The way to get rid of such crimes was to 'remove the opponent against whom this feeling exists and to rule strictly, firmly, and fairly', which England had not done. Gordon questioned in particular the administration of the Relief Fund, which advanced loans to landowners for agricultural development. Much of this money, he alleged, was squandered by the landlords and never reached the Irish peasant whose lot it was intended to improve. And for his pains he was roundly attacked by the Fund's administrators, who turned out to be former brother-officers of the Royal Engineers, who took his censures as impugning their personal integrity.

After a month in Ireland, Gordon's restless spirit moved him on to new pastures. This time he chose the home of the Rev. Horace Waller at Thywell Rectory, near Thrapston in North-amptonshire, who had been a friend and correspondent of his since his days at Gravesend, when Waller had been a curate at nearby Chatham. To begin with, Gordon's intractable aversion to the established Church and its ritual seems to have brought him into conflict with his reverend host. But after a few weeks, at the beginning of 1881, a remarkable transformation took place in his spiritual thinking. Suddenly revealed to him was the inner meaning of Holy Communion. No longer did he feel the sacrament to be a mere religious rite, serving as little more than a rector's roll-call of the faithful among his flock. From now on he experienced through Communion a state of union with God and Christ. 'Through the working of Christ in my body by His Body and Blood, the medicine worked,' he wrote exultantly to Augusta. 'Ever since the realization of the sacrament, I have been turned upside down. I may say that I never could have thought so many holes and corners would have been searched out. Scarcely a quiet day elapses without something being brought out which I had thought did not exist. As it were, I used to walk through my heart and find nice walks and splendid palaces in which I reposed. Then came the downfall of my Egyptian palace. It was worldly, faded, and despicable. Too many earthly motives were discovered, and I turned from the ruins in disgust. Then I wandered into the last visit of the China palace and it was splendid. However, only two or three weeks ago, that appeared tattered and mildewed and so I have no pleasure in that ruin.' Here at last was 'the antidote to the poison in my body. . . . I go not to the Table for salvation or in fear. I go . . . to realize this great weapon for warfare against the flesh.'

So with his 'realization' of the sacrament, Gordon's mysticism deepened. From now onwards he spent more and more of his life on earth living in the next world in an ever-increasingly close union with God. Whether on leave or on duty in some remote corner of the globe, he wrote regularly, sometimes as often as two or three times a week, to his sister, telling her how fortunate he was in being able to hold this intimate communion with his Maker. 'Between man and God is a wall; life and freedom were given to man to reunite with God [but] some reunite while on this earth and consequently are able in the future life to enjoy Him.' And he was one of those lucky ones.

Yet despite his discovery of this vast new reservoir of contemplation, Gordon could not settle down in England, whether at Thrapston or in London, where he spent a couple of months in the early spring of 1881. And in May he arranged with the War Office to take the place of a friend of his, who had been appointed Commander, Royal Engineers, in the island of Mauritius, a distant British colony in the Indian Ocean, 500 miles east of Madagascar. 'I believe this pilgrimage to M. will be blessed to me,' he wrote, 'for I believe I was hanging about Jordan, i.e. wishing for death and not caring to conquer the promised land.'

The blessings of Mauritius, however, turned out to be somewhat mixed. First, Gordon discovered that the job he had undertaken was a virtual sinecure. There were only five Royal Engineers for him to command in the whole island, plus three-quarters of a battery of artillery, and three companies of infantry. The only post worth having was that of Garrison Commander, and he persuaded himself soon after his arrival that he had been cheated of this in favour of a seventy-year-old, General Murray, who although well over the retiring age had been specially requested to stay on in Mauritius until the following year. The request had come from Queen Victoria's Army C.-in-C., H.R.H. the Duke of Cambridge, who Gordon firmly believed was victimizing him because of his many eccentricities. Added to these petty jealousies, he, of course, hated the social life of the garrison and the endless round of tennis and garden parties. 'Fearful ordeals' he called them. His greatest consolation was that his duties of supervising the island's defences were light enough to allow him to explore not only the natural beauties of Mauritius, but further afield as well. From here he visited the Seychelles Islands, 1,000 miles off the coast of Tanganyika where he compiled a long memorandum on the protection of British commercial shipping routes in the Indian Ocean. Here he also discovered the coco-demer tree, which is to be found in its wild state only in these islands. Growing to a height of 100 feet, these trees bear gigantic fruits with aphrodisiac qualities which Gordon contended were the original forbidden fruit from the Garden of Eden—a belief which was strengthened by the discovery that his guide in this natural paradise was called Adam, as had been all his male progenitors!

Less than a year after he took up his appointment in Mauritius he had resigned again, this time to take command of the colonial forces in South Africa, which had been offered to him by the Cape Colony Government. The Cape colonists were having trouble with the tribes of Basutoland on their north-eastern border and Gordon, with his flair for the unconventional type of military and diplomatic operation, seemed to be the man they required to settle the issue with the unruly Basutos. To Gordon the assignment offered a new challenge and he soon set off, entirely alone, to beard the Basuto chief, Masupha, in his den. He managed to impress himself sufficiently on Masupha to bring the Basutos to discuss terms for a settlement. But when he returned to Cape Town he failed to persuade the authorities to ratify his terms. And so in October 1882, after serving the Cape Colony for less than five months, he asked to be relieved of his command. As always when subjected to this type of frustration, he compared his current employers unfavourably with his previous associations. And, forgetting all the harsh words he had used about the Egyptians and Sudanese, he wrote home to say: 'I scarcely like these people here as I like the Arabs or peoples of the Sudan. . . . I found the Cape government a feeble invertebrate formation and I could do no good there.' Still, his sudden liking for the Arabs did not go so far as to draw him back to Egypt or the Sudan. 'Egypt moves me no more,' he wrote as he prepared to leave South Africa for England. 'I would not go back even if I could. . . . It is odd how little I think of Egypt or the Sudan; it is all now passed from me.' And back in England in November, he lost no time planning his next move, which was to take him for a year's visit to Palestine.

CHAPTER 16

REVOLT IN EGYPT AND THE SUDAN

HOWEVER Gordon might protest his disinterest in Egypt and the Sudan, the fact is that while he was wandering about the world from India to China and from Mauritius to Palestine between 1880 and 1882, a chain of events was being created which was to lead inexorably to his last and fateful mission in Khartoum. In Egypt, by a series of half-measures designed to keep the peace and protect British interests without evoking long-time responsibilities, Britain was being drawn step by step into undertaking the very commitments which she was seeking to avoid. By her first intervention in 1876 to protect the interests of the bondholders and creditors of the Khedive, she had undertaken together with France the responsibility of controlling Egypt's finances; and within the next six years Britain was to find herself, against her own better judgement, in physical occupation of the country and in control of every major facet of Egyptian policy, internal as well as foreign. And less than two years after that, when the current breakdown of the Egyptian administrative machine and disintegration of the Army coincided with the Mahdist revolution in the Sudan, she found herself compelled, again with infinite reluctance, to order the Khedive to withdraw from his Sudanese dominions and to despatch Gordon to Khartoum to execute this policy.

How did this dangerous drift come about? It is worth recalling this sequence of events in some detail. Soon after Gordon resigned from the Sudan, it became clear to Britain's principal representatives in Cairo—Sir Frank Lascelles, Vivian's successor as Consul-General, Rivers Wilson, and Baring—that the substitution of Tewfik for Ismail on the Khedival throne had, to say the least, not solved any of the more chronic problems of Egypt. The country was bankrupt and discontent was widespread. The population hated their Turkish rulers for their cruel and arbitrary systems of government and taxation. And the Turkish ruling class distrusted the Europeans because they suspected that they wished to reform not only the finances but the Constitution of Egypt as well. Moreover, there was some reason for these suspicions, so far as the British were concerned. British policy had undergone a significant change since the days when Lord Palmerston proclaimed in 1857 that while 'it is very possible that many parts of the world would be better governed by France, England, and Sardinia than they are now ... we do not want to have Egypt.... We want to trade with Egypt and to travel through Egypt, but we do not want the burthen of governing Egypt.' Now, as Lord Salisbury had put it at the time of Ismail's deposition, the view of the British Cabinet was that 'The geographical situation of Egypt, as well as the responsibility which the English Government have in past times incurred for the actual conditions under which it exists as a state, make it impossible to leave it to its fate. They are bound, both by duty and interest, to do all that lies in their power to arrest misgovernment before it results in the material ruin and almost incurable disorder to which it is evident by other oriental examples that such misgovernment will necessarily lead.'

From not wanting 'the burthen of governing Egypt' Britain had been led in the space of twenty-two years 'by duty and interest ... to arrest misgovernment' in Egypt. And as a first step towards arresting that misgovernment, it was decided that the Khedive should no longer be his own Prime Minister and should not, save in exceptional circumstances, preside at meetings of his Cabinet, and that control over public expenditure should in future rest with his constitutionally appointed ministers. As a corollary to this attempt to democratize Egypt, the British and French Governments accepted that the Anglo-French Controllers-General should in future concern themselves with investigation only and should be shorn of administrative functions, although they could not be dismissed without the agreement of their Governments.

For a brief interval this modified system of dual control worked well enough. Riaz Pasha, the Prime Minister, although he resented any foreign interference, recognized the need for it, and Baring was able to gain his confidence and that of his Ministers, and to break down some of the suspicions felt by the Turkish ruling class towards the Europeans. The rate of interest on the

Unified Debt was reduced from 5 per cent. to 4 per cent. and a number of taxation reforms were carried out, including the abolition of punitive taxes on agriculture. Nevertheless, the burden of repaying her creditors continued to weigh heavily upon Egypt's economy. Half the total revenue of £E.8½ million was earmarked for paying the interest on the debt, which left nothing to spare after the costs of administration and the annual tribute to the Ottoman Sultan had been paid. In particular, there was no money to improve the pay and conditions of the Army, and among the large number of officers, who had been placed on half-pay for reasons of economy in 1878, discontent was rising to boiling-point. The fact that the Government appeared to have singled out Egyptian, as opposed to Turkish, officers for such pay-reductions served to aggravate matters still further. If only within the Army, therefore, an explosion was inevitable.

On January 15, 1881, the explosion came when an Egyptian Colonel of peasant origin, Ahmed Arabi, placed himself at the head of the discontented officers in an attempt to repeat the pressure tactics which had proved so successful in forcing the hands of Nubar and Rivers Wilson in February 1879. A petition was presented to Riaz demanding the dismissal of the Minister of War, Osman Rifki, as the Minister responsible for this discriminatory treatment of the Khedive's Egyptian officers, and insisting that promotion should be by merit only. Arabi and his associates were promptly arrested and put on trial. But when their regiments marched to the Khedive's palace and demanded the dismissal of Rifki and the release of their officers, Tewfik gave way and conceded their demands. Mahmoud Sami, a politician in sympathy with the Army, was appointed in place of Rifki, and a commission was set up to enquire into the officers' grievances, with Arabi as one of its members. The Army had won yet another round in the developing struggle of Egyptian nationalism against Turkish rule. And for a while quiet reigned. But it was a deceptive calm. For underneath a dangerously combustible combination of fear and arrogance kept the cauldron of discontent simmering. On the one hand, Arabi and his friends were certain that the Khedive was planning to get even with them for their mutinous conduct. At the same time, the Army had learned for the second time that the surest way to redress their grievances was to show fight.

In July Arabi's fear complex received a further jolt when Tewfik replaced Mahmoud Sami with his own brother-in-law as War Minister. And such was the prevailing atmosphere of suspicion that two months later, on the strength of a rumour that he had been secretly condemned to death, Arabi decided to strike before he was struck. On September 9, with 2,500 men and some artillery, he marched to the palace, where he formed his men into a square and demanded to see the Khedive. Tewfik walked out into the square of mutinous soldiers and, after asserting his fast-disappearing authority by ordering Arabi to sheathe his sword, demanded to know the meaning of the demonstration, to which Arabi replied that the Army demanded a complete change of Government. Faced with overwhelming *force majeure*, the Khedive had no alternative but to submit, and Cherif Pasha, who was known to favour a constitutional system, was appointed Prime Minister, with Mahmoud Sami reinstated as Minister of War. Arabi and the Army were now the arbiters of Egypt's destinies. And, as he triumphantly proclaimed to his troops, 'A new era has just opened for Egypt.... You now have power in your hands and united you will be invincible.'

At this point the Ottoman Sultan, who until now had been content to let the European powers sort out their problems with the Khedive, so long as they offered no threat to his ultimate sovereignty over Egypt, awoke to the danger of an Egyptian nationalist revolt leading to yet another secession from his fast-contracting empire. The Sultan now proposed to Britain and France that he should send Turkish troops to keep order in Egypt. Britain was prepared to look at the problem sympathetically, but the French objected violently that a Turkish intervention in Egypt would raise the Sultan's prestige in Algeria and Tunisia, which they had only recently wrested from Turkish control. If foreign intervention were necessary, France favoured an Anglo-French occupation, an idea which Mr. Gladstone's Liberal Government in their turn greeted with horror and alarm. Nevertheless, Britain allowed her French ally to make the running, and through her Ambassador in Constantinople, Lord Dufferin, supported the French objection, whereupon the Sultan agreed to drop his proposal.

Meanwhile, Ahmed Arabi continued to go from strength to strength, drawing reinforcement from the incipient nationalist movement within the Chamber of Notables—Egypt's nearest approach to a national parliament—and from the Press and public opinion, where he came increasingly to be accepted as the spearhead of the struggle against the Turkish ruling class. He inveighed against the Europeans as infidels who sucked the blood of the Egyptian people and he fertilized the seeds of anti-Turkish feeling. Demonstrations and sporadic acts of violence followed in many parts of the country; and with no army on which they could rely to keep order, Tewfik and Cherif were eventually driven in January 1882 to the desperate step of bringing Arabi into the Government as Under-Secretary for War.

At this point, a new French Government, headed by Gambetta, decided the time had come to let the Khedive know that France and Britain, having engineered his accession, would not stand idly by while an upstart Army Colonel destroyed his authority and ousted all European influence and interest. And on January 8 Sir Edward Malet, the British Consul-General, joined with his French colleague in presenting a note to the Khedive, declaring the determination of their Governments to maintain him on his throne, as being 'alone able to guarantee for the present and the future the good order and development of general prosperity in Egypt'. In an obvious allusion to the Arabi revolt, the joint note went on to warn that the elements threatening his authority would 'find England and France united to oppose them', and concluded by saying that the Khedive should 'draw from this assurance the confidence and strength which he requires to direct the destinies of Egypt and his people'.

On the face of it, such language might seem unexceptionable enough. But in the highly charged atmosphere of Cairo at the height of the Arabi revolt it exploded like a bombshell. Tewfik naturally expressed his sincere gratitude; but Cherif was thunderstruck and, two days later, protested to Malet that the joint note would be interpreted by Arabi and the nationalists as meaning that Britain and France wanted to put the clock back by encouraging the Khedive to oppose all reform and by threatening to intervene with military force. And Malet duly reported to London that the only effect of the note had been to strengthen Arabi's hand 'in protesting against what he is represented to consider as unjust interference'.

Arabi was not alone in protesting. The Chamber of Notables

also decided to assert their authority against European intervention by reaffirming their claim to vote the administrative budget. But the French Government insisted through Cherif Pasha that the Chamber's claim was incompatible with the system of Anglo-French control of Egypt's finances and therefore unacceptable. Matters were now brought to a head, and on February 2 the Chamber sent a deputation to the Khedive to demand a change of government. Tewfik once again bowed to the inevitable, and three days later Mahmoud Sami was appointed Prime Minister, with Arabi as Minister of War.

Arabi and his nationalist supporters in the Chamber were now more than the arbiters of Egypt; they were running virtually every facet of government. Appeasement of a mutinous Army was the order of the day. Soldiers' pay was increased; officers were promoted by the hundred; new battalions were raised. A new wave of anti-European feeling swept the country as the extremists demanded first dismissal and later death for all European Government employees. Public disorder increased and the local governors in the provinces lost all authority.

Yet, despite their dominant position, Arabi and his associates could not rid themselves of their earlier fears of Khedival retribution. And in April, after another rumour had reached him that Tewfik was planning to have him murdered, he ordered the arrest of some fifty people, including Osman Rifki, who were summarily convicted by a secret tribunal and sent into exile in the Sudan. Acting on Anglo-French advice, Tewfik at last asserted his prerogatives and commuted the sentences. But his defiance only served to widen the breach between himself and his Arabist ministers, and a few days later Mahmoud Sami tendered the Government's resignation. Deadlock ensued and, although the British and French Consuls-General said that they would accept any Prime Minister except Arabi, the impotent Khedive was unable to find anyone who would serve him. Then the Army and police officers at Alexandria threatened violence if Arabi and his friends were not promptly reinstated. And when the Chamber, together with the Moslem elders, the Chief Rabbi and the Christian Patriarchs, all warned Tewfik that his life would be in danger if he persisted in trying to form a non-Arabist ministry, he finally relented and accepted the reinstatement of the Government, with Arabi once more as War Minister.

While Tewfik was losing this further round in his vain struggle against the Army and the nationalists, it was becoming painfully clearer to Gladstone's Government with every report from Cairo that the experiment in constitutional government had boomeranged badly, and that sooner or later foreign intervention was going to be necessary to restore order and safeguard British and other European interests in Egypt. But although Gambetta's Government had recently given way to another of considerably less chauvinist views, there was still no enthusiasm in Paris for the use of Turkish troops in Egypt. It was therefore decided to make the gesture of sending an Anglo-French naval squadron to Alexandria, where the majority of the European colony in Egypt lived and where Arabi's influence was, if anything, even stronger than in Cairo.

This action brought matters to a head. Two weeks later, on June 11, fifty Europeans were slaughtered in Alexandria after Arabist agitators had inflamed the mob with cries of 'Kill the Christians'. And over the next two weeks similar massacres took place in different parts of Egypt. A mass exodus of Christians, both European and Egyptian, followed and before the end of June, when 20,000 had fled the country, it was clear that the whole commercial fabric of the country was on the point of collapse. Europe and the Arabists were now set on a collision course. Directly after the arrival of the Anglo-French squadron in Alexandria, the Egyptian Army, defying the express orders of the Sultan, began to erect batteries for use if necessary against the foreign warships lying off the harbour. Early in July, therefore, the Admiral commanding the British fleet was told to stop the construction of the batteries, if necessary by force. The French Government were invited to send similar orders to their naval commander, but, not possessing the aggressiveness of a Gambetta, the French Premier declined to do so.

The writing was now on the wall for Arabi and his followers, with Britain about to use her naval might to storm his barricades. And when the Alexandria garrison stubbornly refused to stop work on the batteries, the British warships opened fire on the morning of July 11. The Egyptians returned the fire, but by the following day the batteries were silenced. The Egyptian garrison withdrew and Alexandria was occupied by British forces.

The British Government now accepted the unpalatable fact

that, if the Arabi revolt was to be crushed, they must now do the crushing. France was a non-starter, fearing among other things to commit to Egypt troops which she needed to defend herself against the German menace in Europe. As for Turkey, the Sultan had recently demonstrated by the despatch of agents to Egypt to intrigue against Tewfik that his principal aim was to restore his own authority and not the Khedive's. And so, as Arabi proclaimed from his headquarters outside Alexandria that 'irreconcilable war exists between the Egyptians and the English', a British force of 5,000 men was despatched from India to Egypt under the command of Sir Garnet Wolseley. Soon after arriving at Alexandria, Wolseley marched on Ismailia to take the Suez Canal under his protection. Then on September 13, as he made for Cairo, he encountered Arabi's forces. After a brief engagement, the Egyptian Army was routed, and the following day a British advance guard under Colonel Watson, Gordon's former helpmate in Equatoria, occupied the Citadel of Cairo. Arabi and his associates surrendered and were handed over to the Khedive. And after a brief trial, at which the British authorities arranged that he should plead guilty to the charge of rebellion, be sentenced to death and then have his sentence commuted to perpetual exile, Arabi was deported to Ceylon.

*   *   *

The revolt was over; but Egypt's and Britain's troubles were not. Egypt was faced with the mammoth task of picking up the pieces and repairing the catastrophic damage done during the past twenty months that Arabi had been on the rampage. The state of the economy was worse than ever, the prestige of the Khedive and the Turkish ruling class had been sorely discredited, and the Army had ceased to exist as a cohesive and dependable force. And by reason of the fact that British troops now occupied the key centres of the country and that British representatives sat in the seats of power, it was clearly up to Britain to clear up the mess.

This unhappy conclusion placed Gladstone's Government in a most awkward dilemma. On the one hand, they believed that it was Britain's duty to 'arrest misgovernment' and introduce reforms in Egypt. Yet they also devoutly hoped for an early end to the military occupation, into which they had been drawn and upon which France, equally with the Sultan, now looked with the utmost suspicion as being directed against French and Turkish influences in Egypt. In an attempt to square this circle, the British Government despatched Lord Dufferin to Cairo to report on what should be done to restore order, prosperity, and the Khedive's authority 'for the judicious development of self-government and the fulfilment of obligations towards the powers'. But any hopes for a quick end to Britain's new and unwanted commitments were soon shattered when Dufferin reported that reform and/or solvency in Egypt would be impossible to achieve unless the Government were placed under British tutelage. Without such assistance, the Egyptians would once again 'quickly become a prey to dishonest speculators, ruinous contracts, and delusive engineering operations'. Only 'the strong hand of a master' could restore order and equilibrium and, since Arabi's revolt had virtually destroyed the Egyptian Army, it was unthinkable in these conditions to withdraw the British occupation force. The Egyptian Army had to be recreated, and this task must be undertaken by British officers. Finally, the question arose as to who should direct this delicate and difficult exercise of British tutelage —the man who would provide the 'strong hand of a master', while calling himself Her Majesty's Consul-General, in recognition of the Ottoman Sultan's continuing sovereignty over Egypt. The obvious choice was Baring, who had already served for three years in Egypt helping to control the country's finances, and who had been fortuitously absent for the whole of the Arabi revolt, during which period he was on transfer to the Government of India. Thus in September 1883 Baring returned to Cairo to begin his historic mission as the *de facto* ruler of Egypt for the next twenty-four years.

An approach, albeit not the one which Britain's Liberal Government would have chosen, had been found to the eventual solution of Egypt's internal and financial problems. But at the very moment when Mr. Gladstone's Cabinet was reluctantly shouldering this 'burthen' and pretending hopefully that it would only be a temporary affair, an even more far-reaching revolution than Arabi's was unfolding across the Khedive's Sudanese dominions away to the south and threatening to uproot Egypt's sovereign authority and thereby to involve Britain in yet another dangerous, unsolicited responsibility. In the Sudan, while Arabi was raising the standard of nationalism in Egypt, the son of a Nile boat-builder from Dongola, named Mohammed Ahmed, had risen against Egyptian rule and had proclaimed himself the 'Mahdi' who had come, in fulfilment of the Prophet Mohammed's promise, to guide all true Moslems in the way of the pure faith and to deliver them from oppression.

Even before Gordon left the Sudan at the end of 1879, such a revolution had become inevitable. Discontent among the Sudanese people and hatred for their Egyptian rulers was widespread. Nearly every Sudanese had a reason for hating the administration: some because its attempts to stop the slave trade had threatened their livelihood, undermined the economy and drained the country's agriculture of its labour force; others because the taxation and penal system, despite Gordon's efforts at reforms, had often been unjust or because they resented the violence done to their country by the Egyptian occupation. After Gordon's departure, the administration had fallen back into its former corrupt ways and degenerated into moral and material decrepitude. Raouf Pasha, the former Governor of Harar, who, astonishingly enough, was selected to succeed Gordon as Governor-General, was neither willing nor able to arrest this deterioration. And with a total garrison strength of 40,000 troops spread about this vast country in small pockets of from 3,000 to 5,000 each—only Khartoum had more than 5,000—and with the Government in Cairo totally absorbed in dealing with greedy creditors and rebellious nationalists, the administration's weakness became daily more transparent. It therefore only needed a dynamic leader to unite all the various rivers of popular discontent into a single torrent of rebellion and to rally slave-trader, peasant, and tribesman alike in throwing off the Egyptian yoke.

The chosen leader, Mohammed Ahmed, had been born in 1844 of a family which, despite a humble way of life, claimed descent from the Prophet Mohammed. Early in his youth he showed promise as a student of religion and, after several years of strict Moslem education by the local elders, he decided at the age of seventeen to settle for an ascetic life within the mystic sect of Islam known as Sufism. Seven years later, after further religious instruction, he became a sheikh of the Sufi order and set up his headquarters at Abba Island in the White Nile, about 200 miles south of Khartoum, where his piety and, still more, the power of his personality soon won him a large following among the local tribes. But his success aroused the jealousy of his religious superiors, and some eight years later, when Mohammed Ahmed ventured one day to reproach one of the elders for impiety, they seized on his act of arrogance to expel him from the order. Not being one to take this reverse lying down, Mohammed Ahmed withdrew to a village on the Blue Nile to decide his next move. And as he contemplated his future, he recalled that in the Sudan there was a widespread belief that the promised coming of the Mahdi would take place at the end of the thirteenth Moslem century, and that this century was to end in less than five years' time. This, then, would be the signal for the rising of all pious Moslems against sacrilege and for overthrowing the hated 'Turks', as he termed his country's Egyptian rulers.

Legend has it that, while he sat dreaming of the great political and spiritual revolution that was to come, Mohammed Ahmed was visited by an Arab from Darfur, Abdullah ibn Mohammed, who was later to become his deputy and successor and to find fame as the Khalifa—and that at their first meeting Abdullah addressed him as the expected Mahdi. Be that as it may, Mohammed Ahmed soon returned to Abba, declared himself to a small circle of his tribal followers as the Mahdi, and then went to El Obeid to spy out the land and assess the readiness of the people of Kordofan for revolution. Having satisfied himself that Kordofan was ripe for revolt, he once again confided to a small group of notables that he was the expected Mahdi and, on their accepting him as such, made them swear an oath of allegiance.

Three months later, back at Abba, Mohammed Ahmed cast off the veil of secrecy, publicly assumed the title of Mohammed el-Mahdi, and called on all true Moslems to rally to him to reassert the true faith which the sacrilegious Turks had profaned and to reclaim their land from those who had seized it. Then, deliberately re-enacting the story of the early struggles of the Prophet to introduce the Moslem faith, he ordered his followers to accompany him on a *hijra*, or flight, to Kordofan to prepare for the day of liberation. At first the Khartoum authorities regarded Mohammed Ahmed's threats as the ravings of a harmless eccentric. But when it became clear that these preachings were making an impression on the public, Raouf decided to arrest the self-styled Mahdi, and sent a squad of soldiers to bring him to book. On August 12, 1881, the expedition reached Abba, where Mohammed Ahmed was waiting for them. And, although his followers had only spears and sticks to fight with, Raouf's troops were caught in an ambush and sent scuttling back to their steamer.

Such a victory against trained soldiers with overwhelmingly superior arms seemed like a miracle and, as Mohammed Ahmed set out for Kordofan with his followers, whom he named Ansar, after the supporters of the Prophet, his claim to be the expected Mahdi began to find a wide acceptance, with no less than 8,000 tribesmen joining his *hijra*. Moreover, to show that the Abba incident was not an isolated fluke, the Ansar dealt a similar blow four months later to a much larger Egyptian force which sought to drive them out of Kordofan. Raouf then appealed to Cairo for reinforcements. But Cairo was thinking of other things, with the Arabi revolt in full swing; and the only response he got was an order dismissing him as Governor-General, and in his place, appointing Abd el-Kader Hilmi, a Sudanese by birth, who had served with Baker in Equatoria and commanded his bodyguard, the 'Forty Thieves'.

But even as the new Governor-General was proceeding to his post, the administration suffered another crushing defeat. Giegler Pasha, a German official in the Khedive's service, who was then acting Governor-General, sent a force composed of units from the garrisons of Khartoum, Sennar, and El Obeid to round up the Mahdi and compel his surrender. But to the Egyptian commander's request for his submission, Mohammed Ahmed contemptuously retorted, 'We are not under your command, but you and your superiors are under Our command. . . . There is nothing between Us and you save the sword.' Urged on by their leader's fiery words, the Ansar then fell upon the Egyptians and massacred them almost to a man.

The Mahdi had won his third successive victory against the 'Turks' and, as the news spread like wildfire throughout the west and south of the Sudan, sympathetic risings took place in Darfur and Bahr-el-Ghazal. Now he declared a *jihad*, or holy war, against the infidels and profaners of Islam who ruled over the Sudan in the Khedive's name. 'I am the Mahdi,' he declared, 'the successor of the Prophet of God. Cease to pay taxes to the infidel

Turks and let everyone who finds a Turk kill him, for the Turks are infidels who transgressed the command of God's apostles and of His Prophet ... insulted the Faith and placed poll-tax on your necks and dragged away your men and imprisoned them in fetters and took captive your women and children.' And as this message, judiciously blended to appeal equally to men with piety or with revenge in their hearts, swept through the towns and villages and desert encampments of the Sudan, the Mahdi and his Ansar set off in July to attempt their first important capture—the capital of Kordofan, El Obeid.

Here he was to suffer the only serious rebuff in all his long campaign. Failing to realize that Egyptian forces defending a fortified city could not be stampeded into submission as were those whom he had encountered in open desert, he sought to take El Obeid by storm with sticks and spears, eschewing the use of the rifles and guns which the Ansar had captured in large numbers from their thrice-defeated enemy. The Prophet, he asserted, had won his victories armed only with spears and the true faith, and he would do likewise. The result was a bloody reverse; and for a moment the future of the Mahdist revolution hung in the balance. But Mohammed Ahmed's personal leadership turned the scale and, on advice from his lieutenants, he decided to starve El Obeid into submission and at the same time forego old-fashioned virtue and use in future whatever modern weapons he possessed. With such overwhelming numbers, the result was inevitable. And in January 1883, after a four months' siege had reduced the garrison and population to eating palm fibres and the leather covers of sofas and chairs, the Governor of Kordofan surrendered and the Mahdi entered El Obeid. The town was systematically plundered and £100,000 worth of coin and valuables was seized for the Mahdist treasury, and subsequently divided between the 'state' and the individual soldier in the same proportions, as was done at the time of the Prophet.

The Mahdi took good care to see that from now on his politico-spiritual revolution should in every way be based on the Prophet's teaching. He declaimed that, before God, all men were equal and, although he defended the institution of slavery, he insisted, as the Prophet had done, that slaves should be treated as members of their owners' families. Also he told his Ansar that all worldly goods were to be despised. 'Look on the things of this life with a piercing eye,' he enjoined them. 'Be sure of the nothingness of it, turn your hearts to things above and devote yourselves to God and abstain from worldly pleasure and enjoyments.' And to ensure that his injunctions were obeyed, he ordained a penal code which provided the severest punishment for any infractions of the Koranic law. For drinking wine an offender would receive eighty lashes with the *kourbash*, and for tobacco smoking a hundred. Desertion brought about the loss of a hand or a foot; profanity was punished by death. Dancing was forbidden, women had to be veiled, and any show of luxury, such as banquets or rich clothes, was taboo. From now on the rough *jibbeh*, or smock, with patches sewn on it as a mark of poverty and hence of virtue, became the uniform of this extraordinary man's extraordinary army, and was worn by all his followers, including even their children.

The fall of El Obeid had a cataclysmic effect throughout the Sudan. In Darfur, which, as Gordon had found, had long been a hotbed of revolt, the Austrian Governor, Slatin, had for the last year been fighting a losing battle to hold the allegiance of his province. Leaders of the principal local tribes had joined the Mahdi's *jihad*, and his Deputy Governor, who was a cousin of Mohammed Ahmed, was busily intriguing against him from within his citadel at Darra. In a desperate effort to uphold his waning influence, Slatin became a Moslem and took the name of Abd el-Kader Salatin. But with El Obeid and most of Kordofan in Mahdist hands, he was now cut off from Khartoum. And as the tribes moved in to lay siege to Darra, it was clearly only a matter of time before he would be overwhelmed. Nor was the position much better in Bahr-el-Ghazal, where the young English Governor, Frank Lupton, was barely holding out with a garrison of 3,000 troops, which he shared with Emin Pasha in Equatoria. Finally, although the main Mahdist pressure was being concentrated in the west and south, the revolt had begun to spread eastwards along the Blue Nile, and Sennar was being besieged by local Mahdist forces.

Abd el-Kader Hilmi, the new Governor-General, moved with speed and determination to relieve the Sennar garrison and temporarily to pacify the Blue Nile valley. But a few weeks later, in February, this energetic soldier-administrator was rewarded for his successes by dismissal for giving vent to criticisms of the

Egyptian Government. The functions of the Governor-General were then divided, and a seventy-five-year-old Circassian, Suleiman Niyazi, was appointed Commander-in-Chief, with a retired English officer as Chief of Staff, Colonel William Hicks, while the civil administration was entrusted to Ala el-Din Siddiq. At the same time the Khedive's Government, now disburdened of the Arabi menace, ordered an all-out effort to crush the Mahdi and restore the situation in Kordofan. But the new command arrangements soon proved unworkable and Hicks informed the Egyptian and British authorities in Cairo that he could not co-operate with his aged superior, who was hopelessly unsuited to command the projected operations in Kordofan. Five months of bitter argument followed, and it was not until July that Hicks was given full powers as Commander-in-Chief of the expeditionary force. At length, on September 27, Hicks, accompanied by Ala el-Din Siddiq, marched off towards El Obeid with a force of 8,000 Egyptian soldiers.

It would be hard to imagine a more unhappy expedition than that which Hicks was doomed to lead. Bitter discord and dissension existed between him and his officers. Few among them knew the country, and they were at the mercy of guides secretly in sympathy with the Mahdists. Cumbersome artillery pieces slowed down their progress in the intense heat and the Ansar, kept constantly informed of their route of march, blocked the wells on which they relied for water. For two months they plodded on through the desert towards their objective; morale slumped to zero, as each day they grew more desperate from the miseries of heat and thirst; and then, when they finally got within striking distance of El Obeid, the Mahdi marched out to meet them on November 1. Four days later, in a forest near the village of Shaykan, a few miles south of El Obeid, 50,000 Ansar fell upon them. The result was a massacre. Hicks and Ala el-Din Siddiq perished with all but 250 of their men. As the Mahdi returned in triumph to El Obeid, the sound of war-drums reverberated across the Sudan.

Like a great tidal wave, the Mahdist message swept outward. A month later Slatin surrendered in Darra, and soon afterwards El Fasher succumbed to its Ansar besiegers. Lupton in Bahr-el-Ghazal was invaded by a force of 10,000 Ansar. And in the east a former slave-trader, named Osman Digna, rose for the Mahdi and swept away every vestige of Egyptian control along the vital communication route between Suakim on the Red Sea and Berber on the Nile. The days of Egypt's dominion in the Sudan were now numbered. Mahdism was marching to victory, and there was nothing that anyone could do to stop it.

CHAPTER 17

DEUS EX MACHINA

ONE immediate result of the Hicks disaster was to change the policy of the British Government. Up to this point Britain had tried to pursue a policy of rigid non-interference in the Sudanese crisis. Having drifted into the unhappy situation of occupying and virtually governing Egypt, the last thing Mr. Gladstone and his Ministers wanted was to get involved in the Sudan. Britain had no interests there; the Egyptians had got themselves into this mess with the Mahdi; and, as Gladstone had made very clear, they would have to get themselves out of it without calling on British support. Besides, if Britain were now to assume any responsibility for the Sudan, she might well prolong indefinitely the period of her tutelage in Egypt, and it was a cardinal principle of Gladstone's policy to withdraw from Egypt as soon as possible. Even as late as November 1883, a few days before news of the Hicks disaster reached London, Gladstone had proclaimed at the Lord Mayor's Banquet: 'We are about to withdraw. The order has been given. That withdrawal will include the evacuation of Cairo.'

The utmost that Britain would undertake towards the Sudan was to send a British Hussar officer, Colonel D. H. Stewart, an expert in Arab affairs, to report on the state of the country in the light of the Mahdist revolt. After spending the winter of 1882–3 in the Sudan, Stewart told his Government in no uncertain terms that the Egyptians had lost out and would be well advised to 'abandon large portions' of the country. The Treasury was exhausted; their troops were ignorant, untrained, and disloyal to the Khedive; and the Sudanese battalions were infected with Arabist sympathies and filled with 'superstitious ideas of the power of the Mahdi'. In these circumstances Stewart felt that the projected expedition to recover Kordofan involved 'a very great risk' against a well-equipped fanatical enemy flushed with success. Recommending that the western Sudan should be abandoned, he suggested that Slatin in Darfur be instructed to destroy his stores and withdraw to the south before he was completely cut off.

Dufferin, who was still in Cairo drawing up his report on Egypt, supported Stewart's views, and unofficially told the Egyptians that they would be wise to consolidate their position in the eastern Sudan and withdraw from the west. But when he sought authority from London to repeat his advice officially on behalf of the British Government, he was forbidden to do so, and firmly told that 'Her Majesty's Government are in no way responsible for the operations in the Sudan, which have been undertaken under the authority of the Egyptian Government, or for the appointment or actions of General Hicks.' So afraid were the British Cabinet of getting involved in the Sudan that they even objected to Hicks using the British Consul-General in Cairo as a channel of communication to the Egyptian Government. And when Malet wrote to congratulate Hicks on his appointment as Commander-in-Chief in place of the septuagenarian Suleiman, he felt constrained to add: 'The act is spontaneous on the part of the Egyptian Government for ... I am debarred by my instructions from giving advice ... the policy of Her Majesty's Government being to abstain as much as possible from interference with the action of the Egyptian Government in the Sudan.'

It was a disastrous policy. As Baring truly stated when reviewing the part played by the Foreign Secretary, Lord Granville, in the tragic sequence of events which led to Gordon's final martyrdom in Khartoum: 'Had he, acting on the views expressed by the various British authorities in Egypt, stepped in and forbidden the despatch of the Hicks expedition to Kordofan, not only would thousands of lives and the large sums of money, which were subsequently squandered, have been saved, but he would have saved his own country from that interference which he so much dreaded and which was eventually precipitated by the negative policy adopted in the early stage of the proceedings. Lord Granville appears to have thought that he effectually threw off all responsibility by declaring that he was not responsible.... The result was that the Egyptian Government blundered on headlong to their own destruction and that the British Government, like the frail beauty of Byron's poem, while vowing that they would ne'er consent to a policy of intervention in the Sudan, consented but a short time afterwards to a degree of intervention far greater than would have been necessary, had the true facts of the situation been in the first instance recognized.'

Nor was Baring only wise after the event. For as soon as he returned to Cairo as Consul-General, three days after Hicks's expedition started for Kordofan, he set himself out to modify his Government's policy of 'no advice, no involvement'. His first opportunity occurred in mid-November, when in the course of an interview the Egyptian Prime Minister, Cherif Pasha, remarked that he supposed that Britain would not like to see the Turks intervene in the Sudan. Baring took this to be a subtle hint that the Egyptians were hoping for British and/or Indian troops to help crush the Mahdi, and telegraphed home to say that he could not, if confronted with a request for troops, continue to refuse either discussion or advice. If Hicks should fail to crush the Mahdi, he felt he should at least tell the Egyptians to 'fall back on whatever point on the Nile they can hold with confidence'. At this point the news of Hicks's defeat had not yet percolated to Cairo or London; but the Government had recently learned that the British Consul at Suakim had been killed in an affray with the Mahdists in the eastern Sudan, in which a force of 500 Egyptians was routed. And Granville, who was beginning to have second thoughts about the wisdom of Britain's negative policy, promptly replied to Baring: 'We cannot lend English or Indian troops.... It would not be for the advantage of Egypt to invite Turkish troops into the Sudan. If consulted, recommend the abandonment of the Sudan within certain limits.'

Baring had made a small dent in the British Cabinet's armour of neutrality, and two days later, when the news broke that Hicks had been overwhelmed, he telegraphed home that the British military authorities in Egypt as well as the Governor-General in Khartoum thought that, with the Suakim–Berber route cut, Khartoum could no longer be held against the Mahdi and that the Egyptian Government should be told to get its garrisons out of the Sudan. The Egyptians, he said, would no doubt find such advice 'very unpalatable'; but, if they were left to their own devices, they would blunder on from one disaster to another. For reasons of prestige, they could not bring themselves to a decision to withdraw and were currently talking of asking the Sultan to bail them out with a Turkish expeditionary force.

At first Granville still hesitated to proffer such far-reaching advice, and on November 25 he told Baring that 'the Egyptian Government must rely on their own resources' and that it seemed reasonable to conduct 'defensive operations' against the Mahdi. However, as reports from Khartoum became more alarming, with *The Times* correspondent, Frank Power, telegraphing to his paper that 'it is perfectly useless to attempt to hold this place', the British Government came round to the view that the Egyptians must withdraw from all but the eastern provinces, which could be supplied and defended by sea. And after Osman Digna had inflicted yet another devastating defeat on the local Sudanese forces in the Suakim area, Granville telegraphed to Baring that Britain would not object to a Turkish force being sent to Suakim to hold the eastern Sudan, provided the cost did not fall on the over-stretched revenue of Egypt. As for the rest of the Sudan, the Government recommended the Egyptians 'to come to an early decision to abandon all territory south of Aswan or at least of Wadi Halfa'. To this sudden change of view, Cherif reacted like a kicking mule. And a week later he told Baring that the Egyptian Government 'cannot agree to the abandonment of territories which they consider absolutely necessary for the security, and even for the existence, of Egypt itself', and that they hoped that Britain would help them to obtain Turkish assistance in holding the Sudan.

Baring telegraphed this reply to Granville, commenting that, while he felt sure that the Sultan would not agree to send troops and that the Egyptian Army was incapable of holding the Sudan, 'no amount of argument or persuasion will make the present ministry adopt the policy of abandonment'. The Government must therefore face the possibility of 'appointing English ministers temporarily', if they insisted on an Egyptian withdrawal. Baring added that it would also be necessary to send 'an English officer of high authority to Khartoum with full powers to withdraw all the garrisons' and to make the best arrangements possible for the Sudan's future government. But the idea of accepting this much responsibility found no favour with Gladstone's Cabinet. And Granville promptly replied that, if the Sultan refused to help, the eastern Sudan should be 'given back to the Porte' and that Cherif must be told to withdraw 'from Khartoum itself, as well as from the interior of the Sudan'. Waxing still more admonitory, he added that 'ministers and governors must carry out this advice or forfeit their offices'. To appoint British ministers would be most objectionable, but no doubt Baring could find 'Egyptians who will execute the Khedive's orders under English advice'.

But Cherif was not such an Egyptian, and when he realized that the British who were occupying his country were determined to enforce their advice, he tendered his resignation to the Khedive on January 7, 1884. Tewfik, as usual giving in without a struggle, sent for Nubar, and on January 8 Baring was able to telegraph to Granville that a new Government had been formed which 'entirely concurred in the wisdom of abandoning the Sudan, retaining possession of Suakim'. But the government, although nominally Egyptian, was in reality no more than a puppet, a ventriloquist's dummy, with Baring, under orders from London, telling it what to do and say on all matters, domestic and foreign. And henceforth Britain found herself committed, not only to running and reforming Egypt and recreating her Army, but still more to directing the policy of evacuating the Sudan, retaining only the Red Sea coast around Suakim. Gladstone's Cabinet had drifted into the very position which they had sought so strenuously to avoid. And as they pondered on their new commitment, their thoughts turned inevitably to Charles Gordon as the *deus ex machina* of the day, the only man with the necessary experience and reputation to extricate them from these unwelcome responsibilities.

*   *   *

While these cataclysmic events were building up to the final denouement, Gordon was in Palestine exploring the Holy Land, Bible in hand, in a feverish attempt to escape from what he called the 'doles'. 'We generally when in the doles go and try for something to fill the gap,' he had written to his sister. And 'to fill the gap' and banish the 'doles', he plunged into an abstruse series of researches and investigations of biblical history, topography and theology, visiting every shrine and monument—Jewish, Christian, and Moslem—of the thrice holy city of Jerusalem and walking for miles across the Wilderness of Judaea. Determined that the accepted theories as to the site of Calvary were all wrong, he insisted that Christ had in fact been crucified on a hillock opposite the Damascus Gate which happened to be shaped like a skull and must therefore have been the real Golgotha. He further proclaimed that a nearby tomb, known today as the Garden Tomb, was the sepulchre where Christ's Body was buried. (Sometimes also known as 'Gordon's Tomb', from his discovery, this place has not infrequently led to some confused twentieth-century tourist remarking that he never knew that Gordon had been buried in Jerusalem!)

Less creditably, he also indulged in helping himself to pieces of the mosaic from Jerusalem's famous seventh-century Dome of the Rock Mosque and selling them as souvenirs, an action which seems strangely at variance with his scrupulous integrity in handling public funds and his insistence on slashing the salary offered to him in the Sudan by the Khedive. The explanation of this extraordinary lapse probably lies in the fact that he was at the time very hard up and, as his letters to his brother show, was also in debt. In fact, throughout the last ten years of his life his letters reveal that he was continually agitated about his finances and fussed interminably about the payment of his bills and debts. Even in his last letter from Khartoum, when he wrote to his old friend Colonel Watson to say 'the game is up' and that he expected a 'catastrophe' within ten days, he concluded by saying, 'Mind and let my brother (68, Elm Park Road, Chelsea) know what I owe you'! And in his final adieu to his sister, he wrote apologetically to say that 'pecuniarily' his affairs were 'not over bright', but that Henry would take care of her financially.

Always a prolific correspondent, Gordon excelled himself in letter-writing during the eleven months he spent in Palestine. To Augusta he wrote nearly 100 letters in this period, and to a recent ecclesiastical acquaintance, the Rev. Barnes of Exeter, he sent a further forty-seven, in addition to keeping up a regular correspondence with his brother Henry and other friends. The bulk of all this prodigious correspondence dealt with spiritual and not temporal matters, although he did also maintain desultory communications with the ex-Khedive Ismail and with Emin in Equatoria, and sometimes wrote hectoring letters to Malet in Cairo, telling him to force Tewfik to be more energetic in suppressing the slave trade. But in his letters home he seldom mentioned the tribulations of Egypt or the Sudan, beyond occasionally saying that he had foreseen the rebellions that had occurred, but that nobody had listened to him. And to his brother and sister he washed his hands of the whole unhappy business. To Henry he wrote: 'I think little of Egypt, that country is never again for me.' And to his sister: 'From what I hear I am very glad I have done with Egypt. . . . I would feel a great repugnance to go back to the Sudan.'

Delving deep into his mysticism, Gordon felt closer to God, and to Jesus Christ, during his time in the Holy Land than at any other period of his life. This sense of true communion was for him a living reality. 'Christ is life or the existence of every life,' he wrote. 'By Him all things subsist or hold together. Life is the essence of God and everything that lives must be vivified by His life.' He was, of course, speaking of life eternal and not of earthly existence. For his sense of close communion with God made him feel he was at 'the summit of life or rather the dawn of resurrection', so that he longed all the more earnestly for his release. 'Death would be a blessing at any moment,' he wrote to Augusta from Jerusalem in January 1883. 'It is *through death* that He will, and we in Him will, destroy the wiles of the Devil.' Then in May he wrote: 'I have a very great desire for death.' And again in November: 'I wish it were given to all to look on death . . . as a thing to be desired.'

Daily his mystic sense grew stronger, occupying more and more of his thoughts: 'I feel more strongly than ever the next world will be no new world to us.' He even attributed mystical powers to the Devil. 'I truly believe,' he told his sister in September, 'that every word I speak against anyone is mystically conveyed to that person by Satan and though that person may not know it, yet he is impelled to speak against me.'

Then one day in October came a summons from King Leopold to go to the Congo. Gordon leapt at it. Here at last might be the answer to his fervent prayer for release. He admitted that he saw 'no great or beneficial result to be obtained by the King's expedition'. But he added enigmatically that 'there may be some result which may be unseen to me and which God may rule for good purpose'. And with this wishful thought in his mind he confided to a friend, Laurence Oliphant, who lived near Haifa, his conviction that he would never return from the Congo, having finished his work for God on this earth.

His only fear was that the British Government might not allow him to accept Leopold's invitation, lest the French—with whom relations had seriously deteriorated since Britain had become the paramount power in Egypt—should suspect that Gordon's appointment concealed a conspiracy against French interests in Central Africa. Late in November this fear seemed to be confirmed when he heard from London that the Foreign Office refused to give their blessing to his appointment in the Congo, and that the War Office would not give him a pension if he resigned his commission to circumvent the Government's veto. But Gordon had made up his mind that if the Government refused him leave as a serving officer—he was now a Major-General—he would resign from the Army and rely on Leopold to compensate him for any consequential financial loss. So, after leaving Palestine in mid-December, he made straight for Brussels, where he arrived on January 1, 1884. The next day he saw the King, who agreed to his terms and signed a blank cheque to honour his undertaking. Whereupon Gordon hastened to London to send in his resignation to the War Office in a letter, which he could not resist ending with the sarcastic comment that 'H.M. King Leopold II has most kindly assured me that H.M. will compensate any pecuniary loss I may incur in leaving Her Majesty's Service'.

The Foreign Office's reason for refusing Gordon permission to go to the Congo was, of course, only partly fear of French repercussions. They were more anxious that he should not go and bury himself in Central Africa at a time when his special knowledge and reputation might be needed in the Sudan. Over a year earlier, Lord Dufferin had suggested that 'some person like Colonel Gordon' should be found to take over the administration of the Sudan. And more recently, when the news broke of the annihilation of the Hicks expedition, a letter had been written by a R.E. Colonel to the Inspector-General of Fortifications which found its way on to Lord Granville's desk, and which said quite simply: 'There is one man who is competent to deal with the question—Charlie Gordon.'

Although it was four weeks before Baring himself was to recommend the despatch of 'an English officer of high authority' to withdraw the Sudan garrisons, Granville decided to ask his representative in Cairo whether Gordon 'would be any use to you or to the Egyptian Government and, if so, in what capacity'. Baring consulted Cherif, and on December 2 replied that the Egyptian Government were much averse to employing Gordon for fear that, with a religious revolt on their hands, the appointment of a Christian in command would alienate those tribes who had not yet gone over to the Mahdi. Baring also had his own reasons for opposing Gordon, who to his objective way of thinking was altogether too unpredictable and unruly a character to be of help in this critical situation.

No more was said on this issue for the next five weeks, during which the British Government was more concerned to induce the Egyptians to accept withdrawal from the Sudan than to determine which, if any, British officer should conduct the withdrawal. Then suddenly the whole question was blown wide open by an influential and somewhat chauvinist newspaper, the *Pall Mall Gazette*, whose Editor, Mr. W. T. Stead, decided on January 8— the very day on which the Khedive bowed to the inevitable and agreed to evacuate the Sudan—to seek out General Gordon and ascertain his views on the Sudanese revolt.

Gordon was at first reluctant to give any views, professing ignorance of the situation. He had agreed to go to the Congo and, single-minded as always, had neither time nor inclination to spare a thought for the Sudan. Perhaps too he felt a little guilty about what was happening there, for in one of his rare references to Sudanese affairs he had written from Palestine that his attempts to suppress the slave trade and to encourage the people to stand up to the pashas, such as Zubair, had no doubt contributed to the Mahdi's revolt. But Stead was not to be put off so easily, and drew him out by telling him that Gladstone's Government were insisting in Cairo on total evacuation of the Sudan garrisons. This was too much for Gordon, who vehemently protested that evacuation was both dishonourable and impracticable. 'You have 6,000 men in Khartoum,' he said. 'What are you going to do with them? You have garrisons in Darfur, in Bahr-el-Ghazal, and Gondokoro. Are they to be sacrificed? Their only offence is their loyalty to their Sovereign. For their fidelity you are going to abandon them to their fate. You say they are to retire upon Wadi Halfa.... How will you move your 6,000 men from Khartoum—to say nothing of other places—and all the Europeans in that city, through the desert to Wadi Halfa? Where are you going to get the camels to take them away? Will the Mahdi supply them? If they are to escape with their lives, the garrison will not be allowed to leave with a coat on their backs. They will be plundered to the skin, and even their lives will not be spared. Whatever you may decide about evacuation, you cannot evacuate, because your army cannot be moved. You must either surrender absolutely to the Mahdi or defend Khartoum at all hazards.'

The following day the *Pall Mall Gazette* gave a page and a half to the interview with Gordon, and in a front-page editorial, headed 'Chinese Gordon for the Sudan', argued that, in the light of such expert testimony, the Government must admit that evacuation was impossible and must reverse its policy. They should resolve to defend Khartoum and send Gordon, 'who on more than one occasion has proved himself more valuable than an entire army', to take control of the situation, treat with the Mahdi, relieve the garrisons and 'save what can be saved from the wreck of the Sudan'.

These views, based as they were on the statement of one of Britain's foremost popular heroes and reproduced in every principal newspaper in the land, placed the Government in a quandary. They had themselves suggested sending Gordon to Khartoum; but the Egyptians had objected, and they did not want at that stage to take on the responsibility of forcing him on them. Now their potential *deus ex machina* was publicly proclaiming that the policy of evacuation, which they had got the Egyptians to accept and which they thought he might carry out for them, was cowardly and impracticable. Still, Baring had himself now suggested that 'an English officer of high authority' be sent to Khartoum. And if this meant that, with the malleable Nubar replacing the intractable Cherif, Gordon was no longer so objectionable in their sight, it might be possible to persuade him to carry out a withdrawal, in spite of what he had told the *Pall Mall Gazette*. Granville therefore returned to the charge with Baring, and on January 10 he asked whether Gordon would be of assistance 'under the altered conditions in Egypt'. But the answer was still the same. Baring was at this point urging Abd el-Kader Hilmi to return to the Sudan and conduct the withdrawal and, after consulting Nubar, he replied that Gordon's services would still not be welcome.

However, the British Press was now in full cry, stirred up by the news that, as *The Times* put it, Gordon had been 'compelled at great pecuniary sacrifice to resign' his commission and was to leave for the Congo in two weeks' time. The *Morning Advertiser,* a Liberal paper, painted a horrifying picture of the dangers of attempting evacuation of the Sudan, and asserted that 'no effort... would be too great for securing the safety of the defenders of Khartoum', and that a massacre of fugitives would cause 'an outburst of indignation from the civilized world'. For Gladstone's Government there seemed to be only one way out. No matter what the Egyptians might say, if public opinion in England was to be placated, Gordon must be sent out to the Sudan. Somehow he must be persuaded to supplement Abd el-Kader Hilmi's mission to Khartoum by going to Suakim and using his influence with the tribes to open up the Suakim–Berber route for the withdrawal of the garrisons. The Government could then hide behind the ample skirts of a popular hero in executing their policy of evacuation. The essential thing was to get themselves off the hook on which they were currently impaled by the Press, and to appear to be taking some positive action.

Lytton Strachey, in his portrait of Gordon in *Eminent Victorians,* suggested that there was another more subtle reason why certain members of the current Establishment wished to send Gordon to the Sudan. According to his surmise, the 'imperialists' in Gladstone's Cabinet, led by Lord Hartington as Secretary of State for War, refused to be reconciled to a policy of withdrawal which meant handing over the Sudan to the Mahdi. They therefore wanted to send Gordon to Khartoum, knowing that, once there, he would find some reason to go back on any instructions to evacuate the country which the Government might give him. This would force the Government to send an expedition to relieve him and, while they were about it, to conquer the Sudan and impose upon it the British Raj. Like much else of Strachey's essay on Gordon, there seems to be little foundation for the attribution of such Machiavellian manoeuvres, least of all to Hartington, who Strachey himself admitted 'had no imagination at all' and was incapable of being subtle or profound. True, it was Hartington who later became largely instrumental in forcing Gladstone to send a relief expedition. But that was six months after Gordon had left for the Sudan and two months after he had been bottled up in Khartoum. During the earlier stages of the drama Hartington in fact leaned over backwards to make it plain that the idea of a British rescue or relief force could not have been further from the Government's mind. On the day after Gordon returned to Khartoum, he even went so far as to say in a House of Commons debate that 'we are not responsible for the rescue or relief of the garrisons either in the western or the southern or the eastern Sudan'. And there is no reason to suppose that Hartington or any other member of the Cabinet thought of using Gordon for any purpose other than to extricate the Egyptian garrisons from the Sudan, and hence the British Government from the stocks of public criticism.

Thus, while further pressure was put on Baring to secure Egyptian acquiescence, Sir Garnet Wolseley, now Adjutant-General at the War Office, telegraphed to Gordon on January 12 to come and see him, and an interview was arranged for January 15. Wolseley had written to Gordon a few days earlier to try to dissuade him from going to the Congo and to hint that he should return to the Sudan instead. 'You have had enough of liver-grilling climates,' he said, 'and the world does not seem bounded with the clear horizon that would warrant our very best man burying himself among niggers on the Equator.' And when the two men met, he expressed the hope that, although Gordon had committed himself to the King of the Belgians, he would nevertheless be prepared to postpone his departure for the Congo if, as happened to be the case, his own country urgently needed him to go and report on the situation in the Sudan.

It was a curious situation for Gordon. Three days earlier he had written to a friend apropos the nationwide campaign to send him to the Sudan, and said that he could not break his promise to King Leopold and that he could never serve Tewfik. And when Sir Samuel Baker had joined in the general chorus, he had told him to propose himself for the job. But when Wolseley put the proposition to him, Gordon accepted without demur, and wrote that evening to his sister in his most matter-of-fact way: 'I might have to go to the Sudan for two months and then to Congo. But I shall not go as Governor-General, only as a military officer to report on affairs.' The next day he left for Brussels to break the news to Leopold. The King was much put out by this unexpected postponement. But Gordon's mind was made up, and in response to a further summons to an interview with the Foreign Secretary and other Ministers, he returned post-haste to London on January 18.

Meanwhile, an important change of attitude had taken place in Cairo. Abd el-Kader Hilmi, having suffered one frustrating experience in the Sudan, was not anxious for a repetition, and refused to return to Khartoum. And after further consultations with Nubar, Baring telegraphed that the Egyptian Government now wanted Britain to send out at once 'a qualified British officer to go to Khartoum with full powers, civil and military, to conduct the retreat'. The telegram crossed one from Granville suggesting that Gordon should go to Suakim to report on the situation and should take his instructions from Baring. And in the altered situation brought about by Abd el-Kader Hilmi's refusal, Baring reluctantly, and to his subsequent everlasting regret, gave way and replied that 'General Gordon would be the best man, if he will pledge himself to carry out the policy of withdrawal from Sudan as soon as possible, consistently with saving life'.

The die was cast. Baring had withdrawn his opposition to Gordon, and whether the Egyptians had really waived theirs was of little, if any, importance to London. Britain had taken charge of events, and she was no longer going to be told by the Khedive who should or should not be employed to discharge the responsibilities which the incompetence of his ministers and governors had thrust upon her. Gordon must go to the Sudan; British public opinion demanded it. Whatever course Britain might have ordered in the Sudan—evacuation or resistance—was fraught with danger. But if Gordon were there, his back would be broad enough to take any amount of public opprobrium in the event of a disaster; whereas, without Gordon as an alibi, the Government would have to bear the full brunt.

So on the afternoon of January 18 Gordon went once again to the War Office, where he met Granville and Hartington, accompanied by Lord Northbrook, First Lord of the Admiralty, Sir Charles Dilke, President of the Local Government Board, and Wolseley. And that same evening he left London by train for Calais *en route* for the Sudan, taking with him Colonel Stewart as the most experienced available helpmate in his difficult and dangerous mission. It was a strange and almost comic send-off that he received at Charing Cross Station, which clearly betrayed the anxiety of the Government to see him on his way to the Sudan. No less a figure than Granville himself bought his ticket, while Wolseley carried his baggage and the Commander-in-Chief, the royal Duke of Cambridge, held the door of the railway carriage open for him. Then, as the train was about to leave, Gordon found that he had absent-mindedly forgotten to bring any money with him, whereupon Wolseley emptied his own pockets and handed over all his spare cash, plus his gold watch and chain!

The following day Gordon wrote to his sister and to the Rev. Barnes to explain his sudden change of plans. The Ministers, he said, had made it clear to him that they were determined to evacuate the Sudan and had asked him to 'superintend' the operation. 'I said yes,' he concluded. And a few days later, as he journeyed eastward, he wrote in an official memorandum to the Foreign Office that he understood his mission was 'to arrange for the evacuation ... and safe removal of the Egyptian employees and troops' from the Sudan.

Plan of the Defences of Khartoum

CHAPTER 18

RETURN TO KHARTOUM

It has been said that much of the subsequent misunderstanding between Gordon and the British Government stemmed from a confusion as to whether his functions should be advisory or executive. Certainly Gordon's interpretation of his mission as being to arrange and superintend evacuation went somewhat further than his original instructions. These, as drawn up in Granville's own handwriting, were 'to proceed to Suakim to report on the military situation in the Sudan and ... consider the best move of evacuating the interior of the Sudan and of securing the safety and good administration by the Egyptian Government of the ports on the Red Sea coast'. 'To consider and report' is clearly not the same thing as 'to arrange and superintend'. But to say that this distinction was responsible for the differences which later arose between Gordon and the Government is to miss the whole point of the story.

At the interview of January 18 the Government's main purpose was to appease public opinion by somehow inducing Gordon to drop his Congo plans and go to the Sudan. But Gordon had only a few days before gone on public record as saying that evacuation, which happened to be the Government's policy, was both dishonourable and impossible. It is surely natural therefore that, having persuaded him to go to the Sudan, the Government should not, at any rate initially, have imposed upon him mandatory instructions to execute a policy on which he had poured such scorn. Thus he was told to consider evacuation and report on the situation. At the same time, it was made clear to him that the Government drew a sharp distinction between the interior of the Sudan, which they wished to see evacuated, and the Red Sea ports, which they hoped to 'secure' under Egyptian administration. Then long before Gordon reached the Sudan and even before he arrived in Egypt, the Government learned from his own memorandum that he accepted evacuation as inevitable and that he saw his mission as being to carry it out. Needless to say, nobody was more delighted to hear this than Her Majesty's Ministers, who readily gave their sanction to the change of roles from advisory to executive. And when Gordon arrived at Port Said he was greeted by a letter from Baring which confirmed that he should consider his mission as being to 'arrange for the withdrawal of the Egyptian garrisons'. What created the misunderstanding was not that Gordon adopted an executive instead of an advisory role, but rather, as later became evident from his actions after he reached Khartoum, that he decided for reasons of his own to abandon the policy of evacuation and to adopt an attitude of defiance against overwhelming odds. Gordon had spoken his true feelings to the *Pall Mall Gazette* and, although he pretended otherwise up to the time that he got to Khartoum, he stubbornly adhered to these views right to the end.

What is less simple and obvious is the reason why he gave up going to the Congo and went back to the Sudan, if he never intended to carry out the Government's evacuation policy. Part of the answer is that he probably felt obliged to respond to the call of patriotic duty. Britain's interests had precedence over Belgium's and, rebel though he was against the 'trammels' of soldiering at home, he could never escape so far from convention as to disregard an appeal to serve Queen and country. But uppermost in his mind was more likely the ever-present, constantly-repeated desire for martyrdom and for that glorious immortality in union with God and away from the wretchedness of life on this earth. 'I feel so very much inclined to wish it His will might be my release. Earth's joys grow very dim, its glories have faded,' he had recently written to Augusta. He had wishfully thought that he might die in the Congo, but then suddenly he was asked to go back to the revolt-torn Sudan, where the possibility of 'release' was greater still. If the Congo was a jungle full of hidden dangers, the Sudan was a tiger's cage, and all he had to do was to enter the cage and wait for the tiger to spring.

Exactly at what point Gordon made any conscious decision to march out to meet his fatal destiny is difficult to say. Certainly the suggestions which he telegraphed to London while he journeyed to Egypt convey no other impression than that of a dedicated public servant diligently applying himself to his task in accordance with his instructions. And if some of them exceeded the Government's conception of his powers—such as the suggestion that the Khedive should reappoint him as Governor-General and that he should proclaim independence for the Sudan and restore the power of the former sultans deposed by Mohammed Ali—it no doubt seemed that he was only seeking every opportunity to carry out British policy. Admittedly, Gordon now introduced a new element into his mission, contending that, in addition to evacuating the Sudan, he should try to establish some form of settled government by restoring the authority of the petty sultans who had held sway before the Egyptian conquest. This, he thought, could be done in the tribal areas. But in towns such as Khartoum, Dongola, and Kassala there might be some difficulties. These places had grown up since Mohammed Ali's conquest and there were no former sultans to hand over to. In such cases he thought it might be wise to postpone a decision until the inhabitants could be consulted about their future. Finally, he warned that it could not be supposed that the Mahdi would exactly allow the evacuating garrisons a safe conduct, and there might therefore be some fighting. But to these dark hints Gordon reassuringly added after some caustic comments about the Sudan being a 'useless possession' which the Government were wise to abandon: 'I will carry out the evacuation as far as possible according to their wish to the best of my ability and with avoidance, as far as possible, of all fighting.' All of which appeared to London and Cairo as being in complete harmony with their thinking.

Meanwhile, the situation in the Sudan had continued to deteriorate since the Hicks disaster and the surrender of Slatin. Kordofan and Darfur were occupied by the Mahdi; Bahr-el-Ghazal and Equatoria were cut off; and in the east Osman Digna was carrying all before him. Not only was the Suakim–Berber route cut, but the Mahdists were now closing in on the Red Sea ports. Suakim was threatened and Sinkat and Tokar were under siege. In an attempt to halt Osman Digna's advance, a force of Egyptian gendarmerie had been sent two months earlier to Suakim under a British officer, General Valentine Baker, a brother of Sir Samuel Baker, with orders to reopen the route to Berber, if possible by winning over the local tribes, but if not by force of arms. To assist in this delicate exercise, the Egyptian Government had intended to send Zubair, who, they felt, alone enjoyed sufficient prestige among the Sudanese tribes to counter the growing appeal of Mahdism. But for fear of the powerful and vociferous Anti-slavery Society of Britain, Gladstone's Cabinet vetoed Zubair's mission. At this very moment the new Egyptian Government also decided to cancel that part of Baker's instructions that authorized him to use force if diplomacy failed to re-open the Suakim–Berber route.

It was a difficult situation by any measure. But a further complication lay in the fact that Baker, a courageous officer who had been forced to leave the British Army after serving a prison sentence for indecent assault, clearly looked to his present command as a means of rehabilitating himself in his own country's service by achieving some spectacular success in the field. Knowing this, Baring feared yet another disaster, and felt it imperative that he should consult with Gordon. The blocking of the route to Berber meant that Gordon could no longer go to Khartoum via Suakim, as had originally been decided, and would have to change his route plans, if nothing else. Besides, Granville's instructions had included a blanket clause that Gordon should perform, in addition to those already specified, such other duties as the Egyptian Government—in other words, Baring—might want to entrust to him. And in a rapidly changing situation Baring felt, and on his arrival at Port Said Gordon agreed, that they should concert up-to-date instructions before the latter left for the Sudan.

Gordon and Stewart arrived in Cairo on January 24 and, after a friendly interview with the Khedive, spent most of the next day attending meetings at Baring's house at which Nubar, General Sir Evelyn Wood, who was superintending the recreation of the Egyptian Army, and Baring were present. A full discussion took place on the current position and on the suggestions which Gordon had sent home while journeying to Egypt. In his methodical way, Baring felt that, with so unpredictable an emissary, he should use Granville's authority to dot every 'i' and cross every 't' of Gordon's instructions. Accordingly, he spelt out a set of categorical orders which left no room whatever for misunderstanding. These began with the statement that the Egyptian Government were particularly anxious to ensure the safe retreat of the Khartoum garrison, together with some 10,000 to 15,000 other inhabitants who were Christians, Egyptian employees or their wives and children. The timing and method for evacuating these people was to be left to Gordon's discretion. But the instructions continued: 'You will bear in mind that the main end to be pursued is the evacuation of the Sudan. This policy was adopted, after very full discussion, by the Egyptian Government on the advice of Her Majesty's Government.... I understand also that you entirely concur in the desirability of adopting this policy and that you think it should on no account be changed. You consider that it may take a few months to carry it out with safety. You are further of the opinion that the restoration of the country should be made to the different petty sultans who existed at the time of Mohammed Ali's conquest and whose families still exist.... In this view the Egyptian Government entirely concur. It will, of course, be fully understood that the Egyptian troops are not to be kept in the Sudan merely with a view to consolidating the power of the new rulers.... You are therefore given full discretionary power to retain the troops for such reasonable period as you may think necessary in order that the abandonment of the country may be accomplished with the least possible risk to life and property.' To complete the picture, Gordon was appointed Governor-General of the Sudan and furnished with a proclamation by the Khedive, which declared Egypt's intention to evacuate the country and 'to restore to the families of the kings of the Sudan their former independence', and which he was to issue at whatever he considered the opportune moment.

Nothing could have been clearer or more categorical than the language of these instructions. What is more, it was Gordon himself who insisted on the insertion of the passage which said that the policy of evacuation 'should on no account be changed'. Baring therefore had every reason to believe, as he wrote to Granville, that Gordon 'fully understands that he is going to Khartoum for the purpose of carrying out the policy of evacuation and has expressed to me his fullest concurrence in the wisdom of this policy.... No doubt is left on this point and these instructions were drafted at the request and with the entire approval of General Gordon himself.' And in the light of this assurance Gladstone announced to loud acclamations from Parliament and Press that Gordon had gone to the Sudan 'for the double purpose of evacuating the country by extricating the Egyptian garrisons and reconstituting it by giving back to those sultans their ancestral powers'.

Yet how wrong they were. The instructions might make it crystal clear that the 'main end' of Gordon's mission was to evacuate the Sudan and that the evacuation of the Egyptian garrisons was not to be held up to achieve the secondary purpose of restoring the Sudan to its ancestral sultans. Yet from the moment when he left for Khartoum, Gordon reversed the priorities and insisted that evacuation, far from being the 'main end', depended on the restoration of the former sultans or, where this was not feasible, on satisfactory arrangements being made for the Sudan's future government. In the prevailing state of chaos caused by the Mahdi's revolt, this could only mean that there would be no evacuation within the foreseeable future.

No doubt it would have been wiser if Baring had omitted all mention of 'restoration' from the instructions. To say the least, any plans for restoring the Sudan after evacuation could be little more than pious hopes based on the totally unwarrantable assumption that the menace of the Mahdi would somehow melt away, once the Egyptians had withdrawn. Yet there can be little doubt that, whatever Baring had omitted or included in his instructions, Gordon would have found some pretext for disregarding the evacuation order and for sitting it out in Khartoum until the bitter and bloody end. Even before he left Cairo, he had given Baring a foretaste of the kind of unpredictable behaviour which was to make that cool, level-headed administrator regret so deeply in the coming months that he had allowed himself to be talked into accepting so eccentric and hot-headed an emissary.

The occasion arose when Gordon was selecting a staff to accompany him to Khartoum. Proclaiming that the Mahdi was a false prophet of small account who would not dare to venture beyond his strongholds in Kordofan and Darfur, he declined to take a military escort and insisted that he would be adequately served by the two officials whom he had chosen, one of whom was Ibrahim Fawzi, whom he had dismissed five years before as Governor of Equatoria. He would, however, need one other Sudanese to complete his team and, to Baring's astonishment, he said that he had decided to take Zubair. He claimed to have had a 'mystic feeling' that, notwithstanding his murky past, Zubair would be essential to the 'restoration' of the Sudan after evacuation. (Only a week before, Gordon had been telling Granville that Zubair should be 'well watched to prevent his sending emissaries or letters to the Sudan'!) The two men had met the day after the discussions with Nubar and Baring. Zubair had at first refused to shake hands with Gordon, whom he accused of using forged evidence to convict him of complicity in his son's rebellion. But the quarrel soon subsided when Gordon admitted the possibility that the arch-slaver had been unjustly condemned. Whether at this point Gordon asked Zubair to go with him to Khartoum is not clear. But when he advanced the proposition to his associates, Nubar and Stewart expressed grave doubts about it, and Baring, who did not believe in 'mystic feelings', exercised his veto.

For the moment the subject of Zubair was dropped, and on that same evening, January 26, Gordon and Stewart left for Khartoum by the Nile route, accompanied as far as the Sudan border by General Graham, Gordon's old friend since the Crimean War. Graham strongly advised Gordon not to write the Mahdi off as a 'false prophet' of little consequence, and begged him to understand that his adversary was a man of great strength of character and extraordinary mental powers, who had gained a widespread reputation for sanctity and a large and powerful following among the most warlike tribes of the Sudan. He was not a mere political adventurer, who could be jockeyed into settling for his conquests west of the Nile. On the contrary, the very character of his religious pretensions compelled him to accept no frontier that did not encompass the whole Moslem world. But Gordon turned a deaf ear to this well-reasoned advice. After all, he had crushed the Taiping rebellion and he had nothing to fear from the Mahdi. And when he discovered that Mohammed Ahmed was the nephew of one of his guides from his earlier days in the Sudan, he insisted that a man of such humble origins could not possibly establish a durable claim to be the expected Mahdi. He was a fake; his pretensions to conquer the whole Sudan, let alone the Moslem world, were ridiculous; and anyone who claimed, like Power, *The Times* correspondent, that Khartoum could not be held was an 'alarmist'. The Mahdi would count himself lucky to be left in control of Kordofan.

From this premise, Gordon began to evolve a whole series of policy recommendations which he telegraphed to Baring. Paying only lip-service to the principle of evacuation, he devoted his thinking to the country's future administration. He would go and settle with the Mahdi by offering to recognize him as the ruler of Kordofan. As for the rest of the country, he at first suggested that Egypt should retain her sovereignty, while allowing a wide autonomy to the Sudan—a situation analogous to the relationship then existing between Turkey and Egypt. Then as he approached Khartoum, he changed his mind and recommended that Britain should take over as sovereign power and appoint Zubair as Governor-General. Turning to individual provinces, he suggested that Darfur, the most distant and recent of the Khedive's acquisitions in the Sudan should be handed back to the family of the former Sultan. And Equatoria and Bah-el-Ghazal should be taken by the King of the Belgians and joined to the Congo, as the only way of stopping the slave trade and of giving these provinces a proper system of government. (He even wrote to tell King Leopold of his ideas and suggested that when he had finished his task in Khartoum, he should go to the Equator and take over these two provinces in His Majesty's name!)

Not for a moment did Gordon seem to allow for the possibility that the British Government, who wished to evacuate the Sudan, might not share his enthusiasm for the open-ended commitment into which he was suggesting they should enter. On the contrary; when an Italian merchant at Berber, Giuseppe Cuzzi, whom Gordon later appointed as his agent in Berber, reminded him that in the existing state of war in the Sudan it might be difficult to get the tribes to co-operate in his plans without the use of force, Gordon replied that he was supported up to the hilt by the military might of England. Baring quickly sought to divert him from these dangerous illusions. First, he forbade him to visit the Mahdi, knowing that he would be held a prisoner if he attempted anything so rash. Second, he thwarted Gordon's plans to hand over Equatoria and Bahr-el-Ghazal, telling him not to go anywhere south of Khartoum. But there was unfortunately no way for Baring to prevent another act of folly by which Gordon was to play straight into the Mahdi's hands even before he got to Khartoum.

Gordon reached Berber on February 11 to be greeted with the baleful news that, six days earlier, General Baker's force of Egyptian gendarmerie had been cut to pieces by a relatively small group of Osman Digna's rebels on the Red Sea coast and had lost more than 2,000 men. Just as Baring feared, Baker had disregarded his orders and marched to the relief of the Tokar garrison. But when confronted by a force of 1,000 Mahdists, the Egyptians 'threw down their arms and ran ... allowing themselves to be killed without the slightest resistance', while Baker himself barely escaped with his life. Astonishingly enough, Gordon decided, in the light of this shattering blow, that the moment had come when he should issue the Khedive's proclamation of Sudanese independence. He had pinned great hopes on Baker's expedition being able to destroy the myth of invincibility which was growing up around the Mahdist revolt; and with this setback he now felt that his best chance of weaning the tribes away from the Mahdi was to announce that Egypt was about to withdraw from the Sudan and Britain to take over.

As Stewart was later to record in his diary, this was a disastrous miscalculation, and the effect was to lead everyone to believe that they were to be left 'to stew in their own juice', with no alternative but to make terms with the Mahdi as rapidly as possible. Gordon was warned to this effect, but, stubborn as ever, was not to be gainsaid. He contended that his action would put 'a sharp spur into the Sudanese to organize their own government'. And on the morning of January 12 he sent for the Mudir of Berber, Hussein Khalifa, and, after privately showing him the Khedive's proclamation, ordered it to be posted on the gates of the town, with an addendum stating that the governorate of Berber was henceforth independent of Cairo and subject only to himself as Governor-General and 'Commissioner of the British government'. (It need scarcely be said that for this public invocation of British responsibility Gordon had no authority whatever and that, however much Britain might have forced upon the Khedive the policy of withdrawal, he was the Khedive's and not the British Government's representative.)

Immediately after the proclamation was posted, a deputation of local sheikhs and dignitaries called on Gordon to ask whether it meant that the Anti-slavery Convention of 1877, by which all slaves would be freed in twelve years' time, was now a dead letter so far as the Sudan was concerned. This was an awkward question. To release the Sudanese from all obligations to stop slavery would be certain to provoke violent denunciations in Britain. Yet if the Sudanese were to be independent of Egypt, they would not be held to account for engagements entered into on their behalf by the Khedive. Gordon was therefore forced by the logic of the situation to reply that the treaty would no longer apply to the Sudan. And to leave no doubt about the matter, he issued a further proclamation that, in the interests of 'public tranquility' and of remedying 'the severe measures taken to suppress the slave traffic, henceforth none shall interfere with your property; who-ever has slaves shall have full right to their services and full control over them'. On top of this, he wrote to the Mahdi offering to recognize him as 'Sultan of Kordofan' and inviting him to come to terms and cease hostilities. Then, moving on southward to Metemma, he again proclaimed from the house-tops that Egypt was pulling out of the Sudan and that the rights of slave-owners had been restored. And when he finally reached Khartoum on February 18, he repeated the proclamations yet once more.

As Gordon was soon to discover, nothing could have been more wrong than his belief that these announcements would 'spur' the Sudanese to organize their own government. Coming immediately after the second major defeat of an Egyptian expeditionary force, the declaration of independence, plus the blank cheque for the slave-traders, merely appeared as a desperate attempt to outbid the Mahdi. As a result, they only served to strengthen the Mahdi's hand and enhance his reputation. Tribal leaders from many parts of the Sudan now joined the revolt rather than face the Mahdi's vengeance for supporting a régime which had openly admitted that it could no longer give them any protection. In Khartoum itself—contrary to the popular theory that Gordon was unanimously acclaimed by the populace as their liberator—there was great agitation and anxiety when the news was announced. And when Stewart went a few miles up the White Nile with the Sheikh of Duem and the Cadi of Kalkala to see how the proclamations had been received by the people south of Khartoum, they were met with fusillades from the river bank, and as they turned for home the Cadi promptly deserted the party and joined the Mahdi.

Nor did Gordon's speech in reply to Khartoum's official address of welcome do anything to restore morale. 'I come,' he said, 'without soldiers, but with God on my side to redress the evils of the Sudan. I will not fight with any weapons but justice.' And although he immediately set about honouring his pledge by sending Stewart to the jail to destroy all instruments of torture and release large numbers of prisoners who had long ago served their sentences, he failed to arrest the alarm which he had let loose. Forced to admit defeat after a week had elapsed, he reversed his gears and issued a further proclamation to the effect that 'finding that my advice [to desist from rebellion] had no effect on some people, I have been compelled to use severe measures, so much so that British troops are now on their way and in a few days will be at Khartoum. Whoever persists in wicked conduct will then receive the treatment he deserves.'

This astonishing statement has been explained by some writers as arising out of a telegram from London, received by Gordon on his way from Berber, which asked him whether, after the defeat of Baker's Egyptian force, he felt that the despatch of British troops to Suakim would assist or impede his mission in Khartoum. But Gordon can scarcely have interpreted this message as presaging a British expedition to Khartoum. He knew as well as anyone that, both in Cairo and in London, the clearest distinction had been drawn between the Red Sea coast, which it was intended to hold, and the interior of the Sudan, which he was to evacuate. This distinction had existed ever since Granville drew up Gordon's original instructions before he left England, and it had never been called in question. Besides, Gordon himself replied to the telegram in question that 'I would care more for rumours of such an intervention than for forces. What would have the greatest effect would be rumour of British intervention.'

In the event, the British Government opted for reality rather than rumour and, as Gordon reached Khartoum, informed him that General Graham was being despatched with a force of 4,000 British Indian troops to relieve Tokar and reinforce Suakim. Did Gordon therefore deliberately twist this announcement to claim that British forces were about to advance on Khartoum? Or did he expect that the Government would accept his recommendation that Britain should replace Egypt as sovereign power in the Sudan and would therefore send troops to establish her sovereignty? Either way, his action was as unwarrantable as it was unwise. For he knew perfectly well that Gladstone's Cabinet wanted no part in any such commitment, and that the express purpose of his mission was to extricate Egypt from an untenable position and not to put Britain in Egypt's place. Like all his later pretences that a relief expedition was on its way, this fabrication was to do his cause and reputation nothing but harm and, coming on top of all the talk of withdrawal, it created more confusion than reassurance.

CHAPTER 19

PRETEXTS FOR DEFIANCE

IF anything should have persuaded Gordon that there was not a moment to lose in preparing for the evacuation of the Sudan, it was surely the prevailing atmosphere of fear and confusion which greeted him at Khartoum. But instead of making plans for immediate withdrawal, he merely added to the confusion by adopting a posture of defiance which suggested that his proclamations of independence had been completely fraudulent. As he admitted in a report to Baring early in March, the only people whom he sent down from Khartoum were 400 sick or wounded soldiers, plus a number of widows and orphans. Far from planning any general evacuation, he promptly set about organizing a series of armed reconnaissance raids up the Blue and White Niles, and announced that they were going 'to attack rebels in the vicinity'. And the people of Khartoum not unnaturally began to wonder exactly how the use of Egyptian troops to 'attack rebels' would conduce to an Egyptian withdrawal.

In fact, Gordon never really intended to withdraw once he had reached Khartoum. And his every word and action from now on clearly shows that he was determined to stay put and to use every delaying device and prevaricating argument to justify his doing so. No sooner had the British Government rejected one such argument than Gordon would come up with another; no sooner had an instruction been agreed with him than he would either twist it to suit his purpose or disregard it altogether. Having got the Government to accept that, while the 'main end' of his mission was evacuation, he should also try to create a settled government in the Sudan, he promptly reversed the order of priority. Thus, even before he reached Khartoum, evacuation had become his secondary aim—and a poor second at that—whereas his main purpose was to restore a settled government, which he contended could only be achieved under Zubair. And long after it was crystal clear that Zubair would not be allowed to join him or to succeed him, he continued to reverse the priorities of his mission, until finally evacuation was abandoned altogether.

On February 23 Granville replied as expected, through Baring, to Gordon's proposals that Britain should take over in the Sudan and appoint Zubair as Governor-General. The Sudan was not and should not be Britain's responsibility, he contended. 'Her Majesty's Government,' he said, 'are of opinion that the gravest objections exist to the appointment by their authority of a successor to General Gordon ... in any case public opinion in this country would not tolerate the appointment of Zubair Pasha.' Baring duly passed the message on to Gordon, and at the same time asked him if he could suggest any other name as a successor. With typical petulance, Gordon retorted: 'Telegram of February 23 received respecting Zubair. That settles question for me. I cannot suggest any other.' Then he went on to say that if and when evacuation of the Sudan were to be accomplished the Mahdi 'will not let Egypt be quiet. Of course my duty is evacuation ... [but] if Egypt is to be quiet, the Mahdi must be smashed up. The Mahdi is most unpopular and with care and time could be smashed. Remember that, once Khartoum belongs to the Mahdi, the task will be far more difficult.... If you decide on smashing the Mahdi, then send up another £100,000 and send up 200 Indian troops to Wadi Halfa.... Leave Suakim and Massawa alone. I repeat that evacuation is possible, but you will feel the effect in Egypt and will be forced to enter into a far more serious affair in order to guard Eygpt. At present it would be comparatively easy to destroy the Mahdi.'

Thus, eight days after he reached Khartoum, Gordon was seeking to change his mission from a rescue operation of the Egyptian garrisons to an all-out onslaught on the Mahdi, and to persuade the Government to abandon the one part of the Sudan—the Red Sea coast—which they were willing and able to hold. Whether or not some straight talking at this moment from London or Cairo would have made any difference to him is impossible to judge. Probably not; for however sternly Gordon might have been told to carry out his instructions, he would almost certainly have ignored them. In any case, no straight talking was forthcoming and the only remonstrance that emerged from either capital was a letter from Lord Northbrook to Baring saying: 'What a queer fellow Gordon is and how rapidly he changes his opinion.

"Zubair is to be sent to Cyprus before Gordon arrives in Egypt. Zubair is to rule at Khartoum. The Mahdi is a good kind man whom Gordon is to visit quietly and settle affairs with. The Mahdi is to be Emir of Kordofan. The Mahdi is to be smashed up. The Suakim–Berber route is to be opened up.... Suakim is to be left alone." His telegram does not differ very much from Cherif Pasha's programme of keeping Khartoum upon which you turned him out.'

For his part, Baring decided that it would be politic to support his changeable emissary in one of his projects—the appointment of Zubair. How persuaded he was by Gordon's arguments is not very clear. But he certainly did his best to convince the Government at home that it would be wrong to evacuate the Sudan without making any attempt to leave behind a 'settled government' and that they must face the fact that they had made themselves henceforth responsible for 'any arrangements which are now to be devised for the Sudan'. The most advisable course of action, he said, was that 'Zubair Pasha should be permitted to succeed General Gordon'. Zubair was by no means perfect, but neither he nor Gordon nor Nubar could suggest anybody else. Baring concluded with this slightly acid remark: 'I venture to think that any attempt to settle Egyptian questions by the light of English popular feeling is sure to be productive of harm, and in this, as in other cases, it would be preferable to follow the advice of the responsible authorities on the spot.'

It was a powerful argument and, if nothing else, it shook Gladstone's Ministers into recognizing that not only Gordon but also his successor was their responsibility. Deciding to play for time, Granville replied: 'Her Majesty's Government desire further information as to the urgency of any immediate appointment of a successor to General Gordon.' And in a private letter to Baring he added that, while he had much sympathy with his views and did not doubt that Zubair was 'the only man strong enough to cope with the Mahdi', the Government wished to know what, if any, guarantee could be given that he would not revert to his old slave-trading pursuits or even go over to the Mahdi, if he were sent back to the Sudan.

This was the kind of assurance which any democratic government would wish to have before defying public opinion by appointing so controversial a figure to such a position. And although he knew he could offer no such guarantee, Baring sent on Granville's telegram to Gordon and asked him to 'reconsider the whole question carefully and then state to me in one telegram what it is you recommend'. Gordon replied with a further shower of messages, saying that immediate withdrawal was impossible and that 'the combination at Khartoum of Zubair and myself is an absolute necessity for success'. At the same time he asked for a British or Indian force to be sent to open up the Suakim–Berber route, in addition to the 200 troops which he had requested for Wadi Halfa. 'It is not the number but the prestige which I need,' he explained. 'I am sure the revolt will collapse if I can say I have British troops at my back.'

Gordon was beginning to reveal his real intentions. Zubair had become not merely his only successor, but his indispensable help-mate, and British forces were to be asked to move into the Sudan from the east as well as the north. With Zubair's authority and the 'prestige' of British forces in the Sudan, the Mahdi would then be 'easily smashed'. Evacuation was now obviously far from his thoughts. Yet Baring still tried to help him all he could. And on March 4 he telegraphed to Granville that Gordon was still pressing for Zubair to go to the Sudan at once and that, after reconsidering the whole matter, they both still felt that Zubair should be the next Governor-General and should be sent without delay to Khartoum. The only point on which he withheld his support was Gordon's request for a British or Indian force to open up the Suakim–Berber route. To this he told the Foreign Secretary he should not agree. General Graham's terms of reference were limited to relieving the pressure on the Red Sea ports. And so long as any possibility existed of opening up the road to Berber by diplomacy, whether through the authority of Zubair or otherwise, Baring was opposed to committing Graham's force to any incursions into the interior of the Sudan.

But this intervention was less successful than the one before. Granville replied by return that the Government could 'see no reason at present to change their impressions about Zubair', which, he pointed out, they had formed largely from Gordon's own earlier condemnation of him as an out-and-out blackguard. Nor could they see how the appointment of Zubair squared with the prevention of the slave trade and with the execution of the policy of evacuation.

Baring would have been wise to drop the matter there and then. But, encouraged by Granville's private letter to believe that the Government might yet be open to argument, he telegraphed to Gordon that the Zubair question was 'still under consideration', and invited him once again to give chapter and verse for his claim that only Zubair could answer his requirements, and in particular to say whether some other chieftain, such as Hussein Khalifa, the Mudir of Berber, would not be an adequate substitute. Gordon replied on March 8 that 'the sending of Zubair means the extrication of the Cairo employees from Khartoum and the garrisons from Sennar and Kassala. I can see no possible way to do so except through him, who, being a native of the country, can rally the well-affected around him.... As for slave-holding, even if we had the Sudan, we could never have interfered with it. I have already said that the treaty of 1877 was an impossible one; therefore on that head Zubair's appointment would make no difference whatever.... There is no possibility of dividing the country between Zubair and the other chiefs; none of the latter could stand for a day against the Mahdi's agents, and Hussein Pasha Khalifa would also fall.... There is not the least chance of Zubair making common cause with the Mahdi. Zubair here would be far more powerful than the Mahdi and he would make short work of the Mahdi.... Zubair is fifty times the Mahdi's match. He is also of good family, well known and fitted to be Sultan; the Mahdi, in all these respects, is the exact opposite, besides being a fanatic.'

Baring duly forwarded Gordon's replies to London, adding that in his own view the appointment of Zubair would harmonize with the policy of withdrawal, and that he had always envisaged the need to make arrangements for the Sudan's government after evacuation. He also asked for an urgent decision, in view of a remark made by Gordon in one of his many recent telegrams that he had 'a conviction that I shall be caught in Khartoum'. But any hope that the Government might have relented at the last minute and allowed Zubair to go to Khartoum was now finally shattered by an extraordinary act of folly on Gordon's part. For the last several days, as a result of messages sent by Power to *The Times*, there had been some talk in the British Press about the possibility of Zubair being appointed Governor-General of the Sudan after the Egyptians had withdrawn. This had led to a certain amount of adverse comment from Liberal newspapers and, of course, from the Anti-slavery Society. But so far the question had not attracted too much notice. Now, however, Gordon decided to give an interview to Power for transmission to *The Times*, in which he openly proclaimed his desire for Zubair to take over the government of the Sudan, and divulged the exchanges that had taken place between London, Cairo, and Khartoum on this topic.

Later he contended that he had deliberately committed this 'indiscretion' in order to 'save the Government the odium' of appearing to appoint Zubair of their own volition. But his immodest belief that the British public would take Zubair's appointment lying down, simply because he was Gordon's personal choice, was not to be fulfilled. On the contrary, the effect of this confirmation that so notorious a slave-trader was being considered as Gordon's successor came as an electric shock to British public opinion. The Anti-slavery Society protested vehemently to Granville that such an appointment would be 'a degradation for England' and on May 10 a Liberal Member of Parliament and former Minister in Gladstone's Cabinet, William Forster, clinched the case against Zubair with an impassioned speech in Parliament, warning the Government not to outrage the feelings of the vast majority of the people by an action which would contradict Britain's traditional policy respecting Africa and the slave trade. With an extraordinary insight into Gordon's character, Forster said that it sometimes occurred to him that Gordon was 'weary of life' and that 'it would be the greatest possible delight to him to be a martyr'. And he concluded by saying that, however admirable the qualities of this Christian soldier, neither Government nor Parliament could accept blindly to follow the advice of a man bent on his own destruction.

The Government had had enough trouble already in calming the storm aroused by Gordon's earlier announcement that the Anti-slavery Treaty of 1877 could be considered a dead-letter in the Sudan. Now, faced with the threat that a sizeable number of Liberal M.P.'s would follow Forster if they showed any vacillation, they decided finally to reject Baring's advice and to veto Zubair. On March 11 Granville telegraphed to Cairo that the Cabinet, after carefully weighing all the evidence, 'do not consider that the arguments against the employment of Zubair Pasha have been satisfactorily answered'. He also flatly rejected Gordon's request for British or Indian troops to be sent to Berber. Then two days later he sent a further telegram to Baring, saying that Gordon had authority to stay at Khartoum if in his opinion 'his early departure diminishes the chance ... to establish a settled government'. But if he could not achieve such an outcome, 'he should evacuate Khartoum and save that garrison by conducting it and himself to Berber without delay'.

Meanwhile, at Khartoum, contrary to Gordon's over-sanguine assertions that the Mahdi was so unpopular with the tribes that he would not dare to advance out of Kordofan, a report had come in on March 7 that Mohammed Ahmed's agents were inciting the tribes between Khartoum and Berber to rise and to cut the telegraph linking Khartoum with the outside world. On March 9, the day after he sent his last reply about Zubair, he telegraphed to Baring: 'I shall await your decision; if the wire is cut, I shall consider your silence is consent to my propositions and shall hold on to Khartoum and await Zubair and the British diversion at Berber.' The following day he followed up this unwarrantable assumption with a further shower of messages to the effect that, if Zubair were to be sent to Khartoum and a British force to Berber, it would be worth holding on to Khartoum, but that if neither were forthcoming, he could not hold Khartoum or help the other garrisons. In that case he would withdraw with the Khartoum garrison to Berber and thence to Wadi Halfa, or he would resign his commission, send Stewart to Berber with the Khartoum garrison, and take himself off to Bahr-el-Ghazal and Equatoria and hand these provinces over to the King of the Belgians.

Baring, who at this point seems to have become almost as stubborn as Gordon, was determined to have one more try to persuade Gladstone's Cabinet to accept Zubair. But he was still as resolutely opposed as ever to sending British troops to Berber and, on this score, he felt that Gordon should be disabused without delay. Immediately he received Gordon's telegram saying that he would take silence as assent to his requests, Baring therefore telegraphed: 'So far as I know, there is no intention on the part of the Government to send an English force to Berber.' But before this message, or Granville's final refusal to appoint Zubair and send a British expedition, could be relayed to Khartoum, the telegraph line was cut on March 12 at Halfaya, nine miles north of the capital, by a small force of tribesmen responding to the Mahdi's call to arms. And it was not until four weeks later, when a messenger sent by Cuzzi from Berber got through to Khartoum on April 9, that Gordon received Baring's warning not to expect British troops. As for Granville's telegrams rejecting Zubair and confirming Baring's warning, so far as is known, neither of them ever reached Khartoum.

Gordon, however, was relatively unmoved by this adverse stroke. In a letter to his brother Henry, dated March 15, which was brought by courier via Dongola, he seemed to be happily digging himself in. 'The enemy has established himself,' he wrote, 'about nine miles from here and we hear his drums from the palace. We are well off for food and the people are in good spirits.... We shall D.V. go on for months. The steamers are a great advantage to us and we only await the rising of the Nile in two months' time to be still more powerful.'

Meanwhile, Baring was once again talking back to London and arguing the case for Zubair. He admitted all the difficulties and pressures which Ministers had to contend with at home. But he pointed out that the question to be decided was not whether Zubair was 'objectionable', nor whether he would conduct himself improperly as Governor-General. The issue was quite simply whether any other practical and less objectionable alternative could be suggested. 'I can suggest none,' Baring concluded. But it was no good. The Government had set their face against Zubair, and Baring was told that they were not prepared to change their minds. If, in the circumstances, Gordon felt that the difficulty of establishing a settled government would increase rather than diminish with time and without Zubair, then he should evacuate Khartoum as soon as possible.

Baring now saw that it was useless to continue the correspondence, and on March 17 he telegraphed to Gordon that he should now regard the idea of sending Zubair as finally abandoned and should carry out his instructions to withdraw from Khartoum. The message never got through; but, as it happened, this made no real difference. For, despite his statement of March 9 that he would consider Baring's silence as consent to his propositions, Gordon himself soon came to accept that further argument would be fruitless. Replying on April 9 to Baring's damper about British troops, he said: 'As far as I can understand, the situation is this: you state your intention of not sending any relief force up here or to Berber and you refuse me Zubair.' Gordon then went on to make this astonishing pronouncement: 'I consider myself free to act according to circumstances. I shall hold on here as long as I can and, if I can suppress the rebellion, I shall do so. If I cannot, I shall retire to the Equator and leave you the indelible disgrace of abandoning the garrisons of Sennar, Kassala, Berber, and Dongola, with the certainty that you will eventually be forced to smash up the Mahdi under great difficulties, if you would retain peace in Egypt.' In a further message he added: 'I do not see the force of being caught here to walk about the streets for years as a dervish with sandalled feet; not that, D.V., I will ever be taken alive.'

Gordon's contention that, with Zubair's moral authority and with the military help of British forces at Berber, he could have held Khartoum and smashed up the Mahdi is, to say the least, a highly questionable proposition. But now he knew, or accepted, that he was going to get neither British forces nor Zubair. Yet at this crucial turning-point in the story, he made up his mind completely to disregard his official instructions—which he had himself insisted 'should on no account be changed'—and to resist the irresistible force of the Mahdi's movement. Now he was not even going to evacuate the Khartoum garrison to Berber and retire himself to the Equator. Now he was proposing to hold on to Khartoum and 'suppress the rebellion' with a mere handful of Egyptian troops, who he and Stewart knew full well were in no way adequate either in numbers or in training to take on the tens of thousands of fanatical Sudanese tribesmen who had sworn allegiance to the Mahdi. If proof of their inadequacy were needed, it had been supplied less than three weeks earlier, when a local force of Ansar inflicted an ignominious defeat on his Egyptian troops, and Gordon was obliged to order the execution of the two senior officers whose treachery was held by a court martial to have contributed materially to the disaster.

Much has been made of the breakdown in telegraphic communications by certain of Gordon's more laudatory biographers to excuse his failure to evacuate the garrisons and to explain his decision to stand and defend Khartoum against overwhelming odds. It has even been implied that the relatively small force of Mahdists who cut the telegraph were also able to 'blockade' Khartoum and that, from March 12 until the Mahdi took the city ten months later, Gordon was shut up and unable to withdraw. In fact, none of these contentions stands up to critical examination. In the first instance, Gordon had no justification or authority whatever for his assumption that silence from Cairo should mean assent to his request for Zubair and British forces. On the contrary, before the telegraph was cut, every message sent to him suggested the strongest opposition in London on both counts; and he must have known that, even with Baring backing him over Zubair, the odds against the British Government granting him either request were too heavy to commit himself to 'holding on to Khartoum' and 'smashing up the Mahdi' in default of a final reply. And it is inconceivable that any responsible man in such a position and in such circumstances, who put the lives and safety of the Egyptian troops and officials and their dependents before all other considerations, should at that moment have failed to conclude that immediate evacuation was the only possible policy. Even if there are those who would excuse this failure on the grounds that at the beginning of March Gordon had not been definitely told that neither Zubair nor British forces would be coming to help him, no such excuse can possibly explain away his decision to hold on after he had himself accepted a month later that both his requests had been turned down.

As for his being blockaded, Gordon could, and did, pass his flotilla of ten steamers up and down the Blue and White Niles with no effective interference from the Mahdists for the next six months. If the Mahdists were as easy to 'smash up' as he made out, they could hardly have prevented a determined break out down the Nile. In a letter to General Baker dated April 18, Gordon described the enemy force in the vicinity of Khartoum as consisting of 'some 500 determined men and some 2,000 rag-tag Arabs'. What is more, the river region from Halfaya virtually all the way to Berber was occupied throughout by the fierce Shaggias, the one tribe which refused to join the Mahdi, while beyond Berber the Mahdist writ did not run until much later. Thus, as Baring was later to say in his account of these tragic events, while paying fulsome tribute to the heroism of a gallant soldier, Gordon could have withdrawn at almost any moment between March and May, when the Mahdi took Berber and threatened the escape route to the north. Even as late as September, steamers could still get past Berber, as was shown when Stewart went down the Nile in the

Abbas and met his death after the ship struck a rock some 200 miles downstream from Berber. And on October 1, five months after Berber had fallen to the Mahdi, Gordon himself wrote in his journal that withdrawal, although difficult, was 'not impossible'. Nor did the Nile itself present any insuperable problems. For, as the relief expedition was later to prove, the Nile steamers could navigate the cataracts without too much difficulty, even in the dry season in January. And as the spring of 1884 advanced, every week that Gordon spent in Khartoum saw the Nile growing bigger and more easily navigable.

But instead of evacuating, Gordon stayed put and, to explain his stand, pretended to the people of Khartoum that British troops were on their way and that all they had to do was to wait in patience and the Mahdi would be crushed. It was an extraordinary delusion for a man who only six weeks earlier had been told, while he was in London, that the prime aim of British Ministers was to avoid any military adventures in the interior of the Sudan. But that he should have maintained the pretence, after he had received Baring's message warning him not to expect British troops, was nothing less than a cruel deception. However fervidly he himself may have longed for martyrdom, Gordon's primary duty lay towards the garrisons whom he had been sent to extricate. That some were beyond his reach and had to be sacrificed is not at issue. But, as Baring subsequently remarked, Gordon 'was not sent to Khartoum with orders to secure the retreat of every man, woman, and child who wished to leave the Sudan ... [but] to do the best he could to carry out the evacuation'. And that he ended by sacrificing several thousands of men whom he could have saved, as well as condemning their women and children to years of slavery in the service of the Mahdi's successor, the Khalifa Abdullah, places on him a terrible responsibility before history, which all the undoubted heroism and endurance of his final stand at Khartoum cannot expunge.

CHAPTER 20

THE SIEGE OF KHARTOUM

WHILE the argument about Zubair between London and Cairo was dragging on to its final negative conclusion, two signal events took place in the Sudan. The first was the Mahdi's reply to Gordon's peace offer, which reached Khartoum on March 22. This rejected with contumely the suggestion that he should accept recognition as Sultan of Kordofan and cease all hostilities, and in its turn invited Gordon to become a Moslem and surrender. 'Know that I am the expected Mahdi, the successor of the Apostle of God,' the Mahdi wrote. 'Thus I have no need of the sultanate, nor of the Kingdom of Kordofan, nor of the wealth of this world and its vanity.... The Prophet has informed me that those who declare enmity against me shall fail and be conquered by the power of God.... If you will deliver yourself up and become a follower of the true religion, you will gain honour in this world and in the world to come, and in so doing you will save yourself and all those under you. Otherwise you shall perish with them and your sins and theirs shall be on your head.' With the letter was sent a *jibbeh*—'A filthy patched dervish's coat,' as Gordon termed it—for him to wear as a mark of true conversion to the 'true religion'. Indignantly Gordon threw the *jibbeh* away and replied: 'I have received the letter sent by your three messengers and I understand its contents; but I cannot have any more communication with you.' From now on he regarded himself as formally at war with the Mahdi.

The other signal event was the success gained by the British expeditionary force in the eastern Sudan. Osman Digna's rebels had been defeated twice in a fortnight by Graham. But, important as they were, these victories were not of themselves enough to halt the rebel movement in the east. And it soon became apparent to Graham on the spot and to Baring in Cairo that they would have to be followed up, if Osman Digna was not to rally his forces and strike back at Suakim. This meant at least attacking the Mahdists who were besieging Sinkat, if not an attempt to force open the route to Berber.

Graham was willing, even anxious, to try both courses. But Baring, after consulting the British military commanders in Egypt, Sir Frederick Stephenson and Sir Evelyn Wood, was in two minds about risking British lives in the interior of the Sudan. Having recently received depressing reports from Khartoum about the Ansar's superiority in numbers, he felt it necessary to tell London that it was of 'the utmost importance not only to open the Berber–Suakim route, but to come to terms with the tribes between Berber and Khartoum'. And he warned that failure in this respect might make it necessary to send 'an expeditionary force to Khartoum to bring away Gordon'. But, since Stephenson and Wood both held strongly that to send British troops across hundreds of miles of waterless and hostile territory in conditions of intense heat would involve a 'very great risk', he was less than whole-hearted in urging the Government to give Graham the authority which he sought.

With only feeble pressure from Cairo, London's reaction was a foregone conclusion. Granville telegraphed in the most emphatic terms that 'the Government have no intention of sending British troops to Berber' and that any attempt to reopen the route from Suakim should be confined to using influence with 'friendly tribes'. Not only that; he also ordered Graham to limit his operations to pacifying the district around Suakim. His recent victories against Osman Digna had had a mixed reception in Britain and the Government had been attacked for allowing an indiscriminate massacre of unarmed tribesmen. Therefore Graham was told to bring the operations to 'a speedy conclusion' and prepare for the 'immediate embarkation of the bulk of your force'.

Baring was greatly alarmed by this message. And in his reply he asked Granville to put himself in Gordon's position and, if he could not offer any immediate help, at least to persuade the Government to send an expedition in the early autumn, if Gordon should still be holding out in Khartoum. 'This would at all events give him some hope,' Baring argued, 'and the mere announcement of the intention of the Government would go a long way to ensure his safety by keeping loyal the tribes who may be still wavering. No one can regret more than I do the necessity of sending British or Indian troops to the Sudan; but, having sent

Gordon to Khartoum, it appears to me that it is our bounden duty, both as a matter of humanity and policy, not to abandon him.'

Baring could hardly have done more to argue Gordon's case, and this eloquent and sympathetic plea that his emissary should be saved from the consequences of his own stubborn disregard of his instructions offers a more than adequate answer to the slighting criticisms recorded in Gordon's Khartoum journal that Baring let him down at nearly every turn. ('Baring deigned to say he would support me,' Gordon later wrote in an unworthily sarcastic comment on the exchanges with London about Zubair.) In fact, it would be truer to say that it was Gordon who let down Baring. For while Baring was arguing with London the urgent need to ensure Gordon's safety by sending a British expeditionary force, Gordon was reporting that 'for the present and for the next two months we are as safe here as in Cairo. . . . I wish I could convey to you the truly trumpery nature of the revolt which 500 determined men could put down.' And when he received through Cuzzi early in April a message saying that any attempt to open up the Berber–Suakim route would have to be by negotiations with the tribes rather than by the use of British forces, he confidently told Baring: 'We are all right up here and your telegram to Cuzzi did not give me a "twitter".'

This was hardly the spirit to impress a reluctant Government that the plight of Khartoum warranted the commitment of British forces in the Sudan. And, not surprisingly, it confirmed Gladstone's Cabinet in their decision not to be drawn into further operations against the Mahdi. All that they would concede to Baring was that a British officer, Major (later Field-Marshal) Kitchener, should be sent up the Nile to Berber to maintain contact with Khartoum. As for the eastern Sudan, the relief of Sinkat was shortly afterwards abandoned and the greater portion of Graham's force was withdrawn, leaving only a small contingent to defend Suakim and nothing to reopen the route to Berber. And although Queen Victoria now weighed in with a plea that Indian troops be sent to save Khartoum, the Government were able to quote in reply to her appeal Gordon's own reassuring assertions that Khartoum had six months' provisions and could not be taken by assault.

There is no doubt that Gladstone's Government were extremely tardy in failing to prepare for a relief expedition after they knew that the Mahdi had taken Berber and was sitting astride the Nile escape route to the north. But they can scarcely be held to account for refusing to send troops in March or April when the Nile route was still open for Gordon to carry out his instructions and withdraw and when Khartoum was said to be 'as safe as Cairo' and was known to have provisions for six months. What is more, their hesitation at this time is still more understandable when viewed in the light of Gordon's clear intention to use any troops that might be sent, not to help evacuation, but to 'smash up the Mahdi'. Time and again Gordon reverted to this theme of crushing the revolt. And when Baring told him that no British troops would be sent, he promptly asked for Turkish forces to finish off the Mahdi. 'If you would only put your pride in your pocket and get by good pay 3,000 Turkish infantry and 1,000 Turkish cavalry,' he told him, 'the whole affair, including the crushing of the Mahdi, would be accomplished in four months.'

In a further message to Baring, he said that the Sudan should be handed over to Turkey and that he had telegraphed to Sir Samuel Baker to make an appeal to British and American millionaires to give him £300,000 to engage a Turkish force to 'settle the Sudan and the Mahdi for ever'. And a week later, after addressing similar appeals to the Pope and to the European consuls in Khartoum, he petitioned the Ottoman Sultan direct, saying that 'the presence of 3,000 of Your Majesty's troops supported by the prestige of Your Majesty's name and at a cost of £300,000 would be sufficient to suppress the revolt and destroy the rebels. ... These men will not have to fire a shot; the rebels will dissolve as ice before fire.'

It is incredible that anyone should have seriously suggested that 3,000 troops of any nationality would be sufficient to suppress the Mahdi's revolt, supported as it now was by tens of thousands of well-armed tribesmen. But that Gordon should have advocated the use of a handful of Turkish troops to put down the rebellion shows that he not only underestimated the Mahdi's strength, but that he also took no account of the fanatical hatred of his followers for 'Turks' above all people on earth. Better in their eyes a nation of devout Christians than the sacrilegious Turks, who, while pretending the true religion, had profaned and prostituted the Moslem faith and had oppressed and made prisoners the Arab people from North Africa to the Indian Ocean. Not all the armies of the Turkish Sultan could have pacified the Sudan and stamped out Mahdism, let alone a force of 3,000.

When he arrived at Khartoum in February, Gordon seemed to have understood the bitter feelings that existed in the Sudan against the Turks. In an obvious bid for popular sympathy, he announced publicly that while 'the Sultan had the intention of sending an expedition of strong Turkish troops to subdue the rebellious provinces ... I prevented the despatch of this expedition for the present and I have come in person, praising God, to prevent war between Moslems.' And although his statement was a complete fabrication, it impressed some people that in Gordon they had a champion against Turkish oppression. But all this was forgotten and, in a characteristic volte-face, he was now saying that the Sultan should take over the Sudan and that all that was needed to suppress Mahdism was a brigade of Turkish troops.

There was, however, one man in Khartoum who had never subscribed to the view that the Mahdi's revolt was a 'trumpery' affair. Power, *The Times* correspondent, had described Khartoum's plight as critical ever since the Hicks disaster. And on April 1 a report of his appeared in *The Times* which sent a sudden shock of alarm through Parliament and Press. 'We are daily expecting British troops,' Power wrote, no doubt under the beguiling influence of Gordon's repeated assurances that relief was on the way. 'We cannot bring ourselves to believe that we are to be abandoned by the Government.'

For a brief moment the issue of a relief expedition hung in the balance. Knowing that Power's 'expectations' were based on an illusion and seizing on the word 'abandoned', the Parliamentary Opposition staged an immediate debate, and demanded that troops be sent immediately to relieve Khartoum. But they reckoned without the rhetorical powers of the Prime Minister. Leaping in to defend the Government's policy, Gladstone accused the Opposition of doing Gordon the utmost disservice by spreading alarm and despondency on the basis of a report by a mere Consular Agent (Power combined the duties of British Consul with those of *The Times* correspondent in Khartoum). 'A Consular Agent,' Gladstone pointed out, 'is not an officer responsible to the

Government.... He is perfectly free and in the expression of his opinions he is as unrestrained as are the honourable gentlemen who sit opposite—and I cannot say more. And yet the right honourable gentleman, the Leader of the Opposition, takes the opinion of Mr. Power, transmitted to *The Times*, as virtually equivalent to an official declaration of policy, conveying the mature conviction of General Gordon. Really, sir, it is a farce to treat it in such a spirit ... and out of all proportion to the pressure and urgency of the question.'

This clever piece of rhetoric turned the Parliamentary scale against the despatch of British troops to the Sudan. In the words of one of Gladstone's colleagues, the Prime Minister's retort completely 'withered' the Opposition and made them 'scuttle' before the blast of his bitter irony. But while the Conservative Opposition had been effectively silenced by Gladstone's parliamentary skill, it was not so easy to answer Baring—and Baring was daily becoming more concerned for Gordon's safety. Telegraphing to London two weeks after the House of Commons debate, he warned that Khartoum might not be as safe as Gordon made out and that 'no time should be lost in making preparations' for his relief. He might be able to extricate himself without help from outside, but 'It would be better to run the risk of incurring some unnecessary expenditure than to find ourselves unable to seize the opportunity of moving when the favourable moment arrives.'

These ominous words from the man on the spot made a profound impression on Gladstone and his colleagues, which, if anything, was deepened by the coincidental arrival of a message from Cairo saying that Gordon was now asking for Turkish troops to help him to crush the Mahdi. Their response was prompt. 'Gordon should be at once informed,' they replied on April 23, 'by several messengers at some intervals between each, through Dongola as well as Berber, or in such other way as may be on the spot deemed most prompt and certain, that he should keep us informed, to the best of his ability, not only as to the immediate but as to any prospective danger at Khartoum; that, to be prepared for any such danger, he advise as to the force necessary in order to secure his removal, its amount, character, route for access to Khartoum and time of operation; that we do not propose to supply him with Turkish or other forces for the purpose of undertaking military expeditions, such being beyond the scope of the commission he holds, and at variance with his pacific policy, which was the purpose of his mission to the Sudan; that if with this knowledge he continues at Khartoum, he should state to us the cause and intention with which he so continues. Add expression both of respect and gratitude for the gallant and self-sacrificing conduct and for the good he has achieved.'

It is clear from this message that Gladstone's Government, while still determined to discourage Gordon from trying to crush the Mahdi, were having second thoughts about the need to relieve him. But, alas the 'several messengers' sent to deliver this communication did not reach Khartoum until three months later, on July 29. During this critical period the Government were left without any answers to the questions they had asked. And because, not unnaturally, they attributed this lack of response to Gordon's perversity rather than to a breakdown in communications, they did nothing meanwhile to prepare for a relief expedition from Egypt. On the contrary; when the Parliamentary Opposition returned to the charge on May 12, Gladstone argued that the sending of an army to the Sudan meant 'a war of conquest against a people struggling to be free ... and rightly struggling to be free'. And the utmost that the Government would concede was an assurance by Hartington that if the withdrawal of the Egyptian garrisons and the establishment of settled government could not be achieved, 'then I believe that the country would be prepared to grudge no sacrifice to save the life and honour of General Gordon'.

It was the first public admission by the Government that a relief force might be necessary. Following it up five days later, Granville sent a further message on May 17, saying that evacuation of the outlying garrisons was now out of the question. Reminding Gordon that offensive operations could not be undertaken without the Government's sanction, he asked him to 'report upon, or if feasible adopt, at the first proper moment, measures for his own removal and for that of the Egyptians at Khartoum ... by whatever route he may consider best'. Gordon was to 'make free use of money rewards or promises' to the tribes to ensure the safe passage of the garrison and their families.

But, like its precursor of April 23, this message took three months to reach Gordon, owing to the comparative difficulty of finding messengers prepared to go to Khartoum, as opposed to escaping from it. And long before it arrived—indeed, only nine days after it was sent from London—the Mahdi struck the most serious blow so far in his struggle with Gordon by seizing Berber. The Mudir, Hussein Khalifa, was taken prisoner, together with Cuzzi, who embraced the Moslem faith to save himself and his family from death—for which apostasy he was never forgiven by his uncompromising chief in Khartoum.

Gordon responded to these reverses by intensifying the work which had been going on for the past month to prepare Khartoum for a siege. Land-mines were placed at strategic points along the four miles of ramparts guarding the land approaches to the city. Wire entanglements were set up and the river steamers were equipped with armoured protection. The garrison was strengthened by recruiting a number of volunteers and by forming a force of Negro troops, drawn largely from the former slaves of Sudanese who had gone over to the Mahdi. A Negro commander, Faragh Pasha, was put in charge of this force, which became the most dependable military unit in the capital. To maintain morale among those who fell sick or were wounded, Gordon instituted— probably for the first time in any modern army—a form of occupational therapy. Due to a shortage of specie, a special paper currency was issued bearing the Governor-General's stamp, together with Gordon's personal seal and a facsimile of his signature. The notes, redeemable in six months' time in Cairo or Khartoum, were of every denomination from 1 to 50,000 piastres (of £50 Sudanese). Each was signed 'C. G. Gordon', except for the £50 note, which boasted 'C. G. Gordon, Major-General'. Finally, to reward acts of gallantry, medals were struck in silver-gilt, silver and pewter, bearing the inscription 'Siege of Khartoum'.

A month after the fall of Berber, the Mahdi sent Cuzzi to Khartoum with a further letter inviting Gordon to surrender. But Gordon refused to see his former agent and sent back a reply direct to Mohammed Ahmed, saying, 'As you well know, the Mohammedans who are with me do not wish to surrender. Do you expect that I who am a Christian should set the example?' And, finally, with a cut at the unfortunate Cuzzi: 'If you have letters to send to me again, do not send a European, but some of your own people.' The Mahdi's answer was prompt and vigorous. Abu Girgeh, one of his most trusted army commanders, was sent to clamp a tight blockade on all the land approaches to Khartoum, and from now on the palace, which had hitherto suffered only an occasional fusillade of rifle-fire from the north bank of the Blue Nile, was under more or less constant attack. At the same time, pursuing his tactic of starving his enemies into submission, the Mahdi sought to close the Blue Nile to Gordon's steamers, which had been profiting from the spring rise in the river level to collect corn and cattle from Sennar. But Gordon was not having his river forage lines severed with impunity, and on July 29 he struck with a force commanded by his best general, Mohammed Ali Bey, drove the rebels from their positions near the river banks and cleared a passage for his steamers.

On the same day he received the Government's long-delayed telegram of April 23, asking for information as to his situation and for advice on the need for a relief force, and its timing, routing and strength. So much had changed—and for the worse—since the telegram had been despatched three months before, that some of its contents must have seemed laughable to its recipient. And Gordon, making no allowance for the long delay in its delivery, could not resist carping in a letter to the Khedive that the Government 'do not state what are their intentions and only ask for information and waste time'. Completely forgetting his earlier telegrams about Khartoum being as safe as Cairo, he even more unfairly blamed the Government for the fact that people were beginning to lose confidence in his repeated announcements that British troops were on their way to the Sudan. 'Thus,' he told Tewfik, 'through having so often promised the people of Khartoum that assistance would come, we are now as liars in their eyes.' In the same letter he reverted to the subject of Zubair, whose presence, he persisted, was essential 'to render it possible to extinguish the flame of the false Mahdi before it becomes difficult'. And he said he intended to break out and retake Berber and burn it, and then send Stewart to Dongola, while he himself returned to Khartoum. 'It will be impossible,' he concluded, 'to leave Khartoum without a regular government established by some power. I will look after the troops on the Equator, Bahr-el-Ghazal, and in Darfur, although it may cost me my life.'

In his reply to Granville's enquiries, Gordon was little less carping or unreasonable. 'Be assured,' he began, 'that the hostilities are far from being sought for, but we have no option.' Glossing over the fact that he could have withdrawn at any time between February 18, when he arrived at Khartoum, and May 26, when the Mahdi took Berber, he said: 'You ask me to state cause and intention in staying in Khartoum, knowing the Government means to abandon the Sudan; and in answer, I say I stay at Khartoum because the Arabs have shut us up and will not let us out.' And he concluded his reply with these cheerless comments about a possible route for a relief expedition: 'As for routes, I have told you that the one from Wadi Halfa along the right bank of the Nile to Berber is the best and, had not Berber fallen, would have been a picnic.... But I fear it is too late. We must fight it out by our own means; if blessed by God, we shall succeed; if not His Will, so be it.'

CHAPTER 21

THE RELIEF EXPEDITION

WHILE Gordon was penning these caustic and despondent messages, a crucial debate was raging within Gladstone's Cabinet about the pros and cons of sending a relief expedition to the Sudan. What prompted this heated ministerial discussion was a message sent by Gordon to the Mudir of Dongola in the last week of June, which, after taking nearly a month to reach its destination, was flashed to Cairo and thence to London on July 20. This message, which, for better concealment on the courier, was written by Gordon's Arabic scribe on a scrap of paper no bigger than a large postage-stamp, ran as follows: 'Khartoum and Sennar are well maintained, and the bearer will give you the news when he reaches you. Give him what news you have, especially regarding the direction and position of the relieving force and their number. In Khartoum we have more than 8,000 soldiers and the Nile is rapidly rising. Please give the bearer 100 reals on the State. C. G. Gordon.'

It was scarcely the message of a man *in extremis* and, like Gordon's earlier reports on the situation of Khartoum, suggested an air of confident defiance. But there were several things about it that made Ministers in London very uneasy. In the first place, it was clearly not sent in answer to either of the Government's telegrams of April 23 and May 17, asking for advice and information about the sending of a relief force. Presumably, therefore, neither of these telegrams had yet reached Khartoum. Moreover, if Gordon were really so confident about his situation, why did he enquire about the location and strength of a relief expedition which he had no grounds to expect? Such words from a man who three months earlier had been talking of 'smashing' the Mahdi and suppressing the rebellion suggested a serious worsening of his position.

The first reaction of Ministers was to make one last attempt to contact Gordon and secure a reply to their earlier enquiries. And on July 24 instructions were sent to Cairo to repeat the telegrams of April 23 and May 17 to Khartoum once again, and to tell Gordon that, as he would see from these messages, the Government were concerned for his safety and anxious 'to learn from himself his views and position, so that if danger has arisen or is likely to arise ... they may be in a position to take measures accordingly'. But a nagging anxiety had seized Gladstone's Government and, on the very next day when the Cabinet met, a majority of Ministers expressed their conviction that plans should be made for a relief expedition without further delay. Gordon was clearly cut off, and precious time would be wasted by waiting for him to reply to the Government's enquiries. Nine Ministers, including Hartington, were for immediate action, three were for waiting and one was neutral. But the three included Gladstone and the neutral was Granville. And so for the next four days no action was taken.

Then on July 29, the day when Gordon finally received the Government's message of April 23, Hartington forced the issue. He regarded himself as pledged by his statement to the House of Commons in May that 'this country will be prepared to grudge no sacrifice to spare the life and honour of General Gordon'. And, under a threat of resignation, he insisted that plans should be made for a relief expedition before Parliament was prorogued in August at the end of its current session, when it would be impossible to secure proper Parliamentary authority for the despatch of British troops. Gladstone realized that Hartington's resignation on such an issue would probably bring down the Government. The *Pall Mall Gazette* had already got wind of the fact that a minority of the Cabinet led by the Prime Minister were blocking a decision to send a relief force, and in a recent editorial had asserted that the Government were prepared to 'let Gordon be speared with the garrisons he was sent to save'. Accordingly, Gladstone gave way, and on August 5 he personally moved the motion that, 'a sum not exceeding £300,000 be granted to Her Majesty, beyond the ordinary grants of Parliament of 1884-5, to enable Her Majesty to undertake operations for the relief of General Gordon, should they become necessary, and to make certain preparations in respect thereof'. The motion was carried by an overwhelming majority, and on September 9 Lord Wolseley arrived in Egypt to take command of the expedition.

Meanwhile, in Khartoum Gordon's fortunes were fluctuating. In the month of August his able and courageous commander, Mohammed Ali Bey, gained a series of successes against the besieging Ansar. Penetrating 100 miles up the Blue Nile, he captured a large quantity of arms and provisions. He followed this up by overrunning the Mahdist camp at Halfaya, north of Khartoum, and then went on to deal a heavy blow at the local Sheikh el-Obeid, a powerful new recruit to the Mahdi's cause, whom he forced to abandon his villages and flee into the interior. But as Mohammed Ali and his men set off in pursuit of the fleeing tribesmen, they were caught in an ambush in the thickly wooded area on the right bank of the Blue Nile and were cut to pieces by a horde of shrieking Ansar.

It was a crushing blow, which deprived Gordon both of his ablest commander and of the pick of his troops, on whom he was relying to attempt the recapture of Berber. Now his plans had to be changed and the break-out against Berber abandoned. To make matters worse, news had just reached him that the Mahdi was moving a large new force of his Ansar, equipped with heavy guns, to assist in the siege of Khartoum. During the holy month of Ramadhan, from June 25 to July 25, Mohammed Ahmed had observed Moslem ritual and taken no offensive action. But now he was beginning to close in and, after the reverses suffered by his Ansar in August, he had ordered a general advance from Kordofan with his entire army, and sent his most trusted commander, Wad el-Nejumi, to take over supreme command of his forces investing Khartoum. Two weeks later he sent Cuzzi once more with a summons to Gordon to surrender, and another *jibbeh*; and when the unfortunate Italian was again rebuffed, further pressure was brought by Wad el-Nejumi to persuade Khartoum's defender to give in and save himself and his garrison from being destroyed.

The noose was beginning to tighten, and Gordon now decided to send Stewart down the Nile, together with Power and the French Consul, Herbin, with orders to force his way past Berber and to report by telegraph from Dongola the true position of Khartoum. At the same time, in the last letter that he was to send to Baring, he wrote a gloomy, and reproachful, account of his plight and his need for reinforcements. 'While you are eating and drinking and resting on good beds,' he said, 'we and those with us, both soldiers and servants, are watching by night and day, endeavouring to quell the movement of this false Mahdi.... The reason why I have now sent Colonel Stewart is because you have been silent all this while and neglected us, and lost time without doing any good. If troops are sent as soon as they reach Berber, this rebellion will cease.... It is therefore hoped that you will listen to all that is told you by Stewart and the Consuls and look at it seriously, and send troops as we have asked without any delay.'

On September 9 Stewart, Power, and Herbin left Khartoum in the steamer *Abbas*, carrying Gordon's cypher key to prevent it falling into the Mahdi's hands, together with detailed reports of the strength of the Khartoum garrison, their equipment and provisions. The steamers *Safia* and *Mansura* acted as escorts, and a couple of sailing boats were towed along behind, in case the *Abbas* should be unable to negotiate the Nile cataracts. All went surprisingly well to start with. The three steamers and the two sailing boats traversed the Sixth Cataract with no difficulty and, although peppered by desultory rifle fire near Metemma, managed to pass Berber without interference. So easy was the passage past these danger-points that Stewart felt safe enough to send the escorting steamers back to Khartoum and to cut the sailing boats adrift to enable the *Abbas* to make faster progress. A hundred miles beyond Berber the little steamer seemed to justify Stewart's confidence by negotiating the Fifth Cataract without incident. But then, nine days out from Khartoum and just as success was in sight, disaster struck. Beyond Abu Hamed, where the river divides into two channels, the *Abbas* took the wrong course and stuck fast on a rock. With no sailing boats to come to their rescue, Stewart, Power, and Herbin climbed into a small dinghy and were preparing to continue their journey as best they could, when a man appeared on the river bank with a white flag. Stewart, a credulous and dangerously over-confident character, pulled into the shore and, when the man professed to be a friendly sheikh and offered him camels to take him to Dongola, he and his two companions followed their self-appointed guide to his village. But as they sat in his house waiting to discuss arrangements, a group of Ansar rushed in. After a brief struggle, Stewart, Power, and Herbin were done to death, and Gordon's detailed reports about the situation of the Khartoum garrison were seized and sent to the Mahdi.

The news of this disaster did not reach Khartoum until the beginning of October, when the Mahdi wrote to inform Gordon and, to prove his point, gave particulars of the messages and documents which Stewart was carrying to Dongola. But in the meantime a further blow was struck, when the steamers collecting grain up the Blue Nile suffered a ferocious bombardment from the Mahdi's newly installed artillery. The *Bordein*'s home-made armour-plating proved so thin that, after she suffered a direct hit from the Mahdi's shore batteries, she limped back to base with a hole two feet in diameter just above her water-line. And Gordon reluctantly decided not to hazard this vital arm of his defence on further foraging expeditions. Thus, as the month of September wore on, the tide was turning rapidly against the defenders of Khartoum, the Mahdi was closing in with weapons equal in fire-power to anything possessed by the defending garrison and with vastly superior numbers, and the principal source of the garrison's food supplies had been effectively cut off.

Meanwhile, a message sent by Gordon on July 13 saying, 'We are all well and can hold out for four months,' had reached Cairo, soon after the news that Parliament had voted the appropriation for the relief expedition. And Mr. E. H. Egerton—who was deputizing as Consul-General while Baring was temporarily absent attending a conference in London on Egypt's finances—instructed Major Kitchener, then at Debba, south of Dongola, to tell Gordon the news and to ask when he expected to be in difficulties over provisions and ammunition. Kitchener had, however, anticipated his instructions and, in a letter dated August 22, he informed Gordon that 'the relief expedition is evidently coming this way, but whether they will go by Berber or attempt the direct road from here I do not know'.

This letter reached Khartoum on September 20, together with another from Colonel Floyer, the Inspector of Telegraphs at Dongola, which was more precise and said that three infantry regiments, plus a regiment of cavalry and another of mounted infantry, were under orders to proceed to the Sudan. And two days later, two more letters came from Kitchener telling Gordon that two brigades were to be sent under Wolseley's supreme command and that part of the expedition would proceed overland to

Khartoum from Dongola, while the other part went by steamer to Berber. 'A few words about what you wish done would be very acceptable,' was his final, matter-of-fact comment.

Khartoum received the news with rejoicing. Notices, illustrated with pictures of British and Sudanese soldiers, were posted all over the city announcing that relief was on the way, and the Ansar armies beyond the ramparts were treated to a salute of three rounds from each of the garrison's twelve guns. Gordon himself seized on the news to show that he had been right all along in saying that British troops were coming to Khartoum. And in an even more flagrant distortion of the truth he announced that, whereas 'formerly the Government had decided to transport the Egyptians down to Cairo and to abandon the Sudan, on our arrival at Khartoum, on account of pity for you and in order not to let your country be destroyed, we communicated with the Khedive of Egypt concerning the importance and inexpediency of abandoning it; whereupon orders for abandoning the Sudan were cancelled, and all energy was directed towards smoothing the disturbances and driving away the disturbers. Therefore sufficient troops were appointed, both cavalry and infantry, some time ago and indeed they have reached Dongola and started in three divisions. Each of these divisions is alone sufficient to oppose all the rebels. They will soon be in Khartoum. Be therefore fully reassured as to yourselves, your families, and all your possessions.... If God wills, the siege will be raised and your alarm will pass away.'

But Gordon's expectations for the relief expedition's progress were to prove dangerously over-optimistic. A survey had been done of the Nile in May and June with a view to preparing plans for sending a force to Dongola in case of need, and an advance party had been sent to Wadi Halfa to be ready to make a dash for Dongola at short notice. But, despite these timely precautions, the main expedition was delayed by a dispute between Wolseley and the military authorities in Cairo as to whether it should go by the Nile route or should try to force its way from Suakim across to Berber. This was settled in favour of the Nile route. But then a further delay was caused by Wolseley insisting on transporting the relief force in specially constructed boats similar to the type which he had used on the Red River Expedition in Canada fourteen years earlier, instead of making do with the native boats which had been collected at Dongola for this very purpose. Wolseley argued that these boats would be able to pass the cataracts at low water more easily than the keeled native craft. But his stubborn adherence to this plan meant that the 7,000-strong expedition lost several precious weeks before it was able to embark on the first stage of its journey to the Sudan. And it was not until September 30 that Wolseley reached Aswan with the main force, while on the same day a small advance guard of 250 mounted infantry under Sir Herbert Stewart was entering the town of Dongola.

Gordon had by now decided that, since his steamers could no longer be used for foraging up the Blue Nile, three of them should be sent down to meet the relief force and show the flag to the still loyal Shaggias on the right bank of the river between Khartoum and Berber. But while he pretended outwardly that his action would result in the arrival of British troops within a matter of days, or at least in the recapture of Berber, whose population he claimed were 'never very much inclined to the Mahdi', his innermost feelings were by no means so sanguine. Ever since Stewart's departure on September 9 he had had a strong premonition of disaster. And five days afterwards, in the journal which he now kept—being unable to communicate with any certainty with the outside world and having no Europeans to converse with except the Austrian Consul, Hansal, whom he hated—he wrote this revealing reflection: 'I toss up in my mind whether, if the place is taken, to blow up the palace and all in it, or else be taken and, with God's help, to maintain the faith and, if necessary, to suffer for it (which is most probable). The blowing up of the palace is the simplest, while the other means long and weary suffering and humiliation of all sorts. I think I shall elect for the last, not from fear of death, but because the former has the taint of suicide, as it can do no good to anyone and is, in a way, taking things out of God's hands.'

His strong religious beliefs did not allow him to commit suicide and to 'take things out of God's hands'; but he had been perfectly prepared to force God's hand by holding out in Khartoum when he could have withdrawn and when he knew that holding out meant eventual certain death. And, to underline his determination to die a martyr for his cause, he wrote in his journal on September 24, after receiving Kitchener's messages about the relief force: 'I altogether *decline* the imputation that the projected expedition has come to *relieve me*. It has come to *save our national honour* in extricating the garrison, etc., from a position our action in Egypt has placed these garrisons. I was a Relief Expedition No. 1. They are Relief Expedition No. 2.... I am not the *rescued lamb* and I will not be.'

Thus did Gordon try to salve his conscience about the Egyptian troops and officials whom he had failed to withdraw. And the joy that he felt over the news that relief was on the way was for the garrisons, not for himself. 'I declare *positively and once for all*', he wrote on November 9, '*that I will not leave the Sudan until everyone who wants to go down is given the chance to do so, unless* a government is established which relieves me of the charge; therefore if any emissary or letter come up here ordering me to come down, I WILL NOT OBEY IT, BUT WILL STAY HERE AND FALL WITH THE TOWN AND RUN ALL RISKS.' Let the garrison go back with the relief force, but without him. His search for martyrdom would not permit him to be 'the rescued lamb'.

CHAPTER 22

RECRIMINATION AND REFLECTION

GORDON's efforts to salve his conscience were not really successful. Page after page of his Khartoum journal discloses a sense of personal failure, and the more he tried to blame his blunders on everybody but himself, the more obvious it became that his conscience was troubling him sorely indeed. And how he laid about him against his chosen scapegoats! Interlarded between speculations about the Mahdi's movements and instructions to the relief expedition on how to proceed, the journal contains a ceaseless flow of vituperation against the Government, Baring, his Egyptian troops, the relief force's commanders, the Intelligence Department—even down to the wayward sentries who fell asleep at their posts or deserted the lines to forage in the town. All these elements had combined, consciously or unconsciously, to thwart him in his task. How could he set up a stable government without Zubair? How could he extricate the garrisons with Berber in the Mahdi's hands and without British troops? How could he 'smash the Mahdi' with a bunch of cowards and incompetents for soldiers? Above all, how could he be expected to abandon the other garrisons, such as that at Sennar, for instance, and make an ignominious retreat down the Nile with the garrison of Khartoum? '*On fait ce qu'on peut*' was never Gordon's motto. If others wished to adopt it and relieve only Khartoum, let them come and do so, and at the same time relieve him of his responsibility. He would 'fall with the town'. But let the garrison be escorted to safety by the British relief column if, as he fervently prayed, help should arrive in time. For they must somehow be spared the fate which he wished for himself.

Hence Gordon's journal was pitted with vexatious comments about the slowness of the British advance and the lack of information as to their movements. Baring was singled out for especially harsh criticism for refusing an expedition to open up the Suakim–Berber route and for allowing Berber to fall into the Mahdi's hands. 'If Berber had not been taken, it would have been a picnic. Baring!! Baring!!' he wrote. Baring was responsible for Cuzzi 'betraying Berber' because he had *openly* announced that no troops would come up to Berber'. Baring and the Government were to blame for not saying at the very outset, 'We do not care—we will do nothing for the garrisons of the Sudan; they may perish.' They should have told him, 'Shift for yourself in March, when I could have done so, and not now when I am in honour bound to the people.' Baring had suppressed his telegrams which showed 'up to the 12th March the exact position of affairs up here'. Baring had 'told me I was not to leave Khartoum for the Equator'. Baring was pompous—he 'would never laugh, it is too serious, like jesting in church'—and a time-server who obeyed the Government's instructions to the letter and who would have infinitely preferred the Mahdi to finish off Khartoum and all the garrisons to taking any step to help Gordon which had not been endorsed and re-endorsed by London. And when he came across a reference in an old *Army List* to a book by Baring, written as an artillery captain and entitled *Rules for Conduct of the War Game*, he could not resist the biting comment: 'A nice way he has manoeuvred us and carried on his war game.'

As for the British Government, Gordon delighted in satirizing ministers with imaginary accounts of conversations, sometimes illustrated by cartoons, featuring Granville and others sitting in Parliament or luxuriating in the comfort of their castles and expressing horror and indignation that Khartoum was still, most inconveniently, holding out and that 'that duffer the Mahdi' had not yet bestirred himself to write '*Finis*' to Gordon and his garrisons. So little did they care or know about the Sudan, he suggested, that they could not differentiate between the town of El Obeid and the Sheikh el-Obeid. Typical of his satirical outpourings was this entry for October 23:

'House of Lords. Lord Granville in answer to questions put by the Marquess of Salisbury replied that the noble marquis seemed to take a special delight in asking questions which he knew he, Granville, could not answer.... He frankly acknowledged that the names of places and people were so mixed up that it was impossible to get a true view of the case (a laugh). The noble marquis asked what the policy of Her Majesty's Government was?

It was as if he asked the policy of a log floating downstream, it was going to the sea as anyone with an ounce of brains could see.... His Lordship deprecated the frequent questioning on subjects which, as His Lordship had said, he knew nothing about and further did not care to know anything about.'

The Mahdi's rebellion and the terrible loss of life which it had caused in the Sudan were the fault of such men as Sir Auckland Colvin, Sir Edward Malet, Sir Charles Dilke, and Lord Dufferin, who, by siding with the bondholders, had bled Egypt white and prevented her from taking steps to nip the revolt in the bud. 'Three prominent undeniable facts exist,' he wrote in an unpublished section of the journal on November 18. 'Her Majesty's Government refused to help Egypt with respect to the Sudan, refused to let Egypt help herself and refused to allow any other power to help her.... I can imagine no more formidable indictment against a ministry, and no success with the present expedition can possibly enable Her Majesty's Government to justify their policy, which was alike selfish and inhuman.'

Even the wretched Kitchener, sitting at Debba and trying to communicate with Gordon by courier, did not escape the lash of Gordon's satire, and was frequently blamed for the lack of information about the relief expedition's movements. 'Hurrah! Capital news!' Kitchener was supposed to have said on hearing that the Mahdi was closing in on Khartoum. 'The Mahdi has *him* on the hip! He has gone to Omdurman. Bottled him up now! He will make no more impertinent remarks about the Intelligence Departments.' In fact, everyone was out of step except Gordon; and all his failures were due to a persistent misunderstanding of his motives and policy by the Government at home, by Baring in Cairo and by Kitchener on the Nile. He must be 'perfect poison' to Ministers, he had decided, and so they and their henchmen in Cairo wanted to see him eliminated, and the sooner the better.

Deliberately ignoring the clear distinction which had been made by the Government between the interior of the Sudan, which he was to evacuate, and the Red Sea ports, which they were to try to hold, he wrote on October 8: 'If it was right to let Sinkat perish, it was right to let Tokar; if it was right to relieve Tokar, it was right to see after Berber and thence on to Khartoum, Sennar, Kassala, Bahr-el-Ghazal, and the Equator.' Disingenuously, he added that, if the Government had decided against extricating all the garrisons, then they should have told him so in March and he would have made his own arrangements—'a bolt to the Equator'. 'There would be no dishonour in that for, as I had no relief coming, the only sequel to my staying with them would be to be a prisoner,' he added, overlooking the fact that he never had any reason to expect relief in March and that, as Baring said, he was sent to withdraw as many garrisons as he could.

Added to all this, he continued to harp on about the importance of Zubair. 'We must instal Zubair with a subsidy or give over the country to the Sultan [of Turkey] with a subsidy,' he wrote on September 18. 'There is no option. If it is determined to do neither, but to evacuate pure and simply, then when the Sennar garrison is brought down, give me the steamers and the black troops who are willing to go and let me take them up to the Equator, while the expeditionary force goes down to Berber.... Zubair's coming up when I asked for him would have, I think, saved Berber and greatly facilitated the getting down of *those* garrisons which we only care for because it is a *palpable* dishonour to abandon them.' As late as December 13, when he was about to pen his last letters to the outside world, saying 'the game is up', he was actually engaged in drawing up a detailed memorandum on 'the sort of arrangement I would make with Zubair Pasha for the future government of the Sudan'! And to enable him to appoint Zubair without conflicting with his duties as a British serving officer, he sent with his last letters his formal resignation of his Army commission, together with a reminder to the relief expedition's commander that he was henceforth only the servant of the Khedive, '*Soi-disant* ruler of this land,' who had appointed him Governor-General. In this capacity it was in his power 'to appoint any other person I may select as provisionally Governor-General, subject to the approval of Tewfik Pasha, and to hand over the government to him'. All these elaborate preparations were, he explained, so as to have a plan ready for the arrival of the British relief force which he could promulgate as the Khedive's Governor-General, and so absolve the British Government from any responsibility for appointing Zubair as his successor, while he himself would be free to drive the Mahdi back to Kordofan!

At other times he made out that, if abandonment was to be the policy, Abd el-Kader was the man to succeed him, since he 'would be under no such obligations as I am to the soldiers, etc., of these beleaguered places and Her Majesty's Government could put it all on him if anything was said'. And again, when in a more militant mood, he advocated handing the Sudan over to the Turks with a bribe to the Sultan of £2,000,000: 'The time has gone by when Zubair, almost alone, would suffice; he would now need aid in men, while the Turks would need no aid from us in men. Therefore give the country to the Turks ... and you would get off all responsibility of Kassala and Sennar and the bother of the Equator and Bahr-el-Ghazal, if it has not fallen.... The more I think of it, the more the Turkish solution appears Hobson's choice.'

Also included in the journal were some light touches about the palace turkey-cock, which made a habit of eating its young, and about the horrors of social life in England: 'I would sooner live like a Dervish with the Mahdi than go out to dinner every night in London.' And there were some graphic descriptions of life in Khartoum under siege conditions: 'One tumbles at 3 a.m. into a troubled sleep; a drum beats—tup! tup! tup! It comes into a dream, but after a few minutes ... it is recalled to the brain that one is in Khartoum. The next query is: where is this tup-tupping going on? A hope arises it will die away. No, it goes on and increases in intensity.... At last, it is no use, up one must get— and go on to the roof of the palace; then telegrams, orders, swearing, and cursing goes on till about 9 a.m. ...'

There are also some disarming passages in which Gordon admitted that he 'led officers and officials the life of dogs while I have been up here', and that they trembled before him, so that they could not 'hold the match to their cigarette'. And he was generous in his praise of those who fought the Mahdi with determination and courage, such as his late commander, Mohammed Ali, and Faragh Pasha, who succeeded him, and also the Mudir of Dongola, who had beaten off four Ansar attacks and whom he made a Pasha and recommended for the Order of St. Michael and St. George. But he had no sympathy or understanding for those who betrayed their faith to save their lives. On hearing that some nuns captured at El Obeid had married their fellow captives, who were Greek merchants, to save themselves from being forced to become their captors' concubines, he

252

mockingly remarked: 'What a row the Pope will make about nuns marrying Greeks! It is the union of the Greek and Latin Churches!'

Likewise, he would accept no excuses for Slatin and Lupton. This was not so much because they had surrendered. That he admitted was probably another matter of Hobson's choice, and he was not prepared to credit stories that Slatin had plenty of food and ammunition when he gave up. But he could not excuse their apostasy, even if it were the price of their lives. And when Slatin wrote to tell Gordon that he wished to escape from his captors and join him in Khartoum, he declined to be a party to his break-ing his parole to the Mahdi and denied him even the courtesy of a reply. Then when Slatin later wrote to Hansal, saying that if Khartoum were surrendered he would be tortured and killed by the Mahdists, Gordon scornfully commented on the letters in his journal: 'I have no remarks to make on them and cannot make out why he wrote them.' As for Cuzzi, now called by his Moslem name, Mohammed Yusuf, he had nothing but loathing and con-tempt. 'A vile traitor (like all Italians I ever met), I expect he gave the Mahdi all the cyphers...' he remarked on hearing that Cuzzi was being well treated in captivity and had received money, a wife, a slave, and two horses. And while he blamed Baring for driving Cuzzi to surrender, he could not excuse him for divulging information to the Mahdi, which he felt he must have done to be given such favourable treatment.

But Gordon's journal was not only used for vituperative com-ments about personalities. It was also intended as a means of passing instructions or suggestions to the relief expedition as to the best route of approach to Khartoum and of keeping them informed of his own plans and resources and of the Mahdi's movements. Volumes of the journal were taken down at intervals by steamer to Metemma, there to await the expedition's arrival and to be handed over to the officer in command. (As it turned out, the six volumes covering the period September 9 to Decem-ber 14 had to wait until January 21 before they were delivered into the hands of the advancing relief column.) Meticulous lists of troop strengths, arms and ammunition and food stores were compiled and sent down. Typical of these is the entry for October 19:

No. of black troops, regulars	.	.	.		2,316
„ white troops, regulars	.	.	.		1,421
„ Cairo bashi bazouks	.	.	.		1,906
„ Shaggia	.	.	.		2,330
„ Townspeople enrolled	.	.	.		692

Total	. .	8,665

No. of guns upon lines	.	.	.	.	12
„ steamers	.	.	.	.	11

Rounds of gun ammunition	.	.	.	.	21,141
„ Small arms Remington	.	.	.	2,165,000
„ Arsenal turns out weekly	.	.	40,000

Grain, Ardebs	.	.	.	.	4,018
Biscuits, Okes	.	.	.	.	349,000
Weekly consumption of troops, Ardebs	.	.	500

Money in Specie	.	.	.	.	£2,900
„ Paper	.	.	.	.	£39,195

On September 24, three days after hearing from Kitchener and Floyer that relief was definitely on its way, Gordon drew up his first plan for the advancing troops. 'My view is this, as to the operations of British forces; I will put three steamers each with two guns on them, and an armed force of infantry at the disposal of any British authority, will send these steamers to either Metemma, opposite Shendi, or to the cataract below Berber, to there meet any British force which may come across country to the Nile. These steamers, with this force coming across country, will (D.V.) capture Berber and then communicate with Khartoum.... I would not attempt to pass the *bulk* of British force across country, only the fighting column, to co-operate with the three steamers. No artillery is wanted with either force.... When Berber is taken, I should keep the bulk of the forces there and send up the fighting column to Khartoum ... then in combination with us clear out the rebels—an affair of a week—then decide your future policy.... I cannot impress too much on you that this expedition will not encounter any enemy worth the name in a European sense of the word; the struggle is with the climate and destitution of the country.... A heavy lumbering column, however strong, is nowhere in this land. Parties of forty or sixty men swiftly moving about will do more than any column ... it is the country of the irregular not the regular....'

By the same token, he planned, directly he should hear that Berber had been recaptured, to send down his Egyptian bashi-bazouks and white regulars—the 'Cairo debris' he called them—and keep only his black troops and Shaggia irregulars in Khartoum. And he advised that the best route for the relief force was from Ambukol, thirty-five miles upstream from Debba, to Metemma. This was both the shortest way across the lower half of the great S-bend in the Nile, the Bayuda Desert, and also the one offering the most wells, and should bring at least the advance guard to Khartoum by November 15. Once at Metemma, the force could either divide, with one part turning north to take Berber, 100 miles downstream, while the other came on to Khartoum, 100 miles upstream, or the whole force could undertake both operations. But whichever course they chose, it was imperative not to leave Berber in Mahdist hands in their rear. Then with the force which came to Khartoum and his black troops, Gordon planned to destroy the besieging Ansar army in three stages and open up the road to Sennar, whose garrison was still holding out. 'The result of these operations,' he concluded, 'would be the retreat of the Mahdi's Arabs to Kordofan and the surrender of those in and about Kassala.... The Arabs must have one good defeat to wipe out the Hicks disaster and my defeats.'

To help in speeding these operations, Gordon sent three steamers down the Nile, with the first two volumes of his journal. At the same time, a courier was sent to Debba to inform the relief force's commander that the ships would shortly be at Metemma, with orders to place themselves at the relief expedition's disposal. But his expectations as to the progress of the British force were far too optimistic. For the next month it was the Mahdi rather than Wolseley who made the running with his main army from Kordofan, and on October 21 Mohammed Ahmed arrived at Omdurman with a vast array of warriors, and their wives and families and camp-followers of every description. It was more like a migration of tribes than a military advance. 'The Mahdi has come,' Gordon wrote to Stewart, believing that he was still alive and in Dongola, 'with a strange *état major*—Slatin, priests, nuns, and Greeks. It has brightened me up, for it has been very dull....'

But his cheerfulness was short-lived, for that same day a letter came from Slatin to say that the *Abbas* had been captured and 'Stewart killed with nine men and all the papers captured.' And on the following day confirmation arrived in the form of a letter from the Mahdi quoting from the reports and other documents which Stewart had taken with him. The Mahdi's letter went on to say that Lupton had surrendered Bahr-el-Ghazal in April, which, although six months before, was still news to Gordon, who had no means of communicating with the south. For good measure, the Mahdi rounded off his catalogue of disastrous tidings with a further demand for the surrender of Khartoum. 'As to your expecting reinforcements,' he told Gordon, 'reliance for succour on others than God will bring you nothing but destruction.... If you return to the Most High God and become a Moslem and surrender to His order and that of His Prophet and believe in us as the Mahdi, send us a message after laying down your arms.... Otherwise you will have to encounter war from God and His Prophet.'

Gordon retorted that he did not care whether Lupton had surrendered or not, nor how many steamers had been captured. 'I am here like iron and hope to see the newly-arrived English.... It is impossible for me to have any more words with Mohammed Ahmed, only lead.' But he was badly shaken, especially by the news of Stewart's death and the capture of the *Abbas*. Not only had his reports not reached the relief expedition, but the Mahdi now knew the exact situation of the Khartoum garrison, how much food they had and how many men, guns, rifles, shells, and cartridges. On top of that, he had lost a gallant and efficient officer and helpmate. And to his already bitter pangs of conscience about the fate which he had brought on the Khartoum garrison was now added a feeling of guilt for having sent Stewart on his mission. 'I will own that ... I have never been comfortable since they left,' he wrote two weeks later. And then, with remarkable prescience—for he still did not know the circumstances of Stewart's death—he added: 'I can see in imagination the whole scene, the sheikh inviting them to land ... men going on shore and dispersed ... then a rush of wild Arabs, and all is over.'

Nevertheless, Gordon, on the strength of a report received on October 19 that British troops had passed Abu Hamed on the way to Berber, decided to send down another two steamers, one of them the *Bordein*, to Metemma to meet the relief force and expedite the final stage of their journey to Khartoum. With four of his original eleven steamers now captured by the rebels and another four already at Metemma, he thus left himself with only one old steamer, the *Ismailia*, which had brought Gessi up to Equatoria in October 1875, plus a new ship called the *Husseinyeh* which had been completed a few days earlier in the Khartoum shipyard. It was a big risk to take, for it greatly reduced the fire-power of the Khartoum garrison and its ability to strike with 'mobile' artillery at the Mahdi's forces which now surrounded Khartoum and Omdurman. Nor was the Mahdi slow to press the advantage with which he was thus presented. From now on his attacks both by rifle and shell-fire became more frequent and more intense. Hitherto they had been sporadic—a few shells every day or so and a burst of rifle-fire from time to time. But now the Mahdists began to attack in considerable force, several hundreds at a time, and to keep on firing for three hours or more. Their favourite targets were the palace and the steamers; and by mid-November the *Ismailia* had 2,000 bullet marks on her, while the luckless *Husseinyeh*, after less than a month in service, was stuck fast in the mud at the junction of the two Niles after trying to manoeuvre herself to silence the Mahdi's guns firing from outside Omdurman.

Still Gordon tried to preserve an air of calm and confidence. If the Mahdi kept up this rate of fire, he must soon be very short of ammunition, he reasoned. His main supply had been captured from Hicks's army and he had no means of replacing his expenditure. According to Gordon's spies, he had started with 800,000 rounds of which he 'must have expended in the last week 250,000 to 300,000 rounds'. Whereas the Khartoum garrison had about 2,000,000 rounds left and the arsenal turned out another 40,000 a week. Therefore, even if the British did not arrive soon, the Mahdi might well run out of ammunition before Khartoum ran out of food.

Perhaps inevitably, Gordon believed implicitly in every optimistic report and rejected all bad news or severely qualified it as unconfirmed rumour. He even tried to pretend for a brief moment that the story of the *Abbas*'s capture might have been invented by the Mahdi, despite the irrefutable evidence to the contrary. He religiously recorded every report that the Ansar armies were nothing like as numerous as had been thought—a mere 4,000 in all, he claimed, and that figure was rapidly dwindling as deserters poured forth from the Mahdi's lines. But he seldom counted his own deserters, still less the townspeople of Khartoum who went over to the Mahdi, reducing the population of the capital from 34,000 to 14,000 by the end of the siege. He persisted in his belief that the Mahdi was 'most unpopular' and that his own followers would one day turn on him, led by the unhappy slaves, who saw in Mahdism no end to their enslavement. Above all, he believed that the British relief force must come soon to relieve him of his responsibility for the garrisons: 'Once they communicate with Khartoum they must assume the responsibility of the government of that place ... the decision as to what they will do rests with them.' If it were a dishonourable decision and involved a 'rapid retreat' and abandonment of the Sudan then so be it. He would have no more responsibility for the garrisons and he could then 'fall with the town and run all risks' with a clear conscience.

Day after day, Gordon climbed to the roof of the palace to watch for the smoke of his steamers bringing the relief expedition. Day after day, he scanned with his telescope the horizon beyond the sandpit of Tuti Island and the green palm-fringed bend of the river below the junction of the two Niles, while the ubiquitous kites with their ragged wings and hawk-like heads planed and hovered above him, uttering their plaintive cries, as if in warning not to chance his arm any further. And every evening the sun would set across the featureless plain behind the mud walls of the fort of Omdurman, turning the Nile to silver, to announce the closing of another day with no sign or news of the relief force.

Then of a sudden on November 3, twenty-four hours after Gordon had taken stock of his food-stores and reckoned that there was only enough grain for another six weeks, the *Bordein* was sighted steaming slowly up the Nile below Halfaya. Salutes were fired from the forts and flags were run up to greet her arrival. But a sad disappointment was in store. When the steamer came alongside the pier opposite the palace, not a single British officer or soldier stepped ashore, and, worse still, there was a letter from Kitchener dated October 14, which confirmed the report of Stewart's death and which showed that the relief expedition was making painfully slow progress. 'Lord Wolseley is now at Wadi Halfa,' Kitchener wrote, 'and it is expected that the expedition will definitely start from Dongola on or about the 1st November.' It was a bitter blow. No longer could Gordon contend that relief was bound to come for the garrison and townspeople before they ran out of food. At best, he estimated, the relief force would take thirty-five days from Dongola, and a lot longer if they were to retake Berber *en route*. And this would probably be too late.

On October 13 he had written in his journal: 'It is of course on the cards that Khartoum is taken under the nose of the expeditionary force, which will be *just too late*.' And again, eleven days later, after taking stock of his provisions, he expressed the view that 'if they do not come before November 30, the game is up and Rule Britannia'. From the latest information, it now began to look as if these melancholy forecasts would prove all too accurate.

CHAPTER 23

'SITUATION CRITICAL, ALMOST DESPERATE'

In fact, Wolseley's plans involved an even longer delay in getting the relief force on its way than was foreshadowed in Kitchener's letter. Having had no word from Gordon about the plight of Khartoum since he left Cairo on September 27—the first four volumes of the journal covering the period September 9 to October 21 were still at Metemma waiting to be handed over—Wolseley had spent the month of October at Wadi Halfa organizing the transport and other logistic requirements of the expedition. He did not himself reach Dongola until November 3, the same day that the *Bordein* returned to Khartoum with Kitchener's letter. And he planned to start the expedition on its way south in early December, a month later than Kitchener had indicated. Instead of despatching flying columns, as suggested by Gordon, he was planning to concentrate his whole force of 7,000, at least as far as Debba, where he intended to arrive about December 15. Thence he would move on up the Nile after a further interval for consolidation, reaching Korti around Christmas and from there send an advance guard of Camel Corps and infantry across the Bayuda to Metemma.

Judged in the light of everything we now know of Khartoum's situation at the beginning of November, these plans seem extraordinarily lacking in a sense of urgency. But it would be less than fair to accuse Wolseley of being dilatory or casual in tackling the problem of Gordon's rescue. In the first place, when he drew up his plans he had no inkling of the plight of Khartoum. On September 20 he had telegraphed to Gordon in cypher from Cairo to ask for a report of the situation, including details of the garrison's strength and provisions; but when Gordon finally received the message on November 3, he had no cypher key to decode the telegram and Wolseley therefore received no reply. And early in November a message from Gordon was brought into

Dongola which did not in any way suggest that Khartoum's current situation was critical. True, Gordon stated that he was closely blockaded by some 20,000 Ansar equipped with artillery. But he added that the garrison could hold out for forty days without difficulty.

Besides, Wolseley had his own problems to overcome, especially in the matter of transport, and these were unlikely to become any easier with the passage of time. The last of the 800 specially constructed boats did not leave England until October and soon after they reached Wadi Halfa their light and fragile hulls were to prove all too vulnerable amidst the uncharted rocks and rapids left by the falling Nile. As Gordon had found when exploring the Nile in Equatoria, this meant that they had often to be hauled up river by sheer manual strength, which resulted in the boats taking six weeks to cover a distance of 200 miles. Even on those stretches where there were no rapids, it was often impossible to use steamers to tow the boats, owing to a shortage of coal. And, to add to their difficulties, there were not enough camels for transport and the expedition were weighed down with large quantities of extra provisions which had been brought to feed the Khartoum garrison on the return journey. Thus, even if he had been aware of the urgency of the situation, it is difficult to see how Wolseley could have moved much faster, at least with sufficient strength to take on the 20,000 Ansar besieging Khartoum.

As it happened, due to these delays, it took until December 15 for the advance guard alone—consisting of 500 infantry and 1,500 Camel Corps under Sir Herbert Stewart—to reach Korti, which was to be the starting-point for the crossing of the Bayuda. Then on December 30 Wolseley received another message from Gordon which was to complicate his plans and retard the progress of the main force still further. The message was in two parts. The first was brief and clearly intended to deceive the Mahdi if its bearer should be captured. 'Khartoum all right, 14.12.84. C. G. Gordon' was all it said. But the second part of the message was more specific and ominous. 'We are besieged on three sides,' it said, 'fighting goes on day and night. The enemy cannot take us except by starving us out. Do not scatter your troops; the enemy are numerous. Bring plenty of troops if you can.' Then it went on to describe the acute food shortage in Khartoum and urged that relief must 'come quickly'. But at the same time Gordon advised that, on no account, should Wolseley leave Berber in his rear. 'Keep the enemy in your front and when you have taken Berber send me word from Berber,' he concluded.

Wolseley could hardly have been placed in a more awkward predicament. He had to 'come quickly', because Khartoum was on the verge of starvation, and with 'plenty of troops', because the enemy were 'numerous', and at the same time to take Berber on his route, because of the danger of leaving the enemy in his rear. In the circumstances he did the only thing possible. Telegraphing to Baring that Gordon's message compelled him to postpone his personal arrival in Khartoum, he decided to take the bulk of his force by river to attack Berber and to send Stewart with the Camel Corps, a contingent of infantry and a naval brigade across the Bayuda to Metemma, whence Sir Charles Wilson, the Chief Intelligence Officer, would take a detachment of infantry by steamer to make contact with Gordon in Khartoum.

But before Stewart could leave it was necessary to post guards on the wells at Jakdul, a little over halfway along his route of march, to secure them against seizure or sabotage by the enemy. This precaution took another nine days to complete, so that it was not until January 8 that Stewart was able to set out with his force of 1,600 men and 2,400 camels and horses. On January 12 he reached Jakdul, where, exhausted by the rigours of marching twenty miles a day, both man and beast required a twenty-four-hour halt. Then on January 13 Stewart resumed his march towards Metemma. Needless to say, the movement of his column of 2,000 men and camels had not passed unnoticed by the Mahdi's spies. And on the evening of January 16, as they approached the wells of Abu Klea some twenty miles from Metemma, they found their route barred by a force of several thousand Ansar.

Stewart encamped for the night, preferring not to attack so large an enemy force until his troops had had a night's rest. Then on the following morning he gave the order to advance in square formation. When he had got within a mile of the enemy, the Ansar flung themselves upon his advancing column with such force and ferocity that they penetrated to the centre of the square and up to the line of camels inside it. But as a withering fire was opened on the attackers from the other sides of the square, the initial momentum of their charge began to sag. The camelmen and infantry then closed in, and every Ansar warrior within the square was killed, whereupon the enemy withdrew, leaving over 1,000 dead on the battlefield.

Stewart had beaten off the Mahdi's attempt to block his route to Khartoum. But he had paid no small price himself for his victory, with a casualty list of eighteen officers and 150 men killed and wounded, including his unofficial second-in-command, Colonel Burnaby. And two days later, an even worse disaster was to overtake his column when, with Metemma visible in the distance only four miles away, Stewart himself was mortally wounded by an Ansar bullet in a desultory skirmish. No one had foreseen the possibility of both Stewart and his second-in-command being put out of action and, in the absence of any set prescription, the command of the column duly devolved upon the next senior officer, who happened to be Wolseley's Chief Intelligence Officer, Sir Charles Wilson.

It was a highly awkward situation for the unfortunate Wilson, who had not served in any previous campaign and was more a back-room boy than a fighting soldier by experience and inclination. With no experience of desert warfare—his service in the Middle East had been largely spent on survey work for the Palestine Exploration Fund—he inclined to caution at a time when speed was all-important. Yet it would be grossly unfair to blame him for the fact that his efforts to rescue Gordon were unavailing. For one thing, Wilson was not alone in underestimating the amount of force necessary to relieve Khartoum. As Wolseley later admitted to Henry Gordon, even after he received Gordon's message saying that the enemy were numerous and he should bring plenty of troops, his 'plans were based on the conviction that one or two steamers, with British soldiers on board, would at any time have saved the place'. Moreover, in the journal which Wilson found awaiting him near Metemma, Gordon had himself suggested in several entries, including the last one of all on December 14, that 'no more than two hundred men' might turn the scale. As for the delays which occurred after he took command, it is only fair to say that they were minor by comparison with the earlier delays in getting the expedition on its way. The precautions which this naturally cautious officer took to ensure that his advance up the Nile was not harassed by an enemy force in his rear were no more than Gordon had himself enjoined on Wolseley in his message about the importance of taking Berber.

And it was not Wilson's fault that, from the moment when he took command, the Ansar engaged the column in a running battle, so that the last four miles of the march took two days to cover and it was not until January 21 that he finally forced his way through to Gordon's flotilla of steamers at Gubat, a few miles south of Metemma.

At Gubat Wilson was five days' journey from his objective and, although he could not know it at the time, it was exactly five days later that the Mahdi was to attack and overwhelm the now-starving garrison. What he did know, from Gordon's journal, was that the situation was a lot more urgent than Gordon's verbal, let alone written, messages had admitted. True, his latest message, written on a tiny scrap of paper, said: 'Khartoum is all right; could hold out for years. C. G. Gordon, 29.12.84.' But again this was obviously intended to deceive the enemy should the courier have been waylaid. And from reading the journal, Wilson could see that, for some time and largely on account of the critical food shortage, Gordon had been a lot more anxious than he had admitted in his letter to Wolseley early in November, when he said that after forty days it would be 'difficult' to hold out. Even making every allowance for his kaleidoscopic character and quicksilver changes of mood and opinion, it was clear that since the middle of November Gordon had thought the game might be up at any time after the end of the month. And on December 13, five and a half weeks before the relief column reached Metemma, he had asserted that if help did not arrive 'before ten days' time, the town will fall', which statement was repeated in letters addressed to the Chief of Staff and others which had been sent down with the journal. 'It is inexplicable, this delay,' Gordon wrote; 'one hundred men are all that we require, just to show ourselves. ...' A few sentences later he cut the requirement by half: 'All that is absolutely necessary is for fifty of the Expeditionary Force to get on board a steamer and come up to Halfaya and there let their presence be felt; this is not asking much, but it must happen at once; or it will as usual be too late.' And in his final entry on December 14, he wrote: 'NOW MARK THIS, if the Expeditionary force, and I ask for no more than two hundred men, does not come in ten days, *the town may fall*; and I have done my best for the honour of our country. Good-bye.'

Thus, according to these estimates, Khartoum might have fallen at any time during the course of the previous four weeks. Yet Wilson, respecting Gordon's earlier cautionary advice, felt it necessary to spend the next two days reconnoitring the Nile both north and south of Metemma. Then on the morning of January 24, satisfied that no insuperable enemy concentrations would block his advance, he started upstream for Khartoum, taking with him twenty British soldiers and some 200 black troops in the steamers *Bordein* and *Talatawein*.

Meanwhile, at Khartoum Gordon had spent most of the month of November thinking that the relief expedition had started from Dongola on November 1, as Kitchener's letter had said. And although Wolseley had tried to get word through to inform him that the actual date for the expedition to start southwards would be early December, the message never reached Khartoum. Thus when the *Bordein* was sighted on November 25 steaming once again upriver through a hail of Ansar fire beyond Halfaya, Gordon's hopes rose in the belief that she was bringing the advance guard of the relief force. But once again his hopes were shattered. No British troops had come with the steamer, and the only news she brought was a report from Nushi Pasha, the commander of the steamer flotilla at Metemma, that the expeditionary force was at Korti, which progress Gordon ironically described as 'LIVELY!' (In fact, even this report was overoptimistic, since Stewart's advance column of Camel Corps did not reach Korti until twenty days afterwards.)

Apart from this cold comfort, the *Bordein* brought a number of cypher telegrams, including Granville's message of July 24, expressing the Government's interest in his safety, which Gordon could not read, having sent his cypher books down with the ill-fated *Abbas*. Also, there was a message from the Khedive dated September 21 which revised Gordon's firman and limited his powers as Governor-General to Khartoum, Sennar and the immediate neighbourhood of Berber, instructed him to get the Sennar garrison down to Khartoum, and forbade him to send any expedition to burn Berber, or to relieve the garrisons of Equatoria or of Bahr-el-Ghazal, which had surrendered in April! (This curious communication was the reflection of a decision by Gladstone's Cabinet to restrict Gordon's sphere of operations because of British newspaper reports which had appeared in mid-September, saying that Gordon was expecting the arrival of

200,000 Turkish troops and that he was planning to raid Berber and burn it to the ground—a prospect which filled Liberal ministers with horror, and precipitated the prompt despatch of instructions to Cairo to nip any such wild manoeuvres in the bud.) The Khedive's message concluded by saying that he would receive the British Government's instructions 'through Sir Evelyn Baring and Lord Wolseley', which Gordon misinterpreted with ribald comments in his journal as meaning that 'Baring was bumping his way up here' on a camel. 'Baring to Egerton—', ran a typical entry, 'Metemma at last, after the most fearful sufferings, every bone in my body dislocated with those beastly camels. Found here his journal from which it appears that that duffer, the Mahdi, has at last roused himself, but I fear it is too late. As to the tone of the journal it is *simply deplorable*.... Excuse more, for what with the bumping of the camel and the depravity shown by this scoffer, I am more dead than alive.'

Gordon also misunderstood the intention of his revised firman. According to his reading, Khartoum, Sennar, Berber, and Dongola were to be retained as part of the Khedive's domains under a Governor-General, the Mahdi was to be recognized as ruler of Kordofan, Kassala would be handed over to Abyssinia—he had already heard a wild rumour that Britain had made a deal with King Johannes to this effect—and, finally, Bahr-el-Ghazal and Equatoria were to be left to fend for themselves. As with every other proposal which involved his being asked to abandon any part of the Sudan, he rejected these ideas as unacceptable. He had said all along, he wrote in his journal, that there were really only two solutions: either to hand over the country to the Turkish Sultan or to call in Zubair. And he repeated his threat to 'resign and have nothing more to do with the government of the place or of the Sudan' if he were instructed to evacuate Khartoum and leave the other garrisons to their fate.

All in all, the *Bordein*'s arrival must have been a most depressing moment for Gordon. He was greatly worried about the food situation. Although grain-rationing had been started on September 20, after the Mahdi had put a stop to his foraging expeditions up the Blue Nile, his provisions were running dangerously low. He was also extremely anxious for the garrison of Omdurman, who were now cut off from Khartoum by an Ansar encircling movement, which had established itself on the river bank to the east of the town and driven the defenders to take refuge in the fortified area. He was constantly plagued by the indiscipline of his own sentries on the Khartoum ramparts. And although the townspeople were free to leave the capital and join the Mahdi if they wished—for the fewer mouths he had to feed the longer he could hold out—he had periodically to order the arrest of leading citizens on charges of treachery. Now on top of everything came new, and unacceptable, instructions, together with disquieting and disappointing reports of the relief expedition's progress. Still, he made what he could of the news brought by the *Bordein*, and on November 26 he posted notices in Khartoum announcing the imminent arrival of British troops. 'They have reached Dongola,' he proclaimed, 'and started in three divisions.... They will soon be in Khartoum.... If God will, in the next few days the siege will be raised and your alarm will pass away. Know also that, if Mohammed Ahmed should call upon me for three years to surrender Khartoum, I will not listen to him, but will protect your lives and families and possessions with all energy and steadfastness.'

It was a defiant gesture, but it failed to carry much conviction. For one thing, Gordon had too often before told the people and garrison of Khartoum that British troops would arrive at any moment for him to be believed any longer. For another, the food situation was getting rapidly worse. On November 21 he had been able to claim that not one person had yet died of hunger, but he knew now that, if help were not forthcoming very soon, there would be many deaths from starvation and, as the Mahdi clearly intended, the garrison would be too weak from hunger to resist any longer. And when on December 8 he received a letter from the Khalifa Abdullah, he knew that there was all too much truth in its ominously warning contents: 'You have paid no attention to the counsel and reasonings repeatedly sent to you, but have increased in folly,' it said. 'Your letter [*sic*] has reached us in which you deceived the population saying that the British reinforcement is coming to you in three divisions and that it will soon reach you and give you victory. Thus your letter betrays the greatness of your fear and anxiety and alarm as in your deceit you have caught hold of spider-web ropes and have feared to die at our hands.... Know thou, oh! enemy of God, that the true news is with us and not with you and that the news which has reached us contains nothing to cheer thy eye or uphold thy power. On the contrary, there is no escape from death at our hands and from death by lack of food.... The people of El Obeid were longing for reinforcements like the longing of the thirsty for water and they too were writing deceitful and cheering letters and nevertheless you have heard what befell them. If you are content to remain as you are, then prepare for what shall come, but if you knock at the door of repentance, peradventure it may be opened unto you. Peace be upon those who follow after the right way.'

A week later Gordon sent the *Bordein* back to Metemma with the last volume of his journal and with letters to his sister, to his old friend and associate from Equatorian days, Colonel Watson, and to the 'Chief of Staff, Sudan Expeditionary Force'. As these writings showed, he was now very near the end of his tether. Still believing that the relief force had left Dongola around November 1, he could not understand what had held them up so long, especially since he had heard from November 28 onwards repeated rumours that the British had recaptured Berber and that four steamers were on their way to Khartoum. And as he penned his last letters and final journal on December 14, he evidently thought that the Mahdi would storm Khartoum in a matter of days.

For himself, he naturally had no fears or regrets. This was what he sought, and to his sister he wrote: 'This may be the last letter you will receive from me, for we are on our last legs owing to the delay of the expedition. However, God rules all and as He will rule to His glory and our welfare, may His will be done—I fear owing to circumstances that my affairs are pecuniarily not over bright, but Henry will see you and others do not lose through this affair.' And as a postscript he added: 'I am quite happy thank God and like Lawrence [Sir Henry Lawrence, who died defending Lucknow in the Indian Mutiny] I have tried to do my duty.' But, for the garrison that was going to be overwhelmed and perhaps slaughtered, Gordon's conscience pricked him relentlessly. And in his brief final report to the Chief of Staff of the relief force, he emphasized that the position was 'extremely critical, almost desperate' and that Khartoum might fall at any time after the next '5 to 7 days'. In this same report he said that he had no 'feeling of bitterness to Her Majesty's Government'.

Two weeks later, however, he sent by courier a telegram in a rather different vein, addressed to the sovereigns of Great Britain and Turkey. 'After salutations,' he said, 'I would at once, calling to mind what I have gone through, inform Their Majesties the Sovereigns of the nations of Great Britain and the Ottoman Empire who appointed me as Governor-General of the Sudan for the purpose of appeasing the rebellion in that country. During the twelve months that I have been here, these two powers, the one remarkable for her wealth, the other for her military force, have remained unaffected by my situation, perhaps relying too much on the news sent by Hussein Pasha Khalifa [Mudir of Berber], who surrendered of his own accord. Although I am personally too insignificant to be taken into account, the powers were bound none the less to fulfil the engagement upon which my appointment was based, so as to shield the honour of the governments. What I have gone through I cannot describe. The Almighty God will help me.'

Some allowance must clearly be made for the strain under which Gordon had been living for so long, which was aggravated by the failure of Wolseley's and other messengers to get through to Khartoum with accurate and up-to-date reports of the efforts being made to relieve Khartoum. But even so, this telegram was a masterpiece of misinterpretation, both of the British Government's concern for his safety and of the terms of reference of his own mission to the Sudan. As Gladstone correctly stated in a subsequent comment on Gordon's mission: 'When Gordon left this country and when he arrived in Egypt, he declared it to be—and I have not the slightest doubt that it was—a fixed portion of his policy that no British force should be employed in aid of his mission.' And that Gordon should now imply that he had been sent to quell the Mahdi's revolt, with the promise of British and/or Turkish troops to assist him, is such a travesty of the truth as can only be explained by the fact that, as Nemesis approached, his feelings of guilt towards the Khartoum garrison could no longer be appeased by random satire directed against Granville and Baring in a confidential journal, but required an official and public scapegoat in the shape of the governments of Great Britain and Turkey. Whatever view may be taken of Gordon's actions in Khartoum during the last eleven months of his strange, unhappy life, it is sad to think that his last communication to the outside world should have contained such an unworthy accusation.

CHAPTER 24

FINAL MARTYRDOM

By the beginning of January the food shortage in Khartoum had become critical. Except for some green dura on Tuti Island, there was no grain left and the biscuit supply was exhausted. The garrison and townspeople were reduced to eating donkeys, horses, dogs, rats, gum, and palm fibre. Dysentery became rife and many of the garrison were too weakened by sickness and starvation to take their places in the lines, while others frequently deserted their posts in search of food. Corpses filled the streets and no one had the energy to bury them. And on January 6, in a desperate attempt to reduce the non-combatant population and so to eke out the exiguous food supplies, Gordon publicly proclaimed that any of the townspeople wishing to leave Khartoum might do so, and sent a letter to the Mahdi asking him to feed and deal kindly with those who left.

As for Omdurman, the situation was even worse. Not only were the garrison starving, but they were also desperately short of ammunition. Informed of the position by deserters, the Mahdi decided to step up his attacks on Omdurman as a prelude to the final reduction of Khartoum. And although Gordon tried to relieve the pressure of the Ansar blockade with three sorties at the beginning of January, his troops could not break the Mahdi's stranglehold. Day after day from the roof of his palace, Gordon watched through his telescope the death-throes of the little fort across the river, as the Ansar riflemen picked off its defenders one by one and their artillery pounded its ramparts with a ferocious bombardment, which he was powerless to counter without his steamers. Then on January 5 he was informed by signal from Farajallah, Omdurman's commander, that his men had exhausted their ammunition and food, and with a heavy heart Gordon ordered the garrison to surrender.

The fall of Omdurman was immediately felt in Khartoum. Just as the Mahdi had intended, it was regarded as the prelude to the fall of the capital and, as the already abysmal morale of the garrison and townspeople declined still further, desertions among the troops increased sharply with the exodus of the inhabitants. The Mahdi also gained the important advantage of being able to site his artillery along the Omdurman ramparts and so to increase the severity of his bombardment of Khartoum. Thus he could now concentrate his entire force of 20,000 for the final assault.

Under the cover of his guns, the Ansar reinforcements now swarmed across the White Nile at Kalakala to join Wad el-Nejumi's camp. And just as Gordon was unable to prevent the Mahdi's artillery from pounding Omdurman into submission, so he was powerless to stop the massing of the Ansar armies beyond the southern limits of Khartoum's defences. From the palace roof he could see the constant movement of troops across the river and the growing concentration of forces on the south side of the city. But without his steamers he could do nothing to arrest this massing of the enemy for his destruction.

Yet still the Mahdi did not attack. Instead, he sent Gordon the most remarkable of all his letters, in which he beseeched him to surrender and offered to let him go free, if he would only give in. 'To Gordon Pasha, may God protect him,' the letter began and, after praising Gordon's good qualities, went on to say: 'We have written to you to go back to your country.... I repeat to you the words of God, "Do not destroy yourselves. God Himself is merciful unto you." I understand that the English are willing to ransom you alone from us for £20,000.... If you agree to join us it will be a blessing to you. But if you wish to rejoin the English, we will send you back to them without asking for so much as a farthing.'

This little-known letter shows how far the Mahdi was prepared to go to spare Gordon and to capture Khartoum without bloodshed. But his appeal was in vain. Determined to martyrize himself, Gordon contemptuously ignored this final magnanimous offer.

The die was cast. But even as Gordon's final refusal to save himself was being relayed to the Mahdi, another missive was being delivered, which all but changed the course of history and threatened to send the Ansar armies helter-skelter back to Kordofan. On January 20, word reached the Mahdi's camp of the defeat at Abu Klea of the Ansar force which had been sent to harass

Stewart's relief column. The report spread like wildfire and Gordon, perched on his palace roof, scanning the horizon beyond the bend in the Nile, suddenly saw the unaccustomed sight of Ansar women weeping and wailing over the loss of their menfolk. A while later, in answer to his enquiries, word came through one of his spies in the Mahdi's camp that the British had won a decisive victory on their way to Khartoum.

Gordon hastened to announce the good news. And as a wave of public rejoicing broke over the capital, the Mahdi took counsel with his Khalifas in a mood of sudden fear and dejection. In fact, some reports have it that, so great was the general consternation, he thought it prudent to claim that he had received a revelation from God, ordering him to retire from Khartoum and return to Kordofan, before the British force arrived on the scene and repeated their victory at Abu Klea. All but one of his commanders are said to have agreed; but the one dissentient—Mohammed Abd el-Kerim, the Mahdi's uncle—argued strongly the other way. 'If Gordon, a single Englishman, has caused us all this trouble, what will our condition be if an army of his countrymen join Gordon?' he asked. The course of wisdom, as well as valour, was to attack, not to retreat, before the British arrived. All reports coming out of Khartoum from spies and deserters, as well as from the fleeing inhabitants, agreed that the town was starving and its defenders too weak to offer any effective resistance. Added to this, a deserter had recently pointed out a specially weak point in the defences where the falling White Nile had left a strip of muddy ground that would serve as a bridge across the defensive moat on the southern side of the town.

With these powerful arguments, confidence began to return to the Mahdi's council and, seeing no signs that the British were hastening to follow up their victory, the Khalifas accepted Abd el-Kerim's advice. A full-scale assault on Khartoum was ordered for the early hours of January 26. And on the eve of the attack the Mahdi crossed the White Nile, silently and stealthily, so as not to arouse the Khartoum defenders by any noise of cheering from his troops. Gathering his commanders together he gave them their instructions for the morrow. In the name of the Prophet they were to take Khartoum and plunder its wealth for the Ansar treasury. But Gordon, he insisted, must be taken alive, for he was by all accounts a good man, whose only fault was that he was not of the Moslem faith. 'Anyone who molests him,' he declaimed, 'will not be one of us.' (Confirmation of this view of Gordon was given to the author by Dr. Tigani el-Mahi, a member of the Presidential Council of the Sudan in 1965, whose grandmother, a resident of Khartoum during the siege, described Gordon as a man who 'if he had been a Moslem would certainly have gone to Paradise'.) But for the hated 'Turks', the Egyptian garrison, who had profaned the true faith and raped and plundered the Sudan, there was to be no mercy. So saying, the Mahdi returned to Omdurman to await the coming battle.

Meanwhile, in Khartoum, in the absence of any sign of the relief column approaching up the Nile, the brief moment of rejoicing over the news of Abu Klea had once more turned to dejection and dismay. And when the Mahdi sent messengers into the town to spread the word that the British victory had been invented to bolster civic resistance and that it was really the Ansar who had triumphed at Abu Klea, many people readily believed this falsehood. Even Faragh Pasha, the garrison commander, began to doubt that the Ansar had been defeated and on January 23, two days before the Mahdi paid his secret visit to his commanders, he advised Gordon to surrender the town, as the garrison were now too weak to hold out any longer. But Gordon angrily refused to consider surrender and, as he carried out his daily inspection of the Khartoum defences, he exhorted the exhausted and starving garrison to make one last effort to hold the town and urged all citizens capable of bearing arms to help in manning the ramparts. 'They must come, they will come, tomorrow or the next day,' he insisted. And on January 25 he climbed to the roof of the palace for what was to be the last time to scan the horizon for some sign of his steamers. But in vain, for at that moment the *Bordein*, with Wilson and his twenty redcoats and 200 black troops aboard her and her sister-ship, was stuck fast upon a rock in the Sixth Cataract sixty miles from Khartoum, and could not be refloated for another twenty-four hours. As for the rest of Wolseley's expedition, the bulk of the advance column was at Metemma and the residue—5,000 out of the total of 7,000—were no nearer than Abu Hamed, 150 miles on the wrong side of Berber.

On the same day Gordon called the Council of Notables to the palace. Again there was much talk of surrender and doubts were expressed as to the truth of the reported British victory at Abu Klea. But when the doubters had had their say, Gordon announced his implacable opposition to surrendering Khartoum. The British relief force was on its way. It would arrive in another twenty-four hours. Why then surrender and present the Mahdi with a victory which another day's resistance would deny him? They were brave and defiant words; but in his heart he doubted their truth. And as the Council adjourned and the Notables dispersed, he turned despairingly to Bordeiny Bey, a Khartoum merchant and a trusted friend. 'What more can I say? The people will no longer believe me. I have' told them over and over again that help would be here. But it has never come and now they must see I tell them lies. If this, my last promise, fails, I can do no more. Go and collect the people you can on the lines and make a good stand. Now leave me to smoke these cigarettes.'

At 3.30 a.m. on the following morning, January 26, the Ansar infantry under Wad el-Nejumi crept forward towards the mud bridge that was to carry the main assault on the city. Despite a bright moon, the defenders on the ramparts saw nothing of their approach. For one thing, they were too exhausted by hunger to be adequately watchful and wide awake; and for another, many of the regular troops had deserted their posts to forage in the town and an abnormally large number of civilians, unused to this kind of duty, had been drafted in to take their places in the lines. Thus no general alarm was given until, as the approaching assault force reached within a few yards of their objective, a furious covering fire was opened by the Ansar artillery. By then it was too late for the defenders to reinforce the weak point in the ramparts, and in a few moments the Ansar infantry had poured across the moat and into Khartoum. Sweeping to the right, they took the defenders in the rear and then, forcing their way along the lines, seized the Messalamieh Gate at the south-west corner of the defences. For a brief moment the other main gate, opposite Buri village on the west, defied the attackers; but as the Ansar poured past the Messalamieh Gate, the troops at the Buri Gate wilted and ran for their lives.

By four o'clock Khartoum had been taken and the streets were filled with Ansar, uttering their blood-curdling shrieks and shooting and spearing the fleeing defenders. Then the cry went up, 'To the palace,' and in a few moments a group of rebels had swarmed into the palace gardens, overwhelming the guards at the gate. Rushing headlong to the outside staircase that led to Gordon's quarters, they were suddenly brought up short by the appearance of Gordon himself, standing quite calmly at the head of the stairs with a look of scorn on his face. He was dressed in a white uniform with a tarbush on his head and his left hand rested on his sword, which was sheathed and hanging from his sword-belt. Except for the fact that he had a revolver in his right hand, he looked for all the world as if he was about to attend some ceremonial parade and had been disturbed in his preparations by a bunch of noisy street-urchins. And in the final fatal moment of his life, he made not the smallest gesture to defend himself, either with his revolver or with his sword.

In the heat of the moment the Mahdi's express injunction that he was to be taken alive was forgotten. With a shout, 'Oh! cursed one, your time is come,' the leader of the Ansar group flung his spear at Gordon's breast. And as he spun round from the force of the thrust, the others rushed up the staircase and plunged their spears into his body. According to custom, his head was cut off and taken to the Mahdi, who, unable to believe that his orders had been disobeyed, sent it to Slatin for identification. Slatin later described the awful moment when the head of his former chief was brought to him: 'The blood rushed to my head and my heart seemed to stop beating. But with a great effort of self-control, I gazed silently at this ghastly spectacle. His blue eyes were half opened; the mouth was perfectly natural; the hair of his head, and his short whiskers, were almost quite white. "Is not this the head of your uncle, the unbeliever?" said Shatta, holding the head before me. "What of it," I said quietly; "a brave soldier who fell at his post; happy is he to have fallen; his sufferings are over." '

Gordon's sufferings were over and he had at last obtained the release that he sought with so much longing from this earthly life. But the sufferings of Khartoum and its inhabitants were anything but over. For six hours after the town fell, the Ansar conducted a systematic massacre of the 'Turks'. During that time about 4,000 people were killed, including the Austrian Consul, Hansal, most of the Egyptian bashi-bazouks, the white regular troops, and the Shaggia irregulars. Only the black troops were spared. Then at 10 a.m. the Mahdi ordered the massacre to cease, and all the surviving inhabitants and soldiers were sent out of the town. The women and children were distributed as slaves among the Ansar's officers and the men were stripped of their belongings, given *jibbehs* to wear and set free to earn whatever meagre livelihood they might in the Mahdi's camp. Then as the killing stopped, the looting began. Everything of value was carried off to be lodged in the Mahdi's treasury and any citizens found trying to hide their wealth were automatically put to death. In fact, very little was found to swell the Ansar coffers, most of the coin and other valuables having been smuggled out of the town by those inhabitants who had already fled. And a number of people, including Faragh Pasha, were said to have been executed for failing to disclose the whereabouts of the no longer existent treasure.

Two days later, as the sun rose upon the ruins of the Sudanese capital on the morning of January 28, the smoke of Gordon's steamers, the *Bordein* and *Talatwein*, was seen beyond Halfaya. As the two ships drew abreast of Tuti Island, where the two Niles meet, a furious bombardment greeted them from the Ansar's mud-walled gun emplacements at Omdurman. Battling onwards through a hail of shot, they turned out of the soupy green stream at the junction of the rivers and headed into the darker waters of the Blue Nile. But they had not gone more than a few hundred yards before Wilson and his men saw the havoc wrought by the sacking of Khartoum. The palace was a smoking ruin and Gordon's flag had gone. There was obviously nothing they could do. So, turning their steamers about, they headed downstream, watched by the incredulous Ansar, who somehow could not quite believe that the much vaunted soldiers of England, the victors of Tel el-Kebir, had not stayed to exact retribution for the killing of their fellow countryman.

Inevitably, there was a ferocious public outcry when the news reached England on February 5 that Khartoum had been taken by the Mahdi and that Wilson had arrived two days 'too late' to rescue Gordon. Queen Victoria, who had been telling her Ministers ever since the previous March that 'Gordon is in danger. You are bound to try and save him,' sent Gladstone a telegram in which she made no secret of her feeling that he was personally responsible for the disaster. In Parliament and in the Press the wildest recriminations were hurled against the Liberal Government, who at that moment were little more popular than the

Mahdi himself. Although confirmation of Gordon's death was still lacking, few doubted that he had been killed, and Gladstone was denounced throughout the land for his failure to send relief in time to save him. In the music-halls the initials G.O.M., for 'Grand Old Man', by which he had for long been affectionately known, were changed to M.O.G.—'Murderer of Gordon'. And less than five months later the Government fell from power, and was replaced by a Tory Ministry headed by Lord Salisbury.

At the centre of the storm, to begin with, was the unfortunate Wilson, whose alleged failure to save Gordon became the subject of a court of enquiry. Rightly, he was exonerated and later received by the Queen at Windsor as a mark of official absolution. His judges took the view that the fault lay not with him, but with those who began so late in the day to plan for a relief force. But perhaps the most perceptive statement of the case came from Lord Dufferin, who, as Viceroy of India, wrote to Wilson in July 1885: 'the criticisms seemed absurd; nor do I think they need give you a thought. Everyone here understands how the case stood, and what was the nature of your mission; and nobody for a moment believes that you either delayed your start or could have done anything more than you did. It is also perfectly well known that you were sent to Khartoum merely to communicate with Gordon and that there was no question of your rescuing him. Had he been alive when you arrived, he certainly would not have consented to have gone back with you.' Likewise, Gladstone, writing to a former colleague several years after the event, said: 'My own opinion is that it is harder to justify our doing so much to rescue him than our not doing more. Had the party reached Khartoum in time, he would not have come away (as I suppose) and the dilemma would have arisen in another form.'

Dufferin and Gladstone were right. Gordon had made it plain that he would *not leave the Sudan until every one who wants to go down is given the chance to do so, unless* a government is established which relieves me of the charge'. And while it has become a convention among Gordon's biographers to say that Wilson arrived 'two days too late', one is tempted to ask: 'Too late' for what? Certainly he could not have saved Gordon or Khartoum, even if he had brought with him the full complement of the advance column, instead of leaving the bulk of it at Metemma. The most he could have brought was 2,000 men against an Ansar force of 20,000. Gordon, it is true, generally underestimated the courage and effectiveness of the Ansar and frequently contended that a handful of British redcoats would soon send them scuttling. But there were also moments, such as after the battle for the Omdurman river-bank on November 12, when he changed his tune and wrote in his journal that, if the relief force came, 'the *Arabs may run away*, but somehow, since a few days, I doubt it'. And there can be little doubt that, had Wilson arrived with his whole column, let alone with 220 men, before the Mahdi attacked, he could have done little more than prolong the agony and delay the moment when Khartoum was overwhelmed by sheer weight of numbers, allied to the unflinching courage of fanaticism. If proof of this were needed, it is not necessary to look further than the Battle of Omdurman fourteen years later, when a British force of 22,000 equipped with modern artillery and machine-guns avenged Gordon's death by defeating the Ansar. Wave after wave of the defenders charged the British guns with such courage that a British war correspondent was moved to write: 'No white troops would have faced that torrent of death for five minutes.' And it was not until 27,000 out of a total of 40,000 Ansar had been killed or wounded that final victory could be claimed.

It would have required at the very least the whole of Wolseley's force of 7,000 to relieve Khartoum and prevent its capture by the Mahdi. And even if that number had arrived in time, as Dufferin said, they could not have saved Gordon. For in his own words he had declined to be saved: 'I am not the *rescued lamb* and I will not be .... I WILL STAY HERE AND FALL WITH THE TOWN AND RUN ALL RISKS.'

CHAPTER 25

AN ASSESSMENT

WHEN the news reached London on February 11 that Gordon had perished in Khartoum, tributes to his heroism began to pour in from many quarters. Queen Victoria, condoling with Augusta, spoke of 'Your dear noble, heroic brother who served his country and his Queen so truly, so heroically, with a self-sacrifice so edifying to the world.' The Khedive Tewfik wrote to Sir Henry Gordon to say: 'In his own death Gordon has lost nothing, but has gained the glorious object he so fervently desired, to the attainment of which his life was so nobly devoted.' Nubar Pasha also wrote describing Gordon as a hero in the noblest sense of the word. Wolseley told Henry Gordon that he would 'never see his like again'. The Chinese Government sent their condolences to Henry Gordon through their Minister in London; Li Hung-chang telegraphed his tribute to the British Minister in Peking; and the Emperor informed Sir Harry Parkes that, in accordance with Chinese custom, a token sum of money (£120 to be exact) would be granted to Gordon's relatives 'as a posthumous testimonial in evidence of our compassion'. The British Parliament went somewhat further and voted £20,000 for Gordon's family, as being the sum to which he would have been entitled if he had taken service with the King of the Belgians in the Congo, instead of answering his country's summons to return to the Sudan.

A day of national mourning was declared, on which memorial services were held at Westminster Abbey and St. Paul's Cathedral and other churches throughout the country. Most of the great and famous figures of the time turned out to pay their respects, including the Princess of Wales, the Duke of Cambridge, Commander-in-Chief of the Army, Lord Granville, the Archbishop of Canterbury, the Chancellor of the Exchequer, and numerous peers of the realm and Members of Parliament. At St. Paul's the Bishop of Newcastle gave the address and, in the course of his panegyric, recalled one of Gordon's own most moving and significant comments on his earlier mission as Governor-General of the Sudan: 'I would give my life for these poor people of the Sudan. How can I help feeling for them? All the time I was there, every night I used to pray that God would lay upon me the burden of their sins and crush me with it, instead of those poor sheep. I really wished and longed for it.'

No doubt at the time the true significance of this quotation was lost upon an audience steeped in the hero-cult of the 'warrior-saint'. Yet, of all Gordon's manifold personal reflections, there can be few which sum up his mystical conception of life more succinctly than the words selected by the Bishop of Newcastle. He wanted to die, and he wanted to die for the sins of the world, or at least of his world, which at the end became the Sudan and its people. From his early twenties, when he went out to fight in the Crimean War, he had been possessed by this desire for martyrdom. And through all the copious correspondence which he maintained with his sister, and with various close friends, from Gravesend, Equatoria, Khartoum, and Palestine, he never tired of telling of his 'very great desire for death'. Moreover, Gordon's actions fully confirmed the desire which he so repeatedly expressed in words. In the Crimea and in the savage hand-to-hand fighting against the Taiping rebels in China, he invited death at almost every step, exposing himself to totally unnecessary risks, unarmed except for a rattan cane. Likewise, in the Sudan he never failed to put his head in the lion's mouth whenever the opportunity occurred. Whether he was tracking down slavers or suppressing a tribal rebellion, he would delight in outpacing his military escort in order to arrive alone in the enemy's lair. And in the final fatal year of his life, in total disregard of official instructions, he courted and met his death at the hands of the Mahdi's warriors.

Thus by word and by deed Gordon supplied the key to the riddle of his refusal to carry out his orders and evacuate Khartoum and Sennar while evacuation was still possible. And the fact that his biographers have chosen to ignore this palpable truth—even in some cases to omit from passages quoted from his letters the constantly reiterated desire for death—cannot any longer be allowed to cloud the issue. Even with the lapse of more than half a century since Gordon's death, during which time his private letters and journals became available for public scrutiny, books were still being written which contended that he stayed in Khartoum for personal glory or because, as a hero in the nineteenth-century mould, he considered retreat to be an unthinkable dereliction of a soldier's duty. Another writer, Lytton Strachey, went to the opposite extreme in his book, *Eminent Victorians*, with the insinuation that Gordon was a drunkard and a shirker, unworthy of the halo of virtue and courage with which he was crowned by his contemporaries. But it is as misleading and inadequate to say that he stayed in Khartoum for glory or heroics as it is slanderous and ridiculous to accuse him of drunkenness and cowardice.

Strachey's charges, which were based on a story told by Chaille-Long to blacken Gordon's name after he had been dismissed from his post in Equatoria, can be easily dismissed. According to Chaille-Long, when their camp in Equatoria was attacked one night by hostile natives, Gordon refused to move from his tent, where he was seated with 'an open Bible and an open bottle of brandy' on the table, and Chaille-Long was obliged to retire, nonplussed, to deal with the situation as best he could. In the first place, there is no evidence to show that Gordon ever drank to excess. On the contrary, all who knew him best, including his friends and servants, agreed that he was very abstemious and drank brandy largely for medicinal purposes when in hot and unhealthy climates. Secondly, there is no evidence to prove that this particular attack ever occurred. Although night raids were made on a number of other occasions, no mention of an attack on this occasion was made in any of Gordon's letters or in the diary of the Austrian explorer, Ernst Marno, who was with Gordon and Chaille-Long at the time. And, finally, Chaille-Long not only had a personal grievance against Gordon, but in several books which he wrote of his travels in Africa and elsewhere was also known to have deliberately distorted the facts to suit his own ends.

As for the theory that Gordon was simply inspired by a desire for glory or by a nineteenth-century sense of heroic duty, it is certainly true that Victorian England admired and extolled heroism and did not always consider discretion to be the better part of valour. But her own greatest hero, the Duke of Wellington, had himself laid down that the best test of a great general was 'to know when to retreat and to dare to do it'. Thus not only because he disobeyed his Government's explicit instructions, which he himself had helped to draft, but because he also failed the test of generalship set by the supreme military authority of the age, he can scarcely be said to have been doing his duty as a soldier by Victorian standards in martyrizing himself and the Khartoum garrison. Besides, far from seeking glory in the eyes of his countrymen, Gordon had repeatedly disdained 'other men's praises'. Typical of his indifferent attitude was the remark in a letter to his brother Henry on his return from the Sudan in 1880: 'I am quite indifferent to whether I am blamed or not, for I feel I only did, but poorly, my duty.... Everything will be eventually known and the best of men will feel but humiliated when their true motives are known. I do not claim or wish to be considered for a moment in that category.... I do not mind the bitter words which may be said of me if they were published. [They] may write of me as if I was dead, for thank God I am partially so with respect to what men say of me.' To his sister he also said that 'to undergo martyrdom you only have to despise men's praise and to the degree you do so, so will you get it'. And again in his Khartoum journal he wrote in bitter contempt of those who search for glory in this life: 'The fact is if one analyses human glory, it is composed of 9/10 twaddle, perhaps 99/100 twaddle.'

But if we accept on the evidence of Gordon's own repeated statements that in most of his life he was motivated by a death-wish and if we reject as facile or mendacious that he was satisfying a search for glory or was merely an irresponsible drunkard, we are still left with the question: What caused the death-wish? Was it simply the natural projection of his mysticism, the impatient longing of a man, who lived only half of his time in this world, to have done with earthly life and live all the time in the next? Or was there some other irresistible psychological compulsion which made him yearn for his 'release'?

It has become fashionable, when examining the motives of such historical figures as Gordon, to impute that they were inclined to homosexuality and that their actions are all to be explained by the feelings of guilt and shame which these tendencies engendered. Lawrence of Arabia, for one, has been the victim of such misrepresentation, despite an overwhelming weight of evidence to the contrary. And Gordon's memory, although in a much lesser degree, has not been altogether untainted. Admittedly the evidence in his case is less conclusive than that regarding Lawrence, partly because there is nobody alive today who could testify from personal knowledge, as is still the case with Lawrence, and because too this was a subject which was almost unmentionable in the Victorian era and certainly would not have found its way into any memoir. Thus, so far as letters, diaries and the testimony of contemporaries go, there is little evidence one way or the other.

Gordon, of course, never married, and it is, to say the least, unlikely that any relationships that he had with women were other than platonic. 'Miss Dykes,' he wrote of a young woman whom he met at Gravesend, 'is the nicest girl I ever saw, but do not be alarmed; the dead do not marry.' Again he once said, 'I could make no woman happy.' Yet, while denying the institution of marriage for himself, he advocated it most strongly for his friends. 'A man who is not married cannot know his faults,' he wrote to his friend, Colonel Watson. 'A man's wife is his faithful looking-glass.... Till a man is married he is a selfish fellow however he may wish not to be so.... To marry is the best thing a man should do and it is one which I recommend all my friends to do.' And to another friend, Major Donnelly, he insisted that he should get married—and to that 'nicest' of girls, Miss Dykes.

Was then his failure to follow his own advice, his inability 'to make any woman happy', due to a preference for homosexual rather than heterosexual relations? All that can be said in answer to the question is that there is no more proof that he ever practised homosexuality than there is that he ever had a sexual relationship with a woman. His interest and care for the ragged urchins of Gravesend proves nothing more than a love of humanity and a certain Scoutmasterish quality which made him want to help young people. 'Looking back on an active life,' he wrote after leaving the Sudan in 1880, 'I do not think I know anything more interesting than the study of the young of human beings. I have quite enjoyed seeing my youth reproduced in my nephew.'

There is, however, one curious and possibly significant remark which occurs in part of Gordon's prolific correspondence during his stay in Palestine. Writing to the Rev. Barnes from Jaffa, he recalled how 'I wished I was a eunuch at 14' and, in the very next sentence, went on to say: 'I went to Crimea, hoping without having a hand in it to be killed. I survived and lived, but not wishing to be too closely acquainted with God, nor yet to leave Him....: Came home from China, saw my father die. Saw if Jesus did really die He must have died for some greater result than that seen in the Christian world ... and one night something broke in my heart, a palpable feeling, and I knew God lived in me—which I have never lost.'

Is this confession the key to Gordon's death-wish? Did he discover at school a homosexual tendency which, coming as he did from the strict, conventional background of a military family, preyed on his mind to the extent that he wished he had been born a eunuch? Did the repression of this tendency cost him so dearly that he hoped to be killed in the Crimean War? Did he seek in his religious belief a form of self-protection and a way of renouncing the lusts of his flesh? 'I like my religious views,' he told his brother Henry; 'they were and are a greatcoat to me.' And was the greatcoat of religion enough to protect him? It seems not quite. Otherwise, it would simply have helped him to say with resignation that, having committed his earthly life and actions to God, he had done his best and could henceforth live at peace with himself and his superiors, both British and foreign. But he never came to terms with the sins of the flesh and the lusts of this world. 'All that the flesh admires is doomed,' he wrote to Augusta from Gravesend. 'Cursed is the man who makes flesh his aim. ... As crucifixion was a slow process, so is our slow death for the flesh. It makes me yearn for complete deliverance.' And from that time onwards, as his letters showed, he went on yearning for complete deliverance, until that January day nearly twenty years later when, as a pale dawn broke over Khartoum, an Ansar spear, plunged deep into his breast, released him from the turmoil of a sinful world to pass through 'the glorious gate of eternity, of glory and joy, unmixed with the taint of sorrow'.

Whether or not Gordon was a repressed homosexual, he was certainly the complete misfit. Unable to tolerate the 'trammels' of British military traditions and the pretentiousness of life and society in England, he seized every opportunity that presented itself to serve abroad and, whenever possible, under a foreign flag. Yet he could say with the most conventional Englishman that 'We would never have been the nation we are had it not been for the insular position which we occupy and which gives us our individuality.' He also had the gall to write to Donnelly and reproach him for 'separating yourself as you apparently have done from your regiment'. And he frequently fretted and stormed when the 'mutinous' Chinese or the 'indolent' Egyptians and

Sudanese under his command resisted his attempt to impose upon them the very 'trammels' of British Army discipline from which he was himself seeking to escape. For however much he might protest that he could never live or soldier in England, he could equally never completely detach himself from his traditional environment and from the innate sense of discipline which sprang from three previous generations of British Army officers. From adolescence he had been a rebel, yet a rebel imprisoned by certain inescapable traditions, who could never quite follow through with his rebellion.

Thus he could never 'go native', could never truly understand or feel at ease with his foreign employers and, in the final analysis, always judged them and their actions as an Englishman and by English standards. And having judged first the Chinese and later the Egyptians and found them wanting by such standards, and being unwilling to serve in his own country, he became a no-man's-lander, incapable of fitting into any setting or society. The effect of this on his life and actions was further intensified by a certain weakness of character. Like many stubborn people, Gordon had a very weak streak, as was shown by his frequent oscillations and self-contradictions. After his break with Tewfik and his resignation from the Sudan, he gave up, and told everyone that his life was over and all his useful work done. From then onwards, as we have seen, his death-wish waxed stronger than ever. 'My likings and my destiny are analogous,' he wrote to Augusta from Mauritius. 'I do not want to hang on.' And in a letter to a friend he said pathetically: 'How I wish *He* would come.'

No doubt, too, Gordon's sense of being a misfit was strengthened by the irony of his position, both in China and in the Sudan. For in truth, in each case, he found himself forced by circumstances into opposing a movement for which he had no little sympathy. Writing from Soochow in October 1863, he said that 'both sides are equally rotten, but you must confess that on the Taiping side there is at least innovation and a disregard for many of the frivolous and idolatrous customs of the Manchus. While my eyes are fully open to the defects of the Taiping character, from a close observation of three months, I find many promising traits never yet displayed by the Imperialists.' The Taiping mandarins were 'without exception brave and gallant men' and between them and Li Hung-chang or any of his Manchu officers, *'there is* no comparison'. Likewise, in the Sudan he deplored many of the Mahdi's actions, including his alliance with slave-traders, such as Osman Digna. But he could not bring himself to describe the Ansar as 'rebels', contending that the Egyptians were in many ways the real rebels, and that they were resisting an endemic nationalist uprising against foreign oppression and a religious reaction against profanity.

In fact, had he and the Mahdi ever been able to meet in a calm and sober atmosphere, free from the bitter animosities which civil war inevitably engenders, they would quite possibly have found much common ground. Both had the interests of the Sudanese people at heart, both had little use for the Egyptians, and each in their different ways wished to see the Sudan gain independence. True, Gordon overrated the power and influence of Zubair and the former sultans to run the Sudan in unity, peace and freedom, and underrated the strength and prestige of the Mahdi. But his mistake was due more to ignorance of local conditions and sentiment than to any irremovable prejudice against the Mahdi. Yet, in the circumstances of the day, no such meeting could take place. Gordon therefore found himself once more the misfit in Khartoum, driven by his own weariness with this world and eagerness to reach the next into a last, hopeless battle on behalf of a régime and a ruler for whom he had little but contempt. And, final irony of all, his wish to die was granted to him by the very people whom he had spent the latter part of his life trying to help against those rulers whom paradoxically, and typically, he despised, yet served to the bitter end.

His whole life was one continuous conflict between an innate idealism and an iron discipline. The idealist resented the discipline, and the disciplinarian made him scorn the idealist. Stretched like a taut wire between these two poles and unable to cast off at either end, he 'yearned for complete deliverance'. Yet deliverance had to be for some cause, else it would deny his ideals of charity and of faith and become suicide, and so be 'taking things out of God's hands'. Service to the point of self-sacrifice had to be the only way out: 'I would give my life for these poor people of the Sudan.' And in his own special way he did.